POLITICAL PARTICIPATION AND ETHNIC MINORITIES

Political Participation and Ethnic Minorities

Chinese Overseas in Malaysia, Indonesia, and the United States

AMY L. FREEDMAN

ROUTLEDGE
NEW YORK   LONDON

Published in 2000 by
Routledge
29 West 35th Street
New York, NY 10001

Published in Great Britain in 2000 by
Routledge
11 New Fetter Lane
London EC4P 4EE

Printed in the United States of America on acid-free paper.
Design and Typography: Jack Donner

Cataloging-in-Publication Data available from the Library of Congress

CONTENTS

LIST OF FIGURES, TABLES, AND MAPS

The idea for this study came to me in the middle of a sleepless night in 1996. I was kept awake worrying about a different research project that seemed to be going nowhere. I had recently read an article about Southeast Asian business networks that discussed the importance of ethnic Chinese firms to economic growth in the region. I was struck by this for two reasons: first, it is well known that Southeast Asian countries, like Malaysia, Indonesia, and Singapore, relied on extensive state guidance in economic development. If the government had a hand in promoting certain sectors or particular players in the economy, why would Chinese businesses be the beneficiaries? Second, the article seemed to argue that ethnic scapegoating and political discrimination based on ethnicity were things of the past.

On one level this heartened me. It would be wonderful if ethnic violence in Southeast Asia was a thing of the past. And if, in fact, ethnic Chinese had been well incorporated into Southeast Asian nations where they lived, might such cases serve as models for other multiethnic societies? It did not take much research to realize that this outlook was far too rosy. I quickly found that there were wide discrepancies as to how Chinese communities outside of China were treated and how they interacted with the larger polity. The puzzle that particularly intrigued me was: How could the Chinese be powerful economically while still being marginalized politically? And why did this seem to be true in places as diverse as Indonesia, California, and Malaysia?

My research was met with some skepticism. One prominent scholar dismissed my gloomy perspective. He argued that economic growth in Southeast Asia had made ethnic issues obsolete. I asked what he thought would happen if the economy were to stumble. I did not really believe at the time that such a change would come in the midst of my work on this project. In early 1996, when I began this research, the economies of the United States, Indonesia, and Malaysia all seemed to be promising further growth. President Clinton was favored to win reelection in the United States, and Suharto and Mahathir, leaders of Indonesia and Malaysia respectively, seemed as entrenched as ever. Then, in the summer of 1997, the economies in Indonesia and Malaysia faltered. In the United States, Chinese Americans were feeling besieged by the media's portrayal of illegal campaign contributions to President Clinton's reelection effort. By the summer of 1998, as I was concluding my research, both Indonesia and Malaysia were in turmoil. Throughout Indonesia riots destroyed Sino-Indonesian property, and an unknown number of Chinese women and girls were raped and abused by roving bands of thugs. The events of the spring of 1998 triggered a huge exodus; Sino-Indonesians who could afford to, fled Indonesia. My research took on a new significance. In Malaysia, calls for *reformasi* caused Mahathir to remove his popular deputy, Anwar Ibrahim, from power. When Malaysian students took to the streets, Malaysian Chinese (for the most part) stayed home and refrained from criticizing the regime. Protests in Malaysia were quickly put down and Mahathir's power, instead of weakening, had, if anything, increased.

This book does not include a detailed account of the financial, social, and political turmoil of the last few years. It does, however, examine the underlying causes of the political inequity between indigenous populations and ethnic Chinese which, I believe, contributed to the conflict over the last two years. To me, the turmoil has very distinct political roots. One cannot be surprised that Sino-Indonesians were targets for violence and looting when Suharto's political system deliberately maintained policies and practices that treated them as different from other Indonesian citizens. Likewise, Prime Minister Mahathir tolerates moderate opposition to his regime, but whenever his legitimacy, or the legitimacy of the dominant party, the United Malay National Organization (UMNO), is questioned, he relies on Malay-based nationalism to vilify his attackers. Lastly, Chinese Americans feel that even in a land of immigrants they are signaled out as suspect Americans. Espionage charges against scientist Wen Ho Lee, and Congressman Cox's report about the accusation, are just the latest incidents that lead Chinese Americans to wonder if they are always to feel removed from American institutions of power.

Clearly there are myriad complex explanations for these current events. I have chosen to focus on the political underpinnings. Although I also discuss cultural- and class-based arguments, to me, a country's political institutions and norms set the tone for how ethnic groups interact with each other and how immigrant groups (even ones who have lived in a country for generations) are incorporated into the political process. I will leave it to others to develop a more complex historical analysis of these countries and events, and I am certain that other scholars can more thoroughly analyze the political meanings and implications of identities and difference within a population.

ACKNOWLEDGMENTS

Many people have made this manuscript possible. I am especially appreciative and indebted to David Denoon for his encouragement and counsel at every stage of this study. I am also happy to express my gratitude to the other members of my dissertation committee; Martin Schain, Stathis Kalyvas, Chris Mitchell, and Anna Harvey, for their advice and input throughout the research and writing of this work. Many improvements have come from their respective comments. Two reviewers also combed through the manuscript and offered suggestions and corrections. I am also greatly appreciative of the professional editors with whom I have worked at Routledge. I have tried to incorporate many of their ideas into the revisions. I am thankful for their attentiveness to detail.

Additionally, I would like to give collective thanks to those who facilitated my research in Malaysia, Indonesia, New York, and Los Angeles. In particular, I am grateful for the Social Science Research Council's invitation and funding to present my work at a conference and workshop on Southeast Asian diasporas held in Singapore in December 1996. Many thoughts and suggestions came out of that experience which helped guide my fieldwork. Likewise, the funding and support I received from the Politics Department and New York University's Graduate School of Arts and Sciences enabled me to complete the first draft of this book. My faculty colleagues at Franklin and Marshall College have been tremendously supportive and have truly made me feel at home in Lancaster, Pennsylvania.

I also want to thank friends from graduate school who helped me sift through initial ideas and methodologies. At the risk of seeming ungrateful to my other classmates, I want to be sure to thank Sarah Davies Murray, Ethel Brooks, Jeff Togman, James Vreeland, Bill Pink, Helen Wu, and Michael Nest; and those further afield: Brigitte Welsh, Ann Marie Murphy, Geoffrey Stafford, and Mike Montasano.

Finally, I wish to thank my husband, Kevin Kopczynski, and my family for all their love, patience, and confidence in me.

All the errors and failings in this work are entirely of my own doing.

Amy L. Freedman
New York City, 1999

AALDEF	Asian American Legal Defense and Education Fund
ABRI	*Angkatan Bersenjata Republik Indonesia*, Indonesia's military
ACCC	Associated Chinese Chambers of Commerce
APA	Asian Pacific Americans
AP3CON	Asian Pacific Policy and Planning Council
APEC	Asia Pacific Economic Cooperation
APU	*Angkatan Perpaduan Ummah*, Movement of Community Unity
BN	*Barisan Nasional*
CCBA	Chinese Consolidated Benevolent Association
CHH	*Chung Hua Hui*
CHTH	*Chung Hua Tsung Hui*, independent Chinese Association in Indonesia
C-PAC	Chinese Political Action Committee
CSIS	Center for Strategic and International Studies
DAP	Democratic Action Party
DNC	Democratic National Committee
DPR	*Dewar Perwalsilan Ralsyat*, People's Representative Council
EEOC	Equal Employment Opportunity Commission
EPU	Economic Planning Unit
FBI	Federal Bureau of Investigation
FEER	*Far Eastern Economic Review*
GPF	Indonesia Pharmaceutical Association
HCTH	*Hua Ch'iao Tsung Hui*, Japanese-created Chinese federation in Indonesia
HUD	Housing and Urban Development
ICMI	Indonesian Islamic think tank
IMF	International Monetary Fund
IMP	Independence Party of Malaysia
ISA	Internal Security Act
KADIN	Indonesia's Chamber of Commerce and Industry
KMT	*Kuomintang*
LA	Los Angeles
MCA	Malaysian Chinese Association
MCP	Malaysian Communist Party
MCS	Malaysian Civil Service
MIC	Malaysian Indian Congress

MPR	*Majelis Permusyawaratan*, People's Consultative Assembly (Indonesia)
NDP	National Development Policy
NEP	New Economic Policy
NGO	Nongovernmental organization
NY/NYC	New York City
NU	*Nahdlatul Ulama*
OCA	Organization of Chinese Americans
PAN	National Mandate Party
PAS	Islamic Party of Malaysia
PDI-P	Indonesian Democratic Party in Struggle
PKB	National Awakening Party
PKI	Indonesian Communist Party
PNI	Indonesian Nationalist Party
PP	Partai Persatuan, the Developmental Unity Party (a Muslim-oriented party in Indonesia)
PPP	People's Progressive Party
PRC	People's Republic of China
PTD	*Perkhidmatan Tadbiran Diplomatik*, Malaysian civil service
PTI	*Partai Tionghoa Indonesia*, Chinese-Indonesian party
SARA	Sensitive issues concerning ethnic, religious, and racial harmony
SEKBERTAL	Spinning Industry Joint Secretariat
TAR/TARC	Tunku Abdul Rahman College
THHK	*Tiong Hoa Hwee Koan*, the Chinese organization
UCLA	University of California at Los Angeles
UCSCA	United Chinese School Committee Association of Malaysia
UCSTA	United Chinese School Teachers' Association
UMNO	United Malays National Organization
UUCA	Universities and University Colleges Act

1

Introduction

I am standing under a harsh fluorescent light as a man, approaching,
unsheathes a meat cleaver. Around me gathers a gang of people, all holding thick wooden sticks, steel pipes or spears. In the street beyond, more
armed silhouettes near. Some are boys as young as 10, learning early how
to play vigilante. Around us, stores in the Chinese-dominated downtown
remain shuttered, the windows above blank and empty behind bars of iron.
A block away, police speed by on screaming motorcycles, the sound echo-
ing down the dirty, deserted alleys. Their passage is a reminder that elsewhere in this city, homes and cars are burning, families fleeing.

—Jose Manuel Tesoro, "How and Why Indonesia's Third-largest City
Descended into Chaos," *Asiaweek*, May 22, 1998

The quote above reflects the recent experience of Chinese in Indonesia,
but it could just as easily be an account of another minority community
(Chinese or otherwise) facing persecution from a more numerically powerful indigenous group venting their anger on a community clearly
marked as outsiders. This work aims to do two things. On a general level
it is about ethnic politics: How do immigrant communities become incorporated into the larger polity? More specifically, this work is about one
group of immigrants: the Chinese. In this regard the study looks cross-
nationally at how and why Chinese communities have accessed the political arena of their adopted countries. The Chinese diaspora is an
interesting group to focus on for several reasons. Chinese communities
can be found in places as diverse as Paris and Mauritius. Approximately
19.5 million ethnic Chinese live outside China, mostly in Southeast Asia
and North America.[1] Throughout the world they have organized a system
of guilds, benevolent societies, *tongs* (secret societies), and name and place
associations which facilitate the group ties that characterize the community and which have given rise to the phenomena of "network capitalism"[2] which once fueled economic growth throughout Asia Pacific.

Chinese immigration to a wide variety of nations, the size of some of the communities and strength of Chinese community associations and ties, along with a perception that they have significant economic clout in their adopted countries, make them a compelling group with which to study the issue of immigrant politicization.

There are two assumptions in popular opinion and in much of the scholarly literature about politics and the Chinese diaspora: that the Chinese are political pawns of either Beijing or Taipei; or that they are politically passive and more interested in prospering economically than they are in wielding influence or power politically within their countries of residence. Even in initial research it became clear that the extent and nature of Chinese overseas political activity has changed over time and in response to events and developments both within their communities and from outside political institutions.

Events in the United States and Indonesia over the last two years[3] might lead one to believe that Chinese political participation consists of wealthy businessmen forging connections to prominent political leaders. This is not the sum of Chinese political activity and it is part of more complex relations between the Chinese community, economic and political elites, and the mechanisms of government. While there is no one set of strategies or goals that can perfectly capture the activity of the Chinese in all four cases, there are some generalizable trends that can be identified at the outset. Chinese in Indonesia, on peninsular Malaysia, and in the United States, certainly want to be free from persecution and want to ensure the protection of their businesses and property. Chinese overseas consistently seek access to education for their children; some of them also want the ability to maintain their cultural identity, and they would like political rights similar to the rest of society. There is great diversity among and within the communities as well as in the tactics used to reach or ensure these objectives. Both this chapter and the case studies will detail how and why Chinese communities endeavor to become equal players in the political process.

THE PUZZLE

This work begins with the observation that for Chinese overseas, levels of political participation do not seem to be correlated with socioeconomic variables like income or education. This poses an interesting question for the literature on political participation, which finds participation closely connected to levels of education and income. In order to understand this gap between the current scholarship and what seems to be the reality for Chinese communities overseas, this study examines the processes and mechanisms through which these groups are incorporated into the political arenas of their chosen homelands. A second concern addressed here is whether community political participation impacts the level of influence that a group has on policy issues that concern them.

In places where the Chinese have achieved economic success, like Indonesia and Malaysia, rates of political participation are still low. Material from the case studies shows that despite middle- and upper-class status in Indonesia, Chinese have been somewhat removed from most avenues of political power. From the middle of the 1960s until 1998 Sino-Indonesians were prohibited from participating fully in political, civic, and military affairs. Although Indonesia's political system was largely closed to any sort of open contestation, Indonesian Chinese, specifically, were prevented from accessing other avenues of participation. Nonetheless, individual Chinese had considerable personal influence in Indonesia under Suharto. In contrast, Chinese participation in Malaysia is institutionalized; however, the degree to which they are politically active or influential is circumscribed. In the United States, where political contestation is fairly open, Chinese groups remain poorly represented in both local and national politics, and wield only modest influence in policies that impact their community.

In order to unravel this puzzle, the following questions are asked: When or under what conditions do Chinese become active in the political process of their adopted countries? Does political influence stem from group participation? And a subquestion that stems from the first two: What role do communal organizations and their leaders play in determining the nature and scope of participation? In answering these questions this work discusses various possible elements that might impact the degree to which Chinese overseas are political actors: socioeconomic status, culture, and institutional or opportunity structures are examined. Ultimately, this work assesses both the goals and objectives of the Chinese community in entering the political fray, as well as looking at the strategies and tactics used in accessing the political arena.

TERMINOLOGY

CHINESE OVERSEAS

With whom is this study concerned? It is always problematic to define one's subject of study. The term "Chinese overseas" is used to refer to all ethnic Chinese living outside Taiwan, Hong Kong, and the People's Republic of China (the term "greater China" is often used to describe this region collectively). This broad description could be taken to include nationals of Taiwan or China living abroad. Many of these migrants may harbor a desire to become more permanent settlers; however, until they choose to adopt citizenship of a country outside greater China, this study is not primarily about them. Because the focus of this work is on political participation through (mostly) legal channels, noncitizens are marginalized in this book. Predominately, this study is concerned with ethnic Chinese who have become citizens of Malaysia, Indonesia, and the United States. As Lynn Pan states in the beginning of *The Encyclopedia of Chinese Overseas*, "Examples of these are the so-called 'hyphenated' Chinese: Sino-Thais, Chinese Americans and so on; people who are Chinese by descent but whose non-Chinese citizenship and political allegiance collapse ancestral loyalties" (Pan 1999:15). Others with Chinese heritage may have, through intermarriage or assimilation, ceased to call themselves Chinese. This work is less concerned with this group of people and, with the exception of Indonesia, there is little discussion about this segment of the "Chinese" diaspora. For this research, identity is self-ascribed and, because the level of analysis is the community rather than the individual, a certain degree of community identification is also necessary.

NOTIONS OF COMMUNITY

Since this work is concerned with community activism as a whole, and with the ability of individual leaders or activists to mobilize the community, it is less concerned with the actions of individual community members themselves. Much of the recent ethnic studies literature focuses on problems inherent in defining a "community." Ong (1996) describes two distinct groups of overseas Chinese in the United States: one affluent and tied to the global economy, whom she calls "transnational publics," the other, poor and often illegal, still settles in urban Chinatowns.

> These two types of migratory Chinese communities, so dramatically contrasted in terms of class, points of origin, strategies, and power, are shaped by and in many ways the products of flexible regimes of labor capitalism that cast emigrant elites and labor towards metropolitan centers of capital and prestige. (Ong 1996:2)

Although she distinguishes between the two groups of Chinese, she finds that they are influenced by similar economic processes, and thus both groups can be linked to a larger "imagined community" (Anderson 1991). The "community" is thus held together by transnational practices of travel and economy, and also by ideologically charged themes which shape the diaspora. Conversely, in her study of Philippine women migrants, Christina Szanton Blanc (1996) argues for viewing the immigrants as part of several communities, across multiple diasporas. This author does not take issue with these diverse notions about what constitutes a "community." However, for this study a community is an identifiable, self-ascribed, set of people who share certain common characteristics; these might include, but are not limited to, language, religion, nationality, proximity, and cultural[4] attributes. Not all Chinese in the places chosen for this study want to be identified as part of a "Chinese community." For example, some ethnic Chinese in Indonesia and Malaysia have converted to Islam, changed their names, and perhaps married non-Chinese. Such individuals may no longer share common interests with co-ethnics. In such an instance, it is difficult to see how a study of Chinese overseas politicization and influence applies to them. However, if the dominant society persists in viewing them as outsiders, and if particular state institutions or policies target or affect them regardless of how they self-identify, in other words if they are treated differently than the majority population, then they, like other Chinese, must be concerned with the allocation of resources and values that impact their status in relation to the dominant group.

A slightly different approach is taken by Wang Gungwu (1993) in his work on "greater China" and the Chinese overseas. He argues that there is no single Chinese community abroad, and he suggests dividing the Chinese into three groups according to their political activities. Group A consists of the small number of Chinese who maintain links with the politics of mainland China or Taiwan[5] and who identify with the destiny of these two entities. He finds that this group is more numerous in the United States than in Southeast Asia because interest in the home country is closely correlated with recent migration. Group B has a realistic focus on occupational status and on maintaining an ethnic Chinese identity. Interest in the politics of the host country is limited. Instead there is a focus on economic issues and on professional and communal associations. He finds that most Chinese in the United States and in Southeast Asia fall into this category. The last group, Group C, is committed to its adopted country and to the politics of that nation.[6] A potential Group D would be those Chinese who have become fully assimilated with the larger society. While Wang rightly points out the wide variation among Chinese communities and within them, he does not go beyond analyzing the length of time since migrating in accounting for the differences. This cannot, then, explain why some Chinese in Malaysia and Indonesia who have been there for two hundred years might still be categorized as Group B. Even within a Chinese "community," as he defines it, there is no doubt going to be a variety of levels of political interest and incorporation. This study is more concerned with the collective effort and impact of the group on politics than in classifying individuals.

There is much work still to be done in the area of acculturation of immigrant groups into their new societies.7 Compelling studies have yet to be done on rates of intermarriage and assimilation across countries or across immigrant groups. While there certainly may be differences in political activity among different generations of immigrants, this study is based on the assumption that community membership is self-ascribed and that activity on behalf of the group is the relevant criterion for inclusion in the analysis. For example, if a third-generation Chinese lives outside Chinatown and chooses to play an active role within the Chinese community, either through activism, employment, or through professional organizations, then the study is concerned with his or her role in mobilizing his or her constituents for political activity. Likewise, since the study is concerned with political activity such as voting and personal networking, it is less focused on the role of the most recent immigrants, although they too are members of "the community." This is not to say that newer immigrants do not participate in some types of political behavior, because clearly they do; however, this work is most concerned with the collective action of those who have become eligible and have made the decision to take on more permanent status within a country.

Of the four cases examined here, Indonesia poses the most problems to the treatment of the Chinese as a single community within the larger context. As will be discussed later, there are enormous differences among Sino-Indonesians in wealth, time in country, language use, and religious affiliation. While these differences are also apparent within the United States and Malaysia, because Chinese in these two countries are allowed to (and often encouraged to) identify themselves as Chinese, that is, to celebrate their culture and heritage, the differences are often under the surface of a broader "Chinese" identification. Nonetheless, since both the Indonesian government and the majority of indigenous Indonesians perceive the Chinese to be outsiders, regardless of whether they have changed their name, intermarried, or converted to Islam; and since middle-class shop-owners are sometimes assumed to share something in common with the wealthy tycoons linked to Suharto, then it seems reasonable to try and understand the political strategies and goals of the Chinese as a group in Indonesia. In the case of Indonesia this study will certainly make distinctions among socioeconomic classes within the group.

Anderson (1991) writes of imagined communities, which can link the person and collective identities. The process of within-group identity formation overemphasizes what it is that group members actually share. It gives greater emotional weight to the common elements, reinforcing them with an ideology of linked fate. (Ross 1997:48)

This work perhaps shares the same pitfall, overemphasizing the "common elements" and downplaying the divisions. This is a possible failing of a project that chooses as its subject the whole rather than the individual. The author's compensation for this is to attempt to try to define and clarify who in each case study is being referred to when "the community" is discussed.

POLITICAL PARTICIPATION

In the most basic sense, political participation is action designed to influence government decision-making. As Huntington and Nelson (1976:3) wrote, "participation may be individual or collective, organized or spontaneous, sustained or sporadic, peaceful or violent, legal or illegal, effective or ineffective." In parts of this study, and in the most conventional sense, participation is equated with electoral action. Obviously this is not the only type of political behavior that may influence political decision-making. As the quote from Huntington and Nelson illustrates, political activity can vary across a wide spectrum. In this book the following types of political behaviors will be discussed: voting, interest-group activity, community advocacy and political education, and individual networking.

Voting seems like a self-evident term. When elections are held for political office, eligible individuals go to designated places and cast a ballot for the candidates of their choice. However, voting and elections may have different purposes and implications in various settings. For example, in the United States voting may be done under conditions of anonymity and there may be more than one party contesting a position. In other countries, like Indonesia under President Suharto, elections may have been held for purposes of bolstering the ruling party's power.

Interest-group activity is political organization by those with common interests. The motivating issue could be centered on a narrow business or economic interest, or more broadly on a religious group's beliefs. Interest groups attempt to influence policy-makers on behalf of their members. This can be done through requests and education, through supporting a candidate seeking office, or through lobbying efforts. Community advocacy is not dissimilar from interest-group activity. The main difference is that the organizing principle for communal activism is to meet the needs of the community rather than some specific political interest. Political education is when a group seeks to educate its own members on a particular issue, or when they seek to educate lawmakers on an issue of interest to the community. Individual networking is when elites work with political officials for personal gain rather than for more defuse benefits.

Political participation is fundamentally rooted in collective organization or action. Most participation requires some form of collaborative activity and the rewards go to some type of collectivity. While many of these actions require individuals to choose to participate, this study is largely concerned with group behavior as a whole. Examples of groups around which political participation is constructed include: class, communal groups (based on race, religion, language, or ethnicity), neighborhoods, party (those that identify with the same group trying to win or maintain power).[8]

One of the challenges facing leaders in the Chinese community is how to mobilize this sort of collective action. Some argue that it is difficult to view and to organize the Chinese as a single community because there are divisions within the community based on class, language, country or place of origin, and time within their adopted countries.

OVERVIEW OF CASES

Much has been written about the push-and-pull factors of immigration in general, and of Chinese immigration in particular (Fitzgerald 1972; Chesneaux 1976; Hall, K.R. 1985; Lim and Gosling 1988; Chan 1991; Skeldon 1994). In all three countries immigration has a long history and Chinese have been part of the population for over one hundred years. Although this work discusses the impact of the circumstances of immigration on patterns of settlement, as well as the lasting effects of colonial rule in Southeast Asia on ethnic politics, the main emphasis here will be on the period from the 1960s to the present. This coincides with state-building and national development in Southeast Asia, and a shift in immigration policy in the United States which triggered new waves of Chinese settlement and an increased salience of their voice in a political context. In addition, the 1960s were a time of turmoil both in Southeast Asia and in the United States. During this time in these countries, ideas about who constitutes a citizen and how power is divided among groups in society begin to challenge old political norms.

While violent political and ethnic conflict erupted in both Indonesia and Malaysia, the United States too was undergoing a period of reevaluation of political rights and values that would redefine and reorganize the nation in an attempt to incorporate groups previously disenfranchised. While ethnic conflict has existed for ages, it was not until the 1960s that the conflicts became part of larger struggles for nationalism and post-colonial identity in Southeast Asia. In the United States and elsewhere, notions of political and civil rights gained prominence.

The third and fourth chapters focus on Indonesia and peninsular Malaysia respectively. The level of analysis is national-level politics. The fifth through seventh chapters look at the United States in broad terms and at Monterey Park, California, and New York City for a more specific comparison of Chinese-American involvement in local politics. In these case studies the unit of study is more local-level politics. In order to reconcile the disparate cases, comparisons are mainly drawn between Indonesia and Malaysia, and between Monterey Park and New York City. Both the second chapter and the concluding chapter address the applicability of theoretical explanations across all four cases.

Table 1.1 describes the position of Chinese within each case and captures important variables in illustrating degrees of politicization and influence.

TABLE 1.1: OVERVIEW OF CASES				
VARIABLES	NEW YORK	LOS ANGELES	MALAYSIA	INDONESIA
% of Population	3% of NYC 30% of local district	3% of LA 40% of Monterey Park	29%[1]	3%
Major Cultural Groups	Cantonese	Cantonese	Cantonese and Fukienese	Peranakan/Totok
Leading Type of Assn.	Business	Social service	Business and social services	Business
Focus of Comm. Leader	Business	Coalition formation	Coalition formation	Business
Income	$21,345 – low	$37,256 – high	M$34,740 – high	No data – high
Time in Country	1st influx: 1880s 2nd: 1965–1997	1st influx: 1850s 2nd: 1965–1997	1st influx: 1700s 2nd: 1800–1860 3rd: 1860–1930[2] 4th: 1945–1981	1st: 1567–1800 2nd: 1800–1860 3rd: 1860–1930[3] 4th: 1945–1981
Political System	Open	Open	Relatively open	Newly open
Group Targeting	Little	Moderate	Extensive	None
Individual Targeting	Little	Moderate	Moderate	Extensive
Interest-Group Activity	Little	Moderate	Moderate	Little
Level of Politicization	Low	Moderate	Moderate	No data
% Voter Turnout	27%	32%	68%	No data
Influence	Low	Moderate	Moderate	High

[1] This figure is from the 1990 census and is generally thought to be lower now.
[2] This period saw the greatest numbers of Chinese immigrate to Malaysia (Mackie 1976:xxiv).
[3] As with Malaysia, this was the heaviest period of Chinese migration to Indonesia (ibid.).

THE UNITED STATES

The most significant variation between cases occurs in the nature of the political systems and the focus of community leaders. In the Monterey Park and New York City cases, findings show that there are noticeable differences in efforts to target the Chinese community for political activity, and in the organization and orientation of the Chinese themselves. In New York's Chinatown there are competing, and sometimes overlapping, organizations vying for power and for communal support. As 28 percent of the local election district, Chinese on the Lower East Side of Manhattan could become a political force (Zimmerman, Eu, and Daykin 1993:6). Yet the traditional kinship associations and business groups are primarily internally focused and they still play a dominant role in Chinatown politics. In the last twenty years there has been a distinct rise in the prominence of social service organizations, but these groups are factionalized and have not cultivated a set of leaders recognized by a significant portion of the community.

Despite the "model minority" myth, discussed at greater length in the chapters on the United States, of successful Asian immigrants in the United States, Asian New Yorkers in Community District Three, a subset of the local election district, 95 percent of whom are Chinese, experienced the greatest increases in poverty between 1986 and 1990 (Zimmerman et al. 1993:12). This is largely attributed to increased immigration by poorer Chinese; wealthier immigrants from the PRC, Taiwan, and Hong Kong are settling in Flushing, Queens, rather than in Chinatown (Smith, C. 1992). The median family income for the neighborhood was $21,345 compared to $36,831 for the rest of Manhattan. Horton (1992) suggests that the newer Asian immigrants in metro Los Angeles are both better educated and wealthier than earlier arrivals. Statistics support Horton's assessment, as the median family income for Chinese in Monterey Park is $37,256. Yet socioeconomic status alone does not explain the differences between the two communities.

A transition has taken place in the Los Angeles area in the nature of Chinese community leadership. Instead of inwardly focused business and lineage-based leaders, a set of social service and academic professionals who are experienced in community activism through their work on college campuses and in not-for-profit agencies has come to the forefront of ethnic politics in the Los Angeles area. For example, the Asian American Studies Center at UCLA serves as a place for developing relations with community groups, for generating policy studies, and building linkages with other groups.

In response to America, the Asian American Studies Center forged a commitment to research and social change. Emerging from the civil rights struggles of minorities—Blacks, Chicanos and Latinos, Asians and Native Americans—to define their own history, education and future, the Center was founded in 1969 as part of the movement for ethnic studies. (Taken from the center's brochure)

Traditional organizations still operate in Los Angeles's Chinatown, but political activity is spearheaded by social service groups and more mainstream American political institutions such as local Democratic and Republican clubs in Monterey Park, where the Chinese are 40 percent of the population (Horton 1992). Similarly, institutional aspects, such as the drawing of electoral districts, differ in New York and Los Angeles, resulting in greater coalition-building in the Los Angeles area between Chinese, other Asian groups, and Latino organizations. One very clear impact of this is that in parts of Los Angeles county, such as Monterey Park, a suburban community with greater access to local political offices, the Chinese community has become more politically prominent, winning several seats on the city council as well as the mayoralty. In New York the movement toward greater political involvement has occurred more slowly, and no citywide office has been seriously contested by a Chinese American.

MALAYSIA

Research shows that in Malaysia there has been a shift: once Chinese were politically and economically important, but their political capital has decreased since the late 1960s. One significant reason for this waning is that it comes as a response to institutional changes. While Table 1.1 shows the Chinese as participating in moderate to lower rates than Malays and being moderately influential, this does not fully represent the links between institutions and political activity in Malaysia. Chinese in Malaysia may still wield power and influence, but it is achieved through less formal political channels. The case chapters will better explore the relationship between variables.

In Malaysian politics the Chinese are represented in part by the Malaysian Chinese Association (MCA) which is a partner of the dominant United Malays National Organization (UMNO) in the ruling national coalition. By combining electoral and coercive mechanisms, the Malay-dominated state can insulate itself from widespread political dissatisfaction from the Chinese, despite the fact that they comprise roughly 29 percent of Malaysia's population. In Malaysia, the Chinese are perceived to be the wealthy, urban sector of the population. Chinese average household income was M$34,740 in 1995, as compared to M$19,200 for Malays (with the national average being M$24,240) (Malaysia Yearbook of Statistics 1996). While Malays have benefited from the affirmative action policies enacted as part of the New Economic Policy (NEP), and while from 1971 until 1990 Malays were favored in labor market quotas, government contracts, educational attainment, and access to credit, mean income of Chinese households has continued to outpace Malays'. The passage of the NEP, aimed almost exclusively at the Malay population, shows how the Chinese, even while some were the predominant business elites in the country, were largely at the mercy of the government *despite* their formal political participation. Even with the passage of the NEP, wealthy Chinese maintained their socioeconomic status while an upper (and middle) class of Malays also evolved.

Most importantly, what the Malaysia case study shows is that despite similarities in socioeconomic status and cultural attributes, Chinese in Malaysia wielded greater political influence from the 1950s until 1969 than they have from 1969 to the present. This change is best explained by examining the electoral incentives behind efforts at mobilizing the Chinese community for political participation, and in looking at how the relationship between business elites and political leaders has changed. With the growth of a Malay middle and upper class, there is less need for political leaders to rely on Chinese business support for political funding, and since the ruling coalition has institutionally ensured greater electoral victories, there are fewer electoral incentives to reach out to the Chinese community for votes. These factors, more than economic or cultural factors alone, help explain the nature and position of Chinese politicization in Malaysia today.

INDONESIA

Chinese are only 3 percent of Indonesia's population, and although fairly small numerically, they have an overwhelmingly significant effect on the economy of the country. The Chinese have also been subject to disproportionate harassment and suspicions of ethnic chauvinism. While exact socioeconomic statistics broken down by ethnicity are not available for Indonesia, most scholars and the general population certainly perceive that the Chinese are predominantly middle and upper class. There is much truth to the image of Chinese as an economic elite; reports repeatedly state that the Chinese control upwards of 70 percent of the country's economy, mostly in trading and distribution of goods,[9] and this clearly reflects Suharto's decision to favor the Chinese business elite. The combination of preponderant control of the economy and links to Suharto leaves the Chinese in a strange position politically. A few business tycoons are influential in the government, but the rest of the community is marginalized and persecuted.

While a small number of Chinese have become fabulously wealthy, most Sino-Indonesians have maintained their status as small shopkeepers and traders, yet because they are still identified as Chinese they are ethnically linked to Suharto's rich friends and subject to harassment and violence in times of unrest. This furthers the divide between Chinese and indigenous groups and prevents solidarity within the diasporic community itself.

While various Chinese political parties existed in Indonesia during the period of constitutional democracy that followed the transfer of power in December of 1949, most were dissolved in the aftermath of the 1965 coup (Coppel 1976:44–63). Under the Suharto regime electoral politics was highly scripted. Since there were no Chinese political parties, nor any credible opposition parties contesting for power, Chinese political influence was wielded through the use of informal channels. Coppel (1976) refers to this as "cukong influence," which "is intended to refer to the political influence informally exercised on occasion by Chinese businessmen (or cukong) who are in close contact with Indonesian power-holders" (p. 65). He goes on to say "that members of the Chinese community who wish to see certain policies implemented by the Indonesian government or their application modified are far more likely today than earlier to try to work through these cukongs both because of their greater prevalence and because of the absence of effective alternative channels" (p. 66). For example, in the mid 1990s Liem Sioe Liong was one of the twelve richest businessmen in the world, and a close personal friend of President Suharto. As a result, Liem's Salim Group was one of the largest privileged players in Indonesia's state-driven economy (Seagrave 1995:206). Certain prominent Chinese were active in the establishment of Suharto's New Order almost from the beginning, and the role of these players both within the New Order and within Golkar (the ruling party from the late 1960s until 1999) will be discussed later in the book.[10]

In the wake of Suharto's resignation several new political parties led by Indonesian Chinese announced their formation. Likewise, with the June 7, 1999 elections there may be a renewed need to discuss electoral politics in Indonesia. Clearly, with less than 3 percent of the population, an Indonesian Chinese–based party will be forced to play a role as a coalition partner of a larger party. Nonetheless, this does provide an

opportunity for Sino-Indonesians to become more equal political players than they have been for the last thirty years.

SCHOOLS OF THOUGHT

While there may be some merits in the cultural or class approaches to
untangling the question of Chinese immigrant participation, the answer
does not lie in some inherent "Chineseness" that makes them disinter-
ested in political participation, nor does it rely solely on their socioeconomic standing. The answer is better found in looking at the rational
motivations of the political elite, both of the host society's political system
and of particular Chinese community organizations, and at how they act
within the constraints of pertinent institutions.

In answer to the question of when or under what conditions immigrants become active in the political process and what their strategies are
for doing so, three different approaches to the puzzle will be assessed: ethnic, class, and institutional theories all offer explanations for immigrant
participation.

This book's basic hypothesis is that Chinese communities participate
in politics through the mobilization efforts of community leaders when
there are political, economic, and social incentives to do so. The costs of
this orientation toward community participation will depend on existing
institutions. The type of organizations Chinese communities will form to
facilitate political incorporation will depend on the type of problems
needed to be overcome in order to achieve effective mobilization.

To explain briefly, there need to be electoral incentives for political
elites to reach out to the Chinese community for support, and community leaders must feel that their goals can be achieved through negotiation with these political leaders. In the absence of electoral incentives for
participation, either because the Chinese are too small a minority to affect
a candidate's success or because the political system does not rely on electoral contestation, then there need to be economic or social benefits to
group mobilization. Until recently, in the United States traditional Chinese associations were established to provide economic support for immigrants and to mediate business disputes in the community. This gave the
leading businessmen power and prestige within Chinatowns. There were
few incentives to work with local officials. In fact, local governments and
police often expressly told Chinatowns to regulate themselves, confer-
ring the position of "unofficial mayor" of Chinatown on the leader of the
Chinese Consolidated Benevolent Association. Now that there is a more
diversified and less Chinatown-centered economy within the Chinese
community, and since host governments provide money for social pro-

grams, the way that the Chinese community addresses the needs of its members is very different. Social service agencies learn to work effectively with different bureaucratic departments in order to secure funding for various programs. In order to maintain government support for these organizations, they need to nuture a client base that makes community organization necessary for their survival.

Ethnic approaches (exemplified in Jalali and Lipset 1992/3; Glazer and Moynihan 1963; Pye 1985; Huntington 1996; Barth 1969) can sometimes contribute to a better understanding of diasporic politicization by explaining how dominant groups create boundaries between different ethnicities which inhibit a level playing field for political incorporation. Ethnic and cultural explanations are also helpful in providing a better understanding of how attitudes and practices instilled in the homeland may affect behavior in the countries where Chinese settle. However, it then becomes difficult to explain variation among Chinese in different settings; thus approaches that rely on ethnicity as the key variable may explain only part of the dynamic at work. Likewise, social class approaches (exemplified in Verba and Nie 1972; Castles and Kosack 1973; Cerny 1982; Schmitter and Heisler 1986; and Bobo and Gilliam 1990) do an excellent job of showing the relationship between socioeconomic status and rates of political participation. Yet these works downplay the significance of institutional factors or political opportunity structures and the extent to which political elements may shape the behavior and options of community leaders in mobilizing their constituents.

According to class-based assumptions about the connection between socioeconomic status and political participation, the cases where Chinese communities are well-off should see greater participation and influence. In fact, in the overview of the cases above, there appears to be a strong relationship between socioeconomic status and influence. This work should suggest that such a view is too sanguine. While it is true that wealthy Chinese in Indonesia and Malaysia have been able to influence economic policies that affect their business interests, the tight links between business elites and government leaders has come about, in part, as a result of increased state planning in economic development.[11] Instead of focusing just on economic factors, such as growth of gross national product or levels of industrialization, it helps to look at the connection between political and economic factors. For example, one might want to understand how Chinese business growth in Malaysia and Indonesia coincided with increased involvement of state planning as a result of NEP in Malaysia and as a product of Suharto's New Order regime. Within Chinese family businesses there was a shift from internally generated funds to external borrowing and an increased dependence on state or public financing. So Chinese businesses became both more multifaceted and prosperous, and more visible. Companies that flourished often benefited from connections with political officials. Chinese have been wealthier than indigenous groups in these two cases consistently over time, yet their political behavior and levels of influence have varied. It is thus apparent that these political factors need examination.

Class standing may play a role in a threshold of participation, but it will not determine what sort of organizations the Chinese community will form, the modes of participation taken, and how successful their participatory efforts will be. Likewise, one must be wary of the assumption that immigrant organization takes place along ethnic or class lines. Ethnic-based organization, as mentioned above, may be as much an end product of how dominant groups "create" or reinforce minorities by ascribing them certain characteristics based on loose ties (Glazer and Moynihan 1963). Often the first national identity that many immigrants experience develops in the host country (Handlin 1951; Lee, R. 1986). For example, ethnic Chinese from Malaysia, Vietnam, Singapore, and the People's Republic of China have all immigrated to the United States. Once in the United States they become "relabled" as Chinese Americans. Based on these assigned groupings it is not unusual that immigrant groups would form informal and formal cultural and self-help organizations based on ethnic background. However, this "group" need not organize politically along ethnic lines. There are as many splits within the Chinese communities as within the host society at large: language differences; occupational, educational, and economic variation; splits between older and newer immigrants; and vast differences between those immigrating from Taiwan, the People's Republic, and Hong Kong. When they do organize effectively to participate politically, this work argues, it is because host-society institutions provide the framework for them to do so. That is, "host-society institutions have nurtured ethnicity through their policies and practices" (Ireland 1994:10).

This has been especially true in Southeast Asia. Postcolonial states have based their economic development on a successful "combination of democratic legitimization with bureaucratic-authoritarian political control" (Brown, D. 1994:28). This has resulted in a powerful state apparatus that not only controls the economic development process but also shapes the standing and position of different groups in society. For regimes in Malaysia and Indonesia, transnational links have long been suspect as a source of destabilizing influences. This has led to what Brown terms a "garrison mentality" (1994:86), with state measures enacted to ensure that the political loyalties of ethnic Chinese lie within the nation-state rather than the ancestral homeland. The ideologies, policies, and practices of nationalism and state-building in Southeast Asia have thus sought to filter what flows from the outside world to local citizens. At the same time these states have attempted "to accommodate, manage or manipulate" ethnic and religious affiliations within their plural societies so as to control issues that might threaten the survival of the state (Brown 1994:28). In sum, there are remarkable cross-national differences in how diasporan Chinese live in Southeast Asia and the United States. This suggests that the state ideologies, policies, and practices continue to influence and shape how minority populations are incorporated politically.

METHODOLOGY

The case studies are based on fieldwork conducted in Southeast Asia during fall and winter 1996–1997, and on work done in California and New York throughout 1997. In addition to primary source material such as local newspapers and government documents, interviews were conducted with community leaders and local officeholders to get a better sense of what the needs and interests were in each locale. Although there are clear differences in the political strategies and tactics of the Chinese communities studied here, comparative analysis shows that there are distinct patterns that can be discerned.

The cases were chosen because in each place Chinese community leaders are faced with a similar strategic problem: they face uncertainty in the political climate of their adopted countries. Will the Chinese be persecuted or discriminated against, or will they be accorded the same rights and status as other citizens? Both Indonesia and peninsular Malaysia faced colonial regimes that used ethnic criteria to divide and segregate inhabitants. Likewise, both Indonesia and Malaysia faced communist insurgencies at the time of independence and have a history of scapegoating the Chinese minority. In choosing to study Monterey Park and New York City's Chinatown, one can compare communities that share a common challenge in overcoming America's history of keeping minorities on the margins of political contestation. Similarly, in all cases political-minded elites also face competition from within the community from those who believe that the Chinese are better off staying removed from political incorporation with the host society and polity. Given that these inward-looking leaders may be part of an older sojourner diaspora who looked toward Taiwan or mainland China as "home," or as a place they intended to return to, the new generation of elites' assumption of leadership is predicated on them developing the support of the community.

This requires that they can provide for their constituents' needs. Leaders are split into two distinguishable groups: social service elites and business leaders. Business leaders[12] are better positioned to effect influence in the political process, but this does not necessarily result in greater political participation from the community as a group. Social service elites' position rests with meeting the needs of the community through the provision of social benefits and services; this gives them a basis (and often a mandate) for facilitating politicization of Chinese Americans. Yet this mobilization does not necessarily lead to influence. Because not-for-profit agencies receiving government money are required to be nonpartisan, there are severe limits as to the types of political behavior that they can sponsor. For example, they can hold candidate forums, but not endorse any particular party or candidate. These limitations impact the degree of influence that might be achieved, despite efforts at increasing community politicization. These divergent outcomes can be explained in two ways: the first emphasizes the role and motivations of elites, while the other points to consequences of political institutions on their actions.

Before moving on to discuss the framework of this study, it is useful to return to some basic concepts and a discussion of variables addressed in the following chapters. In addition to looking at political participation, this work also uses the term "politicization." As it is used here, politicization pertains to both an awareness of group interests, and to the actions of the community in impacting the selection of government officeholders and the actions they take (Verba and Nie 1972). While politicization is similar to political participation, action directed toward influencing the distribution of social goods and social values,[13] it aims to encompass the community organization necessary to induce participatory events, rather than only trying to estimate individual-level action from aggregate data.[14] Such activities might include holding meetings to plan citizenship and voter registration drives, as well as the more conventional modes of behavior: getting out the vote, holding fund-raisers, and engaging in lobbying or protest activity. Politicization in this study is largely the dependent variable. It may be a function of the following factors: the background and position of Chinese leaders and the nature of the political institutions that shape their interaction with the community, and, to a lesser extent, the percentage of the population that is of Chinese ancestry, their socioeconomic status, their eligibility to vote and partake of political behaviors, and the number of generations that they have lived in the host country. The manner and degree to which the Chinese participate in politics also serves as the independent variable when examining the extent of influence achieved by the community.

Influence is the dependent variable when the effects of politicization are evaluated. Influence can be determined by several indicators: there is the "proximity to power" standard illustrated by levels of representation or close personal ties with crucial figures; successful achievement of benefits for the group through policy outcomes; and at the most basic level, the protection of fundamental rights otherwise enjoyed by the dominant segment of the population. Since there is no absolute standard for measuring influence, one must look at the relative power of different actors in the political sphere and at how well they are able to achieve their goals. In this book, influence will be evaluated within and across cases. Loosely using Dahl's (1970) framework, a paradigm for any comparison of power or influence might be as follows: the Chinese community is more/less influential in one political system versus another with respect to achieving community interests (Dahl 1970:34). In each case study, material from the fieldwork is used to illustrate the interests and goals of the community, and the extent to which the community has been successful in having their interests met is analyzed in each case. The field of political science has an extremely difficult time "proving" influence. One cannot be sure that a policy outcome is the result of specific lobbying attempts, contributions, or desires of constituents. Unless government officials state exactly why they support and choose a particular policy, it is impossible to know if their action is based on their own beliefs about the policy issue, or if they have been swayed because of other factors or players. In the absence of concrete evidence about what "influenced" a certain political outcome, we can follow an issue over time (such as education policy in Malaysia) and draw conclusions about how and why certain actions that affect the Chinese community are taken.

CONCLUSION

Where political institutions are hostile to Chinese communal activity, influence is greater than in places where collective action brings political rewards. This can be explained by the fact that in less-open political systems efforts at individual networking may bring more substantial rewards. In more transparent systems, democratic theory assumes that there needs to be group mobilization to achieve community influence, a difficult task in an ethnic group with internal divisions. The organizations Chinese communities will form to facilitate political incorporation are adaptive mechanisms directly responsive to members' needs and to the demands of the encapsulating political system.

The research here shows that participation is not necessarily predicated on either cultural or class status, but rather on institutional or electoral incentives that increase the likelihood of community mobilization by elites. While the Chinese in both Indonesia and peninsular Malaysia are predominantly situated in the middle- and upper-class segments of the two societies, their modes of participation and effective influence are very different. In Indonesia under Suharto, formal participation was low and influence levels disproportionately high. In Malaysia levels of participation are somewhat lower for Malaysian Chinese than for Malays, and their influence has diminished since the time of Independence. Chinese participate in electoral politics at greater rates when both the ruling coalition parties and opposition parties are seriously vying for their votes. While wealthy Chinese in Malaysia may have been able to protect some of their economic interests, their political influence as a group is moderate and highly dependent on the needs of UMNO during electoral contests. While the Malay dominate the bureaucratic organs of government, the Chinese community still controls vast sums of capital necessary for economic development, and can be mobilized for electoral support. The difference between Indonesia and Malaysia is found in understanding the institutional contexts of the two host societies. In Indonesia under Suharto there were clear economic incentives to work through personal connections for individual economic gain. In a community that is divided between Chinese who have been in Indonesia for generations and those who arrived within their lifetime, those with citizenship status and those without, it is highly difficult to organize communally, and there are few social rewards for championing group rights. In Malaysia, as Horowitz illustrates, there are clear political and economic incentives for Malaysian Chinese Association (MCA) leaders to work within the ruling coalition, even if this means a lesser degree of influence on the politics in the nation as a whole.

The Chinese communities in Indonesia, Malaysia, and the United States neither are apathetic about politics nor are they united in their political goals. Objectives range from protection from rioting and looting in Indonesia to greater representation of group interests in the United States and Malaysia. There is a sense, in the United States and to a lesser extent in Malaysia, that greater political participation and activity will facilitate achieving these goals. Yet this research will suggest that participation alone may not be the most effective way to achieve greater influence. Divisions within these communities may prevent solidarity within the diasporic Chinese, but that does not mean that there is not some basic level of agreement on membership within the group, and that there are certain political and economic goals that *are* shared, such as access to higher education and rights to protect private property and businesses. Ultimately, it also matters how the dominant group defines outsiders. As long as Chinese are considered immigrant populations, they will to some degree constitute a community for purposes of political incorporation.

IMPLICATIONS

This analysis draws much from, and perhaps contributes to, a variety of literature from comparative and American political science. In these fields the role of marginal segments of the population and the nature of institutions and democracy have continually come to the forefront of debates. Immigrant incorporation into the political life of their adopted countries is part of the test as to how well a society copes with diversity. For both democracies and nondemocracies it is vital to understand how groups interact with the mechanisms of power and with each other.

The other important implication of this work for all three nations is how internal relations with Chinese immigrant populations affect the nations' foreign policy with the People's Republic of China. Chinese overseas communities in Southeast Asia have long been suspected of communist sympathies and insurgent organizations. In the case of Indonesia, these charges have been largely propagated as a mechanism of scapegoating a minority population in times of political turmoil. In Malaysia, there was significant Chinese support for the Malaysian Communist Party up through the 1950s, but the more current political issue is the continuation of the Malaysian Chinese as "haves" and the Malays as "have-nots." Rapid economic development and now economic crisis, as well as sparks of growing Chinese military interest in the South China Seas, have caused most Southeast Asian nations to worry about economic competition from China and its possible designs on regional hegemony. That Chinese overseas have played such a large role in economic investments and development in China and Hong Kong may give Southeast Asian governments cause for alarm. This is often reflected in policies and treatment of Chinese living abroad.

PLAN

This work is divided into several segments. Chapter Two looks at the competing explanations in more detail and further analyzes "new institutionalism" and its applications for this study. Chapters Three through Seven present the case studies: peninsular Malaysia, Indonesia, Monterey Park, California, and New York City. Chapter Eight summarizes and offers concluding remarks with a further discussion of the larger implications stemming from this research.

2

Theoretical Approaches
to Understanding
Political Participation and Influence

PRELIMINARY ANSWERS

At first glance there is a surprising degree of consensus in the literature on immigrant participation. In pointing to the factors that cause various groups to become involved in the politics of their host societies, there are two standard reasons given. First, participatory attitudes and behavior develop in stages: there is a shift from temporary migration, or sojourning, to permanent settlement. New groups eventually acquire the language and knowledge necessary to enter the political arena (Handlin 1951; Piore 1979; Ireland 1994). This process has been likened to acclimatization or assimilation. Second, groups might be drawn into the political fray if there is an intensification of discrimination, or threats thereof. If Chinese communities have not adapted culturally to the countries where they reside, one might reasonably understand why they are also removed from the political fray. However, if they are fairly well acculturated with the "indigenous" population (this term will be explained shortly) then one might expect that they would participate in politics to the same degree as other citizens. Thus one of the first tasks of this chapter is to assess to what extent Chinese have become acculturated or assimilated with the populations of Indonesia, Malaysia, and the United States.

ACCULTURATION

Acculturation, as it is used in this paper, is indicated by the adoption of the local language, the indigenization of names, the adaptation of cultural practices, and the possibility of intermarriage. Sociologists, particularly American sociologists, have studied at length questions of immigrant assimilation or acculturation. Early studies posited a normative transition where distinct groups of immigrants became subsumed or absorbed by (superior) "American" values and culture. This was the classic myth of the American melting pot. The phrase "melting pot" was coined by Israel Zangwill in his 1908 play of the same name. Zangwill saw America as a land in which newer groups would meld with those already here into an indigenous "American type." His usage implies both a biological and a cultural merging of the old and new Americans.

The concept of this mixing, however, came to refer to a unidirectional process in which immigrants (European ones) would adopt characteristics of the dominant Anglo-American character. Immigrant groups would arrive on U.S. shores and gradually lose their distinctive ways as they learned English, went to school, and adopted Anglo-American values.[1] This sort of analysis came under attack in the 1950s and 1960s as larger numbers of immigrants to the United States came from places outside Europe. More pluralist models of assimilation evolved. Among these, American sociologist Milton Gordon's (1964) work is particularly comprehensive. Gordon differentiates acculturation from assimilation and Americanization. He sees acculturation as the first stage of assimilation, where a minority group's cultural and behavioral traits become more in line with the dominant group's.[2] For Gordon, structural assimilation, defined as the large-scale entrance into cliques, clubs, and institutions of the host society, is the key criteria in assessing if a minority community has been "assimilated." Acculturation may occur without a further process of assimilation taking place. In the 1960s, Gordon finds that acculturation by many immigrant groups had taken place in America, but not further assimilation.[3]

Glazer and Moynihan (1963), instead of searching for some sign of Anglo-American conformity, as Gordon does, argue that subcultures within both immigrant and more established populations evolve, and groups adapt and are recreated. Using this sort of cultural adaptation approach, Eileen Tamura studies Japanese incorporation into American life in Hawaii (1994). Tamura uses acculturation to highlight cultural adaptation where a Japanese identity is maintained even while the second, third, and fourth generations of Japanese Americans have incorporated American culture and values into their sense of belonging. In this analysis, cultural adaptation is not the same as Americanization, because she finds that Japanese Americans in Hawaii have maintained a distinct sense of their Japanese heritage.[4]

There is a great deal of anthropological literature on cultural maintenance and change, particularly on how cultural practices have changed when faced with new stimuli, such as modern media and communications (newspapers, radio, TV, etc.), global commerce, and urbanization, to name a few of the forces at work. Having stated that culture (and with it, perhaps identity) is malleable, it is important to note that new ethnic or cultural consciousnesses are not formed in response to every new situational factor. Certainly individuals and communities are influenced by affiliations and relationships, by external society and political agencies and norms; however, such elements may only "modify the boundaries or strength or political salience of a prior communal consciousness, rather than creating it anew"(Brown 1994:5). Perhaps most appropriate for this study is the recent wave of scholarship that addresses the concept of diaspora. Such work tackles questions of identity and culture within a context of displacement, migration, and transculturation. Diasporic peoples are viewed in contrast to the territorially based "indigenous" inhabitants, whose identity and culture are often designed or at least reinforced by nation-states.[5] Thus American and Southeast Asian Chinese identity can be seen in relation to legal categories of "citizen" or "native" (the terms for native peoples in Malaysia is *bumiputra,* and in Indonesia it is *pribumi*), where ethnic identity is a political category.

ACCULTURATION IN THE UNITED STATES

In the United States, as the chapters on New York City and Monterey Park will explain, Chinese Americans have been singled out for discriminatory treatment in immigration and repeatedly have had their loyalty and "Americanness" questioned. There are no legal prohibitions against keeping or changing one's name or intermarriage, and rates of both are quite high. Chinese Americans defy easy categorization as maintaining a homeland culture or as acculturated or assimilated. Of the three countries studied here, the United States is the only place where immigration from China, Hong Kong, and Taiwan (and immigration by ethnic Chinese from a third country) still continues and where the Chinese community's population is increasing rapidly. While some Chinese Americans are clearly well acculturated into American society, this adaptation or adoption of cultural characteristics has not necessarily translated into greater participatory action from the community at large. In addition, recent political events in the United States clearly highlight that for even the most assimilated Chinese American, political scapegoating and discrimination occurs. When the Democratic National Committee suspected that some contributions to the 1996 campaign had come from non-U.S. citizens, they returned contributions to a list of Chinese-surnamed DNC donors, even if an overwhelmingly large percentage of those donors were U.S. citizens eligible to give political contributions.

ACCULTURATION ON THE MALAYSIAN PENINSULA

Despite having immigrated more than one hundred years ago, Chinese in Malaysia have maintained a distinct Chinese identity and culture. They are less "acculturated" than Chinese in neighboring countries of Southeast Asia such as Thailand[6] and the Philippines. In Malaysia one has both a cultural and an ethnic identity, and both categorizations serve to delineate members of different groups. The political system reinforces this duel distinction in the way that it separates political parties and many educational institutions. Likewise, stories and practices, patterns of art, ritual, plays, literature, and so forth, link groups to their heritage. These culturally specific histories and practices differ from nations where an officially promulgated narrative describes a common heritage of those who belong to the same territory.[7] In Malaysia, the "common heritage" is the colonial past and the goal of economic growth and prosperity for the future.[8]

From independence in the 1950s until the early 1990s the colonial past was downplayed in an effort to "Malayanize" the country. This ethnicization impacted how Chinese and Indian citizens were incorporated into the larger polity and society. While these two groups are in theory equal players in the political system, in effect they are junior partners of the dominate Malay party—United Malays National Organization (UMNO). That each group is clustered together within an ethnic party only serves to reinforce their separateness despite political slogans promoting unity and a "Malaysian" identity. It is not surprising, then, that Chinese and Indians are less politically active than the dominant Malays and that their political power is highly circumscribed.

SINO-INDONESIAN ACCULTURATION

Of the Chinese of the three countries studied here, the Indonesian Chinese are the most acculturated. Chinese began coming to what is now Indonesia in the sixteenth and seventeenth centuries. Indonesian Chinese are roughly divided into *peranakan* and *totok*. *Peranakan* are Chinese who have been in Indonesia for generations, some dating back to the 1600s. The word *peranakan* suggests mixed heritage and culture. Some *peranakan* may have had *pribumi* mothers and nearly all *peranakan* families adopted elements of Indies culture. Use of the term *peranakan* implies the use of Indonesian as the language spoken at home. What sets the *peranakan* of Indonesia apart from assimilated descendants of Chinese immigrants in Thailand or the Philippines is Dutch colonial policy which segregated the Chinese from the native population in a myriad of ways (this will be discussed at greater length in the chapter on Indonesia). *Totok* Chinese are those who immigrated toward the end of the nineteenth century and in the twentieth century, and who have retained the use of Chinese language, dress, and customs. Another important distinction between *peranakan* and *totok* has to do with their place in Indonesia's political economy. *Peranakan* elite by the nineteenth and early twentieth century had become landowners, revenue farmers, sugar planters, and officials, while *totoks* developed niches in retail and trade networks.

> To the present, the Totoks have continued to emphasize business and self-employment, while the *Peranakan*s drift, if they can, into white-collar occupations. In colonial times, if natives were favored for government positions, *Peranakan*s found themselves as office employees of private firms, foremen for mines and plantations, and with the expansion of the Western education system, in the professions. (Pan 1999:158)

If assimilation or acculturation was the key to political incorporation, one might find high degrees of political incorporation of Indonesian Chinese with the larger Indonesian polity. However, under Suharto this was not the situation. Acculturated or assimilated Indonesian Chinese who had once played a significant role in variety of political parties and action groups were sidelined under Suharto. Interestingly, those with the most political influence during Suharto's New Order regime were *totok* businessmen. So on the surface it does not seem that the degree to which a community is acculturated will impact its political activity or influence. This is something that will be evaluated in more detail when we get to the individual case studies. First we need to turn to other possible explanations for active political participation.

The second explanation for mobilization of a minority community into politics is that persecution pushes them into it. There is little doubt that discrimination can cause a group to unify in order to combat a threat from outside the community. However, this alone cannot explain when and how a group will participate. In Malaysia the violence that occurred in 1969 against the Chinese did not prompt Malaysian Chinese to be more active politically. In fact, one could argue that the opposite occurred. After the spring riots, Chinese acquiesced to Malay leaders' decision to cast the riots as having an economic root rather than a political cause, thus allowing the passage of policies meant to discriminate against the Chinese.

In Indonesia, the Chinese suffered from being the targets of riots, demonstrations, and violence throughout Suharto's regime. Nonetheless, it took Suharto's resignation to prompt Sino-Indonesians to take a more formal and more prominent step of forming new political parties and advocacy groups to assert their interests.

Outside of these two explanations, there are roughly three theoretical approaches used to understand group political mobilization; the first emphasizes social-class characteristics, the second, ethnic or cultural features, and the third points to institutional factors (Ireland 1994:5) as the cause for political involvement. Despite these typologies, as Ireland notes, few efforts have been made to test propositions empirically or to provide a more comprehensive theoretical context to explain the nature of diasporic politics. This chapter will discuss each of these three approaches in turn and will assess their utility in reaching a better understanding of ethnic politicization.

SOCIOECONOMIC STATUS

Social-class-based approaches to immigrant political participation take the group's socioeconomic status as the independent variable in determining participation and influence in the political arena, and there are several variations of this view. Scholars such as Castles and Kosack (1973), Cerny (1982), and Schmitter and Heisler (1986) use a Marxist or neo-Marxist framework to show how capitalism's need for cheap labor, a pull factor in immigration, has resulted in the creation of an underclass made up of marginalized newcomers. Their marginalization thus shapes the immigrant's entry, or lack of, into politics. In support of such an argument, Schmitter and Heisler (1986) discuss how immigrant groups often work in the low-paying, arduous, frequently dirty, or dangerous occupations that native populations disdain. Neo-Marxists like Cerny (1982) view immigrant participation as part of a process whereby indigenous and foreign laborers can find common ground based on their similar class interests. In these approaches race, ethnicity, or immigrant status have become surface categories in which the state has been able to split the working class into fragmented groups, thus "the strategies of business and the state determine whether ethnic and class consciousness are in conflict or reinforce each other, as well as which political tactics are necessary" (Ireland 1994:6). This sort of approach exemplifies a type of analysis that "find(s) the origins of immigrant politics in the structural tensions and contradictions of advanced capitalist society" (ibid.). It assumes that the type of organizations that will be formed in the immigrant community will correspond to the newcomers' position in the economic hierarchy. This sort of analysis, on the surface, should provide a model for Chinese political mobilization in U.S. cities. Newer Chinese immigrants in New York, Los Angeles, and other urban settings have entered the economic system on some of the lowest rungs of the ladder. Chinese immigrants, now as it was one hundred years ago, often work in garment factories, restaurants, and laundries. Poorer Chinese immigrants in the United States often share neighborhoods with other working-class groups, namely Latinos. However, there has been little political organization along class lines either within the Chinese community or across ethnic groups.

Interestingly, Peter Kwong's (1979, 1996) work on Chinatown in New York finds that the splits within the community are largely along class lines, yet this still does not result in political organization that reflects such interests. Economic elites who control the dense web of family and kinship associations maintain their position of privilege by keeping the community internally focused and by emphasizing that disputes should be solved through communal mediation rather than through local government institutions, such as litigation in appropriate courts.

> The purpose of the code of silence is to prevent residents from obtaining help from the larger society. Under the informal political system, working people will not get a fair settlement: in a labor/management dispute, the Chinese elite will side with management. However, when the establishment itself is threatened, the code of silence is not binding; the CCBA might turn an opponent over to the Immigration and Naturalization Service or to the police; the elite monopolizes the community's access to the outside world. (Kwong 1996:95)

While Kwong describes the rise of a new social service elite, he views these leaders, who are mostly second-generation professionals, as only marginally helpful in addressing some social problems in Chinatown. So far, he argues, they have not changed the political power structure within Chinatown (1996:132).

A non-Marxist variant of this class-based argument can be found in the works of John Horton (1992) and Louise Lamphere (1992). Horton looks at the increasing political involvement of the Chinese-American community in Monterey Park, California. He shows how evident economic and demographic restructuring affected the political relationship between newcomers and established residents. The battle for political power in Monterey Park centered around the issue of development and land use. As the percentage of Asians in the population grew and the number of better-educated and wealthy Asians increased in the area, the greater their power in local politics became. Lamphere asks the question, "Are political and economic structures being transformed by immigrants or are institutions merely reproducing older patterns of class, power and segregation?" (1992: 5) She tries to argue that until structures of mediating institutions change, immigrants will remain disempowered. However, Horton describes a situation in Monterey Park where Chinese immigrant groups are able, by virtue of their numerical percentage in the population and wealth, to use existing institutions to their advantage as they become the dominant class. Thus the crucial factor is not that they have changed institutions per se but that the existing institutional structure has been conducive to increased Chinese participation and influence. This finding, if correct, would correlate with what most of American politics literature argues about who participates in the political arena: those with high levels of education and high socioeconomic status. This is discussed below.

In fact, this is not necessarily played out in Monterey Park, California, or in Malaysia, where Chinese have higher levels of education, and higher incomes than other groups (when compared with Latinos in the Los Angeles area and ethnic Malays in Malaysia), yet they vote at lower rates than these groups.

Chinese communities overseas have often been compared to Jewish groups: economically significant but often blamed for a country's problems and persecuted. Like the Jews, Chinese overseas are often small percentages of the population—Malaysia is of course an exception to this—and are viewed as outsiders. Despite these similarities, Jews (in the United States) have some of the highest rates of political participation of any ethnic group. How might this be explained? This comparison merits a short digression. In applying a pluralist model of interest groups, where public policy is an outcome of the free play of group pressures, Mitchell Bard (1988) looks at the influence of the Arab and Israeli lobbies in the making of foreign policy. He finds that pro-Israel groups are more successful than pro-Arab ones. The so-called "Jewish lobby" is made up of AIPAC (American Israel Public Affairs Committee), and a formal lobby group, community organizations such as B'nai B'rith and Hadassah, which do not lobby but are involved in disseminating information and encouraging members to become involved in the political process. Additionally, there are less organized forms of Jewish political activity: voting and impacting public opinion. Bard finds that the Israel lobby enjoys extensive influence and can be viewed as powerful because it has relative access, resources, cohesion, size, social status, and leadership over competing groups. He notes that Jews, although a small percentage of the U.S. population (3 percent, or just under six million), are generally well-off economically and have the highest rate of voter turnout of any ethnic group, and 89 percent of Jewish Americans live in twelve key electoral states (Bard 1988:59). While Bard does not distinguish between class, ethnic, or institutional reasons for pro-Israeli group effectiveness, his analysis implies that status variables play a significant role in their success.

Like Jews in the United States, Chinese tend to live in politically important states. Despite this similarity between Jewish and Chinese diasporas, there may be one significant difference that needs to be studied. The socialization processes through which individuals acquire their civic attitudes clearly varies from group to group. Research on Chinese communities shows that socioeconomic status alone does not impact rates of politicization; however, economic status may be a more important variable when influence is examined. Influence may be achieved because of an individual's socioeconomic status rather than because of a shift in the groups' relative position in society. What neither Horton nor Lamphere discuss about the Chinese groups in Monterey Park is how ethnic organizations within the community played a role in channeling the interests of the group outward into the political arena of the town as a whole.

In the now classic study of participation in American politics, Verba and Nie find that social status determines how much an individual will participate in the political process. The degree to which an individual participates is mediated by the intervening effect of their civic attitudes and the structure of relevant institutions (Verba and Nie 1972:13–14). While they are less interested in the reasons for individual citizen participation than in ways that participation conditions the manner in which political decisions are made, Verba and Nie find that even once the legal impediments to participation are removed, political involvement is not equal. Some people participate more than others, and in the United States there is a class bias in participation (1972:12, 132).

Lester W. Milbrath (1965) also makes broad generalizations about the relationship between socioeconomic status and the increased likelihood of participation. He finds that those who are active in community affairs are more apt to be politically active. A later study by Bobo and Gilliam (1990) on race and sociopolitical participation finds that group consciousness stimulates heightened black participation, even in communities of lower socioeconomic standing. In reading these two studies, Milbrath's from 1965 and Bobo and Gilliam's from 1990, and trying to apply their findings to Chinese overseas participation, we run into a puzzle. Chinese communities overseas are known for the dense webs of community associations that have existed, and many individuals in the communities are active in these organizations. So, too, there is a real sense of identity and difference in Chinese communities outside China. Why, then, are they not more politically active? These variables do not seem to help explain low rates of political participation. Perhaps, as Milbrath notes, the same actions may have different implications in different places. For example, joining a political party in the United States is not the same as joining a political party in Indonesia (Milbrath 1965:19).

So how do social class approaches fare in addressing the questions asked here? The answer to when Chinese communities will be motivated to participate in the political process would be, for Marxists, when they find common cause with other groups. Immigrant groups would form cross-ethnic organizations to overcome the "divide and rule" strategy of the dominant group potentially to win influence. They will be successful in influencing the political process when the objective conditions and contradictions of capitalism are over turned. Alternatively, individual Chinese will participate at greater rates if they have higher levels of income and education. As the following chapters will show, these conditions are not found in Indonesia, Malaysia, or the United States.

Even if all the members of the community voted in elections, it is possible that the group still might not be able to wield political influence (this statement is applicable to the United States at the national level, New York at the local level, and to Indonesian politics). This is because ethnic Chinese generally make up only a small proportion of the population. Malaysia is obviously an exception to this. However there are clearly other means of participation that might result in pronounced effects on policy. From the earlier example of the Jewish lobby in the United States it seems possible that the Chinese could have potential clout through interest or action groups. But there is a further complication. Because Chinese overseas communities are often small numerically, they may not gain the attention of politicians seeking office. If office-seekers do not reach out to a sector of the electorate, then that constituency is less likely to vote. To explain this another way, political participation may be related to whether politicians or political parties reach out to or mobilize voters.

The Chinese will form organizations perhaps because they are too small a percentage of the population to be a target of political party mobilization; thus any efficacy at the political lobbying game would have to be through an interest-group type of organization (Hansen 1991:225–227). While there are obviously extensive debates over how successfully to influence the political process, social-class approaches to participation might be bolstered by works such as Schnattschneider (1935) and Truman (1971), where influence is a by-product of powerful groups that are large, well endowed, and well ordered. These interest groups are favored and others ignored. Hansen (1991) offers a further refinement of this.

Interest-group influence results from elected officials' strategies for deal-ing with electoral uncertainty. A group can wield power when two con-ditions are met: the group enjoys comparative advantage over rivals in meeting reelection needs, and legislators expect the issues and circum-stances that created the comparative advantage to recur (Hansen 1991:5).

ETHNIC OR CULTURAL APPROACHES

Ethnic or cultural approaches assume that the immigrants' identity as a distinct ethnic or religious group is of fundamental importance to under-standing their role in the political process. The myriad of disputes that are classified as ethnic or cultural, such as the wars in Bosnia and Kosovo, unrest in India, and continued strife in Northern Ireland, illus-trate the enduring importance of understanding the significance of group identity and how it can be manipulated for political ends. Many scholars point to the particular traits of a group as the defining characteristic in understanding their participation in the political arena (Glazer and Moynihan 1963; Jalali and Lipset 1992/93; Huntington 1996). This has been the dominant approach used in studying the Chinese diaspora in Southeast Asia.

Freedman (1962), and Crissman (1967) argue that the overall organi-zation of Chinese communities throughout Southeast Asia is based on distinctly "Chinese" characteristics. These classic studies of the Chinese overseas look at the dense networks of kinship associations and posit that Chinese organizations are based on similar groups found on mainland China. While it was certainly true that village life in China, especially southern China before 1949, was organized around lineage groupings, this was less true for urban or trading areas. Likewise, there is extensive variation in where these networks have been recreated and what role they have played in governing the community or in serving as a broker between Chinese communities and the host society.

This argument is supported by Winzeler (1986) and others, who find that in fact Chinese organizations vary considerably depending on what country is studied, whether the Chinese community in question is rural or urban, and how acculturated the community is with the larger society. For example, ethnic Chinese associations in rural Kelantan, Malaysia, are relatively few in number and they play more of a social and economic role rather than a political or brokerage role (Winzeler 1986:141). Where Chinese have been less integrated with the dominant groups, their orga-nizations tend to have more autonomy from the host political system and have more sway within the community. Thus the extent that Chinese form vibrant associational groupings (which are the internal apparatus of political organization) is less a function of ethnicity and more a function of other variables.

Lucian Pye (1985) views politics and the role of leaders and followers as culturally determined by beliefs about the nature of power. He examines the differences in perception about power and the origins of the state in several countries in Asia. He claims that Asians idealize authority and that particular cultural patterns may help or hinder modernization (pp. 23–45). In discussing Malaysian politics, Pye argues that ethnic problems have produced a frail polity where the cardinal rule is to avoid controversy that might inflame the people. Political rhetoric is about nation-building and development in order to legitimize the government and "peace." He says, "The Malays resemble the Indonesians and the Thai in eschewing harshness and seeking gentleness and refinement in human relations" (p. 249). This view overlooks two critical points. First, a focus on economic development as a national goal in Indonesia and Malaysia provided political legitimacy to regimes which reinforced ethnic chauvinism and ethnic inequalities. Second, cultural traits can be manipulated for political ends which may result in tragic consequences, for example the 1969 race riots in Malaysia and the riots and assaults against Indonesian Chinese in 1998.

Pye views the Chinese and Malay cultures as antagonistic in that they deal differently with anxiety, power, and authority. He argues that the tendency of Chinese organizations both in Southeast Asia and in the United States is to shield members from the rest of society so that the inability of Chinese overseas to mobilize politically is accounted for by community leaders' culturally disposed inward focus (pp. 251–252). Although the economic initiatives of Mahathir's government have benefited Chinese and Malay alike, the affirmative action–like policies have raised consciousness and identity of Malays, making the political and cultural distinction between Malay and Chinese more pronounced. Pye is more interested in what he sees as cultural traits of each group as contributing factors to political organization, and for the Chinese this results in a perpetuation of their status as minor players. He argues that Asian dependency culture reproduces childlike conditions of a need for authority and guidance that make authoritarian rule "more endurable" (p. 329). Pye's analysis cannot explain why Chinese overseas communities do participate, but in different ways. For example, there is little discussion about the differences between Malaysian Chinese supporters of the established party, the Malaysian Chinese Association (MCA), and those who favor the Democratic Action Party (DAP), which is a significant opposition party made up mostly of urban Chinese. Pye's cultural framework provides only a justification for the current arrangement of strongman/one party-dominant rule in Malaysia, not an explanation of how the institutions or organizations play a role in either maintaining or breaking down ethnic borders and in facilitating or hampering participation.

Other approaches to studying culture are useful for this project. Barth's (1969) prominent work is more promising for this study in that the focus moves from a description and history of ethnic groups to ethnic boundaries and boundary maintenance. Barth views membership in a group as self-ascribed and as a sharing of cultural values. Culture is not static; it is the dependent variable where the boundary defines the group, not the culture that it encloses. In Malaysia, Indonesia, and the United States, ethnic minorities like the Chinese, are defined by their difference from the dominant group. In this respect, one of the crucial things to study about the Chinese communities overseas is the myriad of organizations established for economic, political, and cultural goals, as well as the socio-economic status of the group, not just because they should be indicators of civic-mindedness, but because they serve as conduits for culture and for socialization. In ethnic or cultural approaches it is natural that immigrants organize and articulate political interests along group lines. What is notable about Barth's argument is that it is not so much the cultural values and practices themselves which impact political behavior, but it is the way that the differences between groups are treated that shapes political actions. Each group's mode of participation has developed from its socialization process within the host country rather than being directly imported from the home country. Ireland builds on Barth's work when he writes:

> Reflecting organizational characteristics developed both before and after emigration, therefore, each of the ethnic groups constituting a given host society's foreign population should exhibit a unique participatory pattern. The immigrants' particular participatory strategies depend on the organizational proclivities of each national group and on its interaction with those of other immigrant groups and the host society. Hence, the ethnicity theory predicts those immigrants of the same nationality or regional background in different host societies will adopt roughly similar forms of participation. (Ireland 1994:8)

Only part of Ireland's assertion seems to ring true: that immigrant participatory strategy depends on the ethnic-based organizations in reaction to others and the host society's institutions. I have not found that this broad relationship results in the adoption of "roughly the same forms of participation" across systems. I have not found that Chinese overseas communities form the same type of organizations in different settings. Similarly, organizational characteristics developed after emigration vary widely in their goals and degree of their political activity.

Cultural approaches provide interesting answers to my concerns here in addressing when a group will be motivated to participate and why its members form the organizational structures that they do, ethnic/cultural approaches look to the immigrant group's experience and practice prior to resettlement (Erie 1988:8). In addition to Steven Erie's work, one can also refer to works by Edward Banfield, James Q. Wilson, and Daniel Patrick Moynihan. Moynihan in particular argues that early-nineteenth-century village life in Ireland laid the foundation for Irish participation through the democratic party machine in U.S. cities.

Ethnic or cultural approaches rely on the nature of civic attitudes derived from a particular culture to understand when one culture will be democratically inclined (Almond 1963). Whether or not communal organizations take the same form in China and in the countries of the diaspora, these institutions certainly shape how and how successfully the Chinese may access the political arena. These organizations, as well as the cultural practices of the communities they represent, are also impacted by state policies and institutions.

David Brown's (1994) work takes a different approach to the "resilience" of ethnicity (p. 5). Instead of ethnicity either as a primordial given or as a situational construct, he finds that ethnic attachment stems from its ability to provide psychological benefits, as would a notion of ethnicity as ideology. As such, ethnicity as ideology provides a psychological formula that mitigates the uncertainties of state-society relations.

> This explanation as to the psychological power of the ethnic attachment provides the basis for explaining the widespread appeal of the political ideology of ethnic nationalism, which translates each of the psychological mechanisms of the kinship myth into legitimatory symbols. (1949:9)

More simply, ethnicity can be manipulated by political elites to mobilize people into ethnonationalist movements or it can nurture the understanding that such divisions are "natural" within society. With or without the negative implications of ethnonationalism, one should not underestimate the importance of communal institutions and informal networks as a means of preserving ethnic identities. Thus in Malaysia and Indonesia the regime can manipulate an ideology of a dominant cultural community that might then be used to legitimate the political order. This use of culture for political purposes has its roots in precolonial history and was reinforced or reconstituted during colonial rule and at independence.

As Nonini (1997) argues, "transnational practices of modern Chinese persons cannot be understood separately from the cultural politics of identities inscribed on them by such regimes[9] in the spaces they traverse and reside in." Through accounts by male, middle-class Chinese, he explores how Chinese seek to transcend these regimes while also being able to navigate them to create practices and transnational family networks of their own.

While Nonini looks at individuals within Malaysian society, this work focuses on the specific policies and institutions that impact and to a certain extent define the Chinese overseas. The political apparatus reflects a desire to manage ethnic cleavages, not to ignore or subsume them. This brings us to the point where we need to unpack and examine the political institutions that shape political participation.

INSTITUTIONALIST THEORY

The third general approach toward studying immigrant political behavior emphasizes the effect of host-society institutions and structures on political mobilization. Institutions are the rules of the game in society. They are formally devised constraints that shape interaction in society; they structure incentives in human exchange. In simpler terms, in addition to understanding the importance of cultural and class variables, certain political systems and organizations make participation easier. Likewise, the nature of a political system (if it is democratic or authoritarian, parliamentary or presidential, multiparty or two-party, etc.) impacts how and whether different ethnic groups are able to assert their interests.

Sidney Tarrow (1994) uses slightly different language to describe the same phenomena. Instead of discussing "institutional constraints," Tarrow writes about the need for "political opportunity structures"(p. 13). He defines political opportunity structures as dimensions of the political environment that provide incentives for people to undertake collective action by affecting their expectations for success or failure (p. 85). For Tarrow (1989, 1994), Tilly (1978), and McAdam, Tarrow, and Tilly (1997) the success of mobilization (or politicization) hinges on the opportunities afforded the group in question. The opportunities present themselves when there is a shift in the institutional structure or the ideological disposition of those in power. For example, the fall of Suharto's regime in May 1998 provided Indonesian Chinese an opportunity to organize and form new political groups.

Most social science begins with the traditional behavioral assumptions about expected utility calculations. That is, people behave in ways that reflect their self-interest. However, ascertaining motivation is somewhat more complicated. For this study, immigrant behavior can be ascribed to the legal conditions and political institutions that have "both shaped and limited the migrants' choice possibilities" (Katznelson 1973:42). Like other research (Erie 1988; Ireland 1994), this work will stress that certain kinds of immigration policies, citizenship laws, electoral districting, and administrative practices seem likely to induce particular kinds of immigrant group activity.

The power of laws and political institutions to shape immigrant politics is immediately obvious in looking at citizenship eligibility. Myron Weiner (1992/93) looks at whether citizenship is accorded on the basis of birthplace or lineage. When the criteria is based on lineage, the migrants are not accorded the same claims to land, employment, education, or political power. For example, the idea of the *bumiputra* in Malaysia is enshrined in the country's constitution and legal system. This ideology of indigenousness shapes the national response to outsiders; thus Chinese are seen as a threat to the dominant culture, and the political system institutionalizes the limited role of the Chinese within the ruling coalition.

Ireland (1994) uses an institutionalist approach to explain the political incorporation of immigrants in France and Switzerland. He largely rejects the cultural- and class-based explanations for immigrant political activity. Instead he argues that the key variable in understanding immigrant politics is how host institutions have both conditioned and responded to immigrant organization (p. 245). The approach used here is somewhat similar. Chinese communal participation can be understood as a product of the institutional structure of the host society, and it is impacted by the strategic mobilization efforts of dominant political elites and Chinese community leaders. These factors are not necessarily independent of other variables, such as culture, class, and historical opportunities. For example, the ability of a group to organize collective action, such as voting consistently as a whole or demonstrating, may be tied to a certain worldview or outlook. However, this view itself does not produce direct effects (Ross 1997:67). Instead, attitudes and options may be mediated through institutions (Laitin 1986: 1995).

There are several components that make up an institutional framework, and it is necessary to understand both the organization's uniqueness as well as the links between the institutions. The aspects that will be examined in the next few chapters include the laws, elected officials and the bodies to which they are elected, party systems, bureaucratic networks, and the associations and leaders of the Chinese community. In this respect it is elites, both in the government and within the community, whose preferences and mobilization efforts go a long way toward influencing the nature of participation of the community.

Rosenstone and Hansen (1993) look at American politics and ask a series of questions about who participates, when, why, and how. Under particular sets of circumstances, participation itself offers a mix of collective and selective benefits (pp. 18–19), but political circumstances are necessary to induce participation (p. 20). They argue that membership in social networks can create selective rewards and thus help overcome the "rational ignorance" that accompanies nonparticipation. These social networks can be mobilized for political advantage, and mobilization is the process through which people are induced to participate (p. 25). For politicians, parties, interest groups, and activists, access to social networks makes mobilization possible. Without the selective benefits offered by membership in such groups, politicians have only collective returns to reward those who participate. For a politician, there is no need to target all people, all the time; thus the strategic calculation to decide whom to target can influence and possibly determine who participates, and when (pp. 33–35). Understanding the institutional structure and the needs of officials within that system can help explain why particular groups may be mobilized and others ignored. Also, from a utilitarian viewpoint, since voting is basically not a rational decision (Olson 1965; Barzel and Silberberg 1973), some other need must be addressed in deciding to vote. Uhlaner (1989) suggests group membership plays a significant role in an individual's decision to vote because the consumption benefits it brings make turning out to vote quite rational. For example, a person might attend a political meeting because a fellow church member sponsored the meeting, or someone might vote because a village elder urged him or her to. In practical terms what this implies for Chinese communities is that the first step in increasing political participation is to overcome the inclination to "do nothing." Voting in elections, giving money to campaigns, attending rallies and political events—none of these activities, on the surface, promises much in the way of a payoff to the individual undertaking the activity. In a nutshell, this is the classic "free rider" problem. Why should any one person bother to vote if the outcome of the election rarely hinges on one or two votes, and when all get the benefit of leaders winning office? Some of the key elements that increase the likelihood of a person voting are if they have a clear partisan preference, or if they are asked to vote for a particular candidate (or attend a meeting, or give money) by a friend or acquaintance. Membership in a civic or community organization has been found to increase the chance that an individual will participate in politics. However, this does not seem to be universally true. Despite the myriad of community associations and organizations, Chinese in the United States and in Malaysia participate at lower rates than the dominant groups.

Wendy Tam Cho's essay on the importance of socialization (1999) also questions the conventional findings that socioeconomic status variables explain political participation. Cho argues that while status variables such as age and education provide skills that facilitate political participation, they may not be as strong a factor as the socialization process that a person undergoes. Cho analyzes rates of voter turnout in America's increasingly heterogeneous population. Since newer immigrant groups are exposed to different forces of socialization (different media channels, civic or community associations, entertainment outlets, etc.), indicators such as levels of income, age, or education may not correlate as strongly with voter turnout. Since socialization processes may differ, and socialization is the mechanism that determines the satisfaction or benefits one receives from voting, then it is not surprising that voter turnout rates differ from group to group.

Since community groups play a significant role in the socialization process, this leads us to look more closely at the nature of the community organizations and at those who lead them. Though often neglected, the leaders of social networks or organizations play a role in passing on the information and overall direction to the groups' members. What are their goals in pursuing a participatory strategy within the larger society, or what do they gain from maintaining a certain ethnic insularity? Studying the Chinese diaspora in different settings helps to answer these questions about strategic mobilization and elite motivations. Even after only an initial review of the literature on Chinese communities overseas, it is clear that the nature of the system of community organizations existing within this population affects the goals and attention toward the larger society. If organizations such as the Chinese Consolidated Benevolent Association, a leading organization in New York City and other U.S. Chinatowns, are focused on mediating within the community rather than on incorporation with the larger society, then political participation will be minimal. Other organizations, such as the Chinatown Planning Council in New York City or Asian Americans for Equality, play an increasingly greater brokerage role between dominant political structures and members of the Chinese community in the satisfaction of political and economic needs. Thus there may be an increasing likelihood of political participation on a wider scale.

In keeping with much of the "new institutionalism" literature, one needs to look past these surface assumptions to understand better how institutional structures, such as the nature of electoral politics and the potential power of groups within society, shape the role of two groups of leaders within the Chinese community. The two broad categories of community leaders are those associated with business networks or individual business leaders, and social activists, most of whom are affiliated with some sort of social service agency. Each case study assesses the role of these leaders in mobilizing the community for particular interests such as education policies, and the chapters examine the extent to which these leaders are able to impact politicization and/or influence on political matters.

There are three broad categories of conditions or incentives that are examined in this study: political, economic, and social incentives structure the relationship between elites and political institutions. Like other immigrant groups, Chinese might expect that participation will result in greater economic opportunity for themselves and the next generation, either through access to government attention to their economic interests or through greater distribution of government largess. This study finds that there needs to be a combination of political, economic, and social incentives in order to bring about both greater politicization as well as greater influence in the form of achieving the desired political and economic outcomes.

Economic rewards are not the only ones that matter to a community. There are social norms and approval that play a significant role in the hierarchy and prestige of individuals within the immigrant group. There can be positive and negative reinforcement for political participation within the immigrant community. Unassimilated elites have an interest in the insularity of their community. To the extent that the community finds itself able to participate in the larger host-society institutions for economic, judicial, educational, and informational services, these elites will lose their constituency. As Laitin explains:

> If a member of the unassimilated community needs to petition authorities for some service, for example, and does so through the minority elite, the minority elite will get some return for the service. By providing such services to the lower strata of the minority community and by helping the dominant society keep basic order (and

political quiescence) in the minority area, minority elites play a crucial political role, which has value to them. (Laitin 1995:40)

When the social stigma of participation is strong, and the internal cen-
sure for doing so is intense, then there is less likelihood of a participatory
strategy. But when there is a mix of both social and economic incentives
to become active, then there is a greater chance of participation.

An institutional approach, or the "new institutionalism," goes a long
way in answering key questions. It is my argument that Chinese communities will be motivated to participate politically when the political
opportunity structures facilitate it and when the costs to doing nothing
are higher than the costs of participation. The costs will largely depend
on the existing institutions and how they facilitate or inhibit particular
forms of participation. For example; from the 1950s until 1969 the parliamentary system in Malaysia, and the need for the UMNO to have a segment of the Chinese community represented within the coalition, gave
rise to Chinese participation in entrenched political parties rather than
through issue or interest groups. Yet, from 1969 to the present, leaders
of various groups within the Chinese community have realized that the
MCA, while claiming the mantle of Chinese representation, also has distinct incentives to maintain their "little brother–like" position in relation
to UMNO. The costs of participating, particularly within the MCA, are
fairly low, and for leaders of the MCA, there are economic and political
incentives to accommodate their coalition partners to maintain their place
in the ruling circle. Yet to achieve a measure of influence over particular
policy areas, for example the right to Chinese vernacular education,
groups outside the MCA have helped win minor victories and have made
it easier for the MCA to achieve compromise positions when Chinese
demands could not be met outright.

Under Suharto, when there was relatively little political openness in
Indonesia, the only two institutionalized forms of participation were voting and interest articulation through state-established corporatist networks. However, there has been dramatic change over the last year or so,
and new networks of political parties and interest groups may help solid-
ify a more democratic polity. Even under Suharto there was some independent expression of influence coming from parastatal organizations,
and semiautonomous nongovernment organizations (Macintyre 1990).
The most powerful example of these seemed to be business associations
and industry groups, something that the chapter on Indonesia will
address more directly. The most often pointed-to form of influence wielding is through personal links with those in power.

In New York the local political institutions, such as the borders of the city council district that encompasses Chinatown, make it necessary for Chinese to assume a measure of unity as well as forming coalitions with other groups in the district. Despite the open political system, until recently there has been little mobilization by elites in power. These two factors have combined to leave the New York community still fractured and marginally influential. In Los Angeles there has been greater cohesion within the Chinese immigrant community and significant coalition-building with other Asians. They have coalesced around issues such as Proposition 187 and minority places in the state university system. The variation seems to indicate that participation does not necessarily translate into influence. In circumstances where elections are not the locus of real political power, individual ties to leaders may be more effective than group mobilization. So, to answer when mobilization will be successful, one must look to both community organizations and the nature of the institutions of power.

CASE STUDIES

MALAYSIA

In Malaysia, neither ethnic nor class approaches alone adequately explain the shift over time in Chinese political influence. Despite the enactment of economic policies designed to improve the economic and social position of ethnic Malays, Chinese per capita income has stayed well above that for Malays or Indians. Yet they participate at lower rates than the Malays and their influence in the political system has diminished. Likewise, it is hard to find that cultural attributes are responsible for these shifts, because if anything, Chinese in Malaysia have increasingly identified as Malaysian citizens of Chinese ancestry. Thus, while they see themselves as part of the Chinese community, they no longer have a "sojourner" outlook that might keep them from participating in the politics of their adopted country. Ethnicity in Malaysia is considered a legitimate basis for the articulation of political interests. Ethnic parties within the ruling coalition seek to balance ethnic interests through communal patronage, but with an overall "racial restructuring" in favor of Malay socioeconomic interests. Likewise, an array of Chinese associational networks voice their interests through the ruling and opposition parties. The key institutional features in Malaysia that affect Chinese participation and influence are the constitution, the nature of the ruling party coalition, and the heterogeneous electoral constituencies. In addition, networks of Chinese associations which address economic, social, and cultural aspects of community life play a significant role in asserting influence in particular

policy areas such as the Chinese education controversies, an issue discussed in the following chapter. Despite internal divisions and fractional
allegiances based on kin, language, or class groupings, most Chinese in
Malaysia (and the same argument will be made for Sino- Indonesians)
would recognize one another as part of a broader Chinese collectivity. In
part this is true because the very nature of Malaysian society and politics
is communally based. The very institutions of state power identify individuals within these larger ethnic communities.

In Malaysia the institutional incentives are geared toward participation
under coalition-building conditions. Active political participation in the
electoral arena does not necessarily translate into influence. Over the last
thirty years the MCA's role in representing Chinese interests and laying
claim to be *the* articulator of communal needs from Chinese Malaysian
has shifted dramatically.[10] In examining the issue of vernacular education
in Malaysia, the focus will be on the important role that community organizations, in this case the *Dong Jiao Zong*, or education movement, and
their leaders play in achieving a circumscribed measure of influence in
national education policy.

INDONESIA

Looking at the wealthy Sino-Indonesians' access to Suharto would seem
to confirm class arguments about the importance of socioeconomic variables in understanding political participation and influence. However,
without understanding the larger developmentalist goals of the state, one
could not understand why Suharto chose wealthy Chinese as the business
elite in the country. And this personal networking between Suharto and
totok tycoons existed at the same time that the majority of Indonesian
Chinese, both *peranakan* and *totok*, were discriminated against in most
Indonesian politics. In Indonesia, the assimilationist policies of Suharto's
regime and the neopatrimonial practices of the state have meant that ethnic groups could not articulate collective interests through ethnic-based
political organizations; thus Sino-Indonesian patrons derive their leverage over their clients through personal ties to state elites.

Although ethnic identification is problematic, official religious communities are recognized by the state and are expected to work through the
appropriate section of the Department of Religion. For some upwardly
mobile Chinese, converting to Christianity has facilitated access to jobs
or capital. A notable example of how this works is found in the hiring and
promoting practices of the Riady's Lippo Group. Employees there have
found it expedient to adopt Christianity, and insiders say that promotion
within Lippo is easier for those who profess born-again beliefs similar to

the Riadys. Yet not all Chinese are Christian, so one can argue that Indonesian Chinese interests have been further divided by the mandate that all Indonesian citizens identify with one of the approved religious groups.

Institutionally, as a mechanism for assessing when Chinese communities become active in the political process, elections from 1965 until 1999 in Indonesia tell us very little. It is important to understand what exists in their place and why it is necessary to work through different channels. While elections are critical to the political regime, it is more useful to look at the economic incentives and conditions that impact Chinese input into the political arena.

Their political vulnerability as an unpopular and unorganized minority leaves Sino-Indonesians in a politically precarious position. Economic wealth does not automatically translate into regularized political participation or influence. The Chinese community is not a monolith, nor can it act as a collectivity. Under Suharto there was little advocacy from the middle and upper class for greater democracy or liberalization of the political system. In part this was due to Suharto's favoring Indonesian Chinese. As a small minority community benefiting from authoritarian rule, Suharto could be reasonably sure that they would not threaten his rule. While neither elections nor ethnically organized groups could serve as channels for participation and influence, there were means of achieving extrastate influence. Macintyre (1990) shows how various industry groups mobilized for particular policy objectives. While the business community as a whole may have little opportunity to project collective political interests, sectorally, business has developed new and somewhat independent political capabilities (Macintyre 1990:3). Individual Chinese have played an active role in how some industry groups have been able to challenge and alter established networks of corporatist representative associations so that there is greater complexity in the coalition-building that goes on inside and outside of the state apparatus.

The differences in how the Chinese have participated politically in Indonesia under changing political circumstances are striking. Under Dutch colonialism, the conditions existed where ethnic insularity and organization not only possible but necessary (Coppel 1976:44–46). Under Suharto's regime, there were significant economic rewards and incentives to work on an individual level for political favors and government largess. Because of the institutional constraints against organized communal activity, the Chinese elite were not compelled to forge a consensus or a sense of unity among what is instead a large number of ethnic Chinese who have been grouped together for predominantly scapegoating purposes. If Sino-Indonesians as a group are to be full participants in society, their choice is to assimilate on an individual basis or to work to secure institutional changes that protect minority rights. I argue that minority groups will be motivated to participate when there is elite mobilization toward political incorporation. Yet, clearly, in Indonesia the incentives for ethnic and indigenous elites are to work through personal connections to achieve economic benefits.[11] There are few social or economic gains to be had by doing otherwise. Ultimately there needs to be a combination of institutional and elite incentives in order to impact participation in the political process. Those conditions may now evolve in Indonesia. After relatively free and fair elections in June of 1999, when forty-eight parties competed, small parties may be able to win seats in Parliament. Since no party won a majority, small parties do wield some power in Parliament and in the surprise election of Abdurrahman Wahid as president in the fall of 1999.

THE UNITED STATES

As the introductory chapter states, the Chinese in the United States are just beginning to organize for greater impact in the political arena. The ongoing controversy over campaign contributions from Sino-Indonesians and Chinese Americans to the Democratic National Committee appears to give weight to those who believe that Chinese culture impacts the way in which Chinese approach politics. Some pundits and commentators argue that the questionable contributions to President Clinton's reelection effort in 1996 were a symptom of *guanxi* (relations or connections) associated with crony capitalism found throughout Asia, and particularly in Indonesia and the People's Republic of China.

In addition to looking at this one recent event through a "cultural" lens, one might also view this from a class perspective; wealthy Asians give money to political campaigns in order to bolster their business standing. But, there is a third way of viewing this: Asian donors such as Lippo Group employees and owners, in seeking influence at home with President Suharto, decided to cultivate an image that they had ties to the President of the United States. Such a relationship is thus instrumental not necessarily in influencing American politics, but in gaining influence in Indonesian politics and greater economic leverage within Asia. This explanation is less threatening to those who fear that U.S. policy interests are being corrupted by Asian donors, but nonetheless it raises questions about economic and political transparency in Asia (and the United States), particularly in Indonesia and China.

Chinese community leaders in New York City and Monterey Park, California, initially dismissed the national-level campaign donations as unimportant for their local organizations and goals. However, as the scandal continued to play out in the national press, local leaders realized that their communities and causes could suffer from the negative publicity. Would the issue provoke a backlash against Chinese Americans and prompt them to withdraw from political activity, or might the issue compel community members to become more assertive of their genuine interests? It is not yet clear which direction the community will go; however, there is some indication that politicization of Chinese Americans will rest on more than just "donor-gate" fallout. Certainly, if Rosenstone's and Hansen's (1993) thesis about the impact of mobilization on political participation is correct, then Chinese-American participation will be hurt if politicians fear reaching out to the community for financial and political support. Yet this may be counteracted by the awareness that Asian Americans are an increasingly prosperous and numerically important constituency, particularly in California.

The U.S. case studies will indicate that the Chinese community in Monterey Park benefits from a suburban political landscape that provides greater opportunities for local political leadership, and that greater efforts at coalition-building in the Los Angeles area between Asian and Latino groups has created a more formidable political force that political elites need to be conscious of. In New York City's Chinatown, there is less coalition-building, and the community has less opportunity for political leadership within the larger institutions of New York City politics. In addition, Chinatown in New York is divided between the authority of the traditional kinship associations and newer social activists. In Monterey Park, a wider array of politically oriented organizations is able to assert community interests.

EMPIRICALLY SPEAKING

For the most part, the remainder of this book is spent discussing four case studies. There is obviously tremendous variation among the three countries: Malaysia, Indonesia, and the United States. As already stated, it is clear that traditional class- or ethnicity-based approaches to understanding the Chinese overseas and their position in the polities of their adopted countries can benefit from comparative analysis which takes institutions into account. Each case chapter looks at the background of Chinese immigrants in that area, the political institutions, and the nature of political and community elites. The relationship between these factors is analyzed by looking at issues of particular importance to the Chinese in their communities; for instance, access to education or the reapportionment of local political districts. On the basis of interviews during fieldwork, and from newspaper accounts, influence is assessed by examining how these concerns are met over time. The concluding chapter reexamines the cases comparatively and discusses the larger implications of this work.

3

Malaysia:
Institutionalized Participation

Malaysian politics is highly ethnicized and it is perhaps the most intriguing country with which to study Chinese political activity outside China and Taiwan. There is a rich diversity of Chinese organizations and institutions which help shape incorporation with the Malaysian polity. These range from long-standing business and cultural associations to political parties organized along communal lines. Few issues are not, in some manner, linked to ethnic relations. This chapter will argue that although the Chinese community is highly incorporated within the Malaysian political system, they vote at lower rates than do ethnic Malays and their influence is constrained by the institutional arrangements that shape and channel all political activity. Their influence is also muted by the diffuse centers of activity within the community itself. Economic power may lead to political influence in narrow instances, but political gains from collective action are muted. The primary goal of this chapter is to explain how and why Chinese in Malaysia wielded greater political influence before 1969 and, despite maintaining a high socioeconomic status, have seen the impact of their political involvement become more circumscribed.

This chapter begins with the history of Chinese politics in Malaysia, explains the competing approaches to understanding Chinese politicization, and then describes the nature of national political institutions and how Chinese incorporation into the Malaysian polity has been shaped and altered over time. Throughout the chapter the debate over Chinese vernacular education is discussed. This public policy issue, more so than any other, can be seen as a barometer of how the Chinese community is faring politically in Malaysia. Finally, the chapter looks specifically at the controversy over Chinese schools as an example of how community associations and their leaders attempt to influence education policy in Malaysia. The discussion about Chinese schools also shows how leaders were able to unify the community behind expanded citizenship rights in the 1950s, but how it has been more difficult to mobilize people for narrower interests such as the protection of Chinese vernacular education. Chinese political participation (as measured by voter turnout) seems to increase when an election is vigorously contested by opposition parties such as the Democratic Action Party (DAP) or when the government has acted against communal interests. It is clear that two different sets of Chinese elites, political party leaders who are tied to business barons and activists from social service sectors, have different constituents and incentives to behave the way they do. While business leaders have a stronger chance of influencing politics, community activists are trapped by the difficulty of organizing collective action. By examining the position of these elites within the Malaysian polity since independence, one can better explain why Chinese are a regular part of the political process in Malaysia without achieving significant influence for the community as a whole.

CONTEXT

Chinese in Malaysia have long been a dynamic economic force, and since they make up close to 30 percent of the population, they have long been perceived as a political threat to the indigenous Malays. The Malay Peninsula has always been ethnically mixed, with indigenous and Malay inhabitants. Chinese and Indian immigrants began coming to the area in large numbers in the first quarter of the nineteenth century, and after World War II strong identities emerged as people begin to think of themselves not just in relation to the colonial rulers but as Malay, Chinese, or Indian. This ethnic feature of Malaysian politics developed as a consequence of the social, economic, and political positions of each group during British colonialism, and was further defined in the decolonization requirements for a multiethnic regime where communal elites would share power (Lee, R. 1986; Horowitz 1985, 1989). Malaysia has often been pointed to as an example of ethnic accommodation. While there has been ethnic conflict—most notably the race riots of May 13, 1969, discussed later in this chapter—Malaysia has not faced the repeated violence and animosity of other multiethnic states such as Sri Lanka or Yugoslavia. Malaysia's political institutions have facilitated ethnic coexistence rather than violence; however, Malaysia's stability and ethnic cooperation have masked the fact that minority groups' political involvement has been increasingly marginalized and the regime has been able to concentrate power in the hands of a few. In many respects Prime Minister Mahathir's government, by focusing on economic growth and by expressly favoring ethnic Malays, has reaffirmed its political legitimacy in the eyes of many Malays. Critics of the regime are portrayed as traitors and as corrupt.

CURRENT SITUATION

After years of record growth, the Asian "miracle" came to a crashing close in the summer of 1997. Economies that had posted 6 to 10 percent growth a year were suddenly on the verge of bankruptcy. The causes of the economic downturn are complex and not agreed upon. In 1997 the heavily intertwined Asian economies such as Indonesia, Malaysia, and Thailand began to slow. They became pressed to repay huge loans to struggling Japanese banks and other international investors. When the Thai government devalued the baht on July 2, 1997, currency speculators began pulling money out of the region. This prompted many of the central banks to attempt to buy up their currencies rather than let them sink. All but bankrupt, Thailand, Indonesia, and South Korea turned to the International Monetary Fund (IMF) for help. Malaysia opted to address the financial crisis without international assistance. The financial crisis sparked political instability as well. While Thailand and South Korea weathered smooth leadership transitions, Indonesia's President Suharto was forced out of office after more than thirty years at the helm.

Unlike Indonesia, however, Malaysia's long-standing leader, Prime Minister Mahathir Mohamad appears to have come out of the crisis with his regime's power intact. In early November, 1999, Mahathir confidently called for new elections to be held on November 27, 1999. Although the elections had to be held before April of 2000, nobody expected Mahathir to announce the general elections when he did. If polling is held on November 27th as expected, it will come on the heels of Chinese Premier Zhu Rongji's visit to Malaysia. This may give Mahathir a chance to boost support among Chinese. Despite the current feeling that the worst of the economic crisis is over, Malaysia's government and rulers have been exposed to greater scrutiny and criticism during the last two years, and the country's reputation for stability and harmony may have cracked.

From 1997 until the fall of 1998, rumors circulated that Prime Minister Mahathir and his deputy prime Minister Anwar Ibrahim were at odds. The whispering got louder as Malaysia confronted the ringgit's loss of value and the reality that the economy would contract in late 1997 and early 1998. Mahathir, long known for his inflammatory anti-Western rhetoric, blamed currency traders and foreign financial forces for Malaysia's economic ills. Meanwhile, Anwar was the one called upon to reassure investors quietly that Malaysia would not invoke some of the (Mahathir-) threatened restrictions on currency trading. In October of 1997 Mahathir returned from a ten-day trip to Latin America and, at a press conference after his return:

> The premier turned to Anwar at one point and exclaimed teasingly:
> "The press is asking questions. I'm answering and tomorrow the
> currency traders will try and push down the ringgit just because Dr.
> Mahathir opened his mouth."
>
> Anwar's laughing reply: "Then I will clarify and they will say
> we're quarrelling." (Jayasankaran October 9, 1997a)

In December 1997 it seemed that Anwar was fully in control of economic
policy. On December 5, 1997, the Deputy Prime Minister announced a
series of belt-tightening measures. This appeared to signal an end to the
megaprojects and aggressive spending that Mahathir had led for more
than ten years. However, by May of 1998 Mahathir was becoming more
assertive about saving large projects and government backing for high-
profile companies in trouble, such as Malaysia Airlines. On June 24, 1998,
Daim Zainuddin was appointed Special Functions Minister and given
the task of overseeing economic policy decisions.[1] This effectively curbed
Anwar's power. On September 1, 1998, Mahathir announced that Malaysia
was imposing capital controls, and the currency was fixed at 3.80 ringgit
to the U.S. dollar. One day later, on September 2, 1998, rumors about
infighting between Mahathir and his deputy were finally silenced. Anwar
was fired from his post as Deputy Prime Minister and Minister of
Finance. Later he was expelled from UMNO and arrested on charges of corruption and sodomy. His expulsion and arrest triggered demonstrations
and calls for political reform.

> Malaysians are perfecting a new form of protest: the "shop-and-
> shout" technique. For the second Saturday in a row, a crowd of what
> looked like ordinary shoppers on October 17 transformed a main
> street in central Kuala Lumpur into a massive demonstration call-
> ing for Prime Minister Mahathir Mohamad to resign. As police
> looked on, several thousand people—mostly Malays, some
> Indians—pumped the air with their fists and chanted slogans call-
> ing for the abolition of the Internal Security Act and demanding jus-
> tice for former Deputy Prime Minister Anwar Ibrahim. (Hiebert
> and Jayasankaran October 29, 1998)

As Anwar's trial got underway later in the fall, protests continued. Some
groups of demonstrators were met with harsh police tactics; police at one
point used water cannons and tear gas. Anwar was sentenced to a six-year
jail term for abuse of power and faced a second trail on June 7, 1999, for
charges of sodomy, a criminal offense in Malaysia. During the protests of

October and November 1998, Malaysian Chinese seem to stay home. Fearing that instability could lead to violence against non-Malays and horrified at the riots and assaults against Indonesian Chinese earlier in the year, Malaysian Chinese seemed to stay on the sidelines of the protests against Mahathir's regime. However, not all Chinese remained out of the fray. A coalition of nongovernmental organizations (NGOs) and opposition parties formed *Gagansan,* or a plan, to hold rallies where speakers condemned the Internal Security Act (ISA) and social and political injustice. Several Chinese, like Tian Chua, a human rights activist, were involved in coordinating the *Gagansan* coalition. After Anwar's trial got underway and once protestors were met with violence and arrests, the movement moved from the streets to private efforts at building a new political party. The result was the creation of the National Justice Party, led by Anwar's wife, Wan Azizah.

While Mahathir's call for elections in November of 1999 did not leave opposition parties much time to campaign formally (there were about two weeks between his announcement and the scheduled date for the election), the National Justice Party is prepared for a fight: "Anwar has always told me that the thing Mahathir fears most is a united opposition. We were getting there, and I think he wanted to nip it in the bud at this nascent state" (Jayasankaran 1999:2). Wan Azizah hopes to win a seat in Parliament from Anwar's former constituency in Penang and she further aims to carry the state. This is less likely. Chinese make up a majority in Penang, and it seems as though they will back Mahathir and the ruling coalition. Mahathir has argued that keeping the National Front in power is a way of preventing ethnic tension, and this view seems to have struck a cord among the Chinese.

In order to understand how Mahathir has been able to maintain his rule and perhaps even to strengthen executive power, and to understand why Malaysian Chinese are marginalized players within the peninsula's polity, it is necessary to place the current turmoil and uncertainty into a larger historical and institutional framework.

BACKGROUND

Chinese began coming to Western Malaysia around 1400, but Chinese settlement in peninsular Malaysia was not significant until the early nineteenth century. Most immigrants came from Guangdong and Fujian and spoke one of five major Chinese dialects: Hokkien, Hakka, Cantonese, Teochiu, and Hainanese. Like elsewhere in the Chinese diaspora, Chinese in Malaysia were organized into a myriad of common-origin associations; for example, the Guangdong Association, Fujian Association, and so on.

In the mid-nineteenth century the most important umbrella organizations were the Chinese Chambers of Commerce. Leadership within the Chinese community came at first from successful merchants. The British colonial administration relied on the Kapitan Cina (Chinese secret society heads with financial power and ties to local Malay chiefs) to administer revenue farms, develop tin mining and plantation economies, and keep the peace in Chinese communities.[2] As the British gained increasing administrative control over Malaya, the Chinese lost some of their ability to govern themselves.[3] The colonial government set up Chinese advisory boards to replace the Kapitans (many were given positions on the advisory boards) in keeping the British informed of events and activities in the Chinese community. Even today, Chinese associations play a role (mostly economic and social rather than political) for the older generation. The Chinese Chambers of Commerce have promoted cooperation across dialect groups.

> Since its formation in 1947, the Associated Chinese Chambers of Commerce has served not only as the bastion of pan-Malaysian Chinese capitalist interest, but has also sought to advance Chinese political and education welfare by working closely with Chinese political parties, in particular the Malaysian Chinese Association. (Pan 1999:173)

Even under British colonial rule, Chinese community elites maintained a considerable degree of autonomy in local matters, particularly in education.

Since 1911, Chinese involvement in Malaysian politics has been linked to fears of Chinese Nationalist or Communist Party influence. To understand this connection, it is necessary to examine briefly the historical mechanism for maintaining overseas Chinese ties to their native land: education. In the middle of the 1880s the Chinese in Malaysia began running local schools for their children. School programs mirrored education in China. In 1911, after the fall of the last imperial dynasty, the Qing, the school curriculum reflected a growing sense of Chinese nationalism. Emphasis was placed on creating military spirit; drilling, uniforms, and patriotic songs were incorporated into the school day. Shortly after the May 4th Movement of 1919 in China, Sun Yat Sen's three principles (nationalism, democracy, and livelihood) became mandatory political components of the already militarized curriculum. This alarmed the British. With the adoption of Mandarin as the medium of instruction, Chinese schools:

were becoming instruments of propaganda for political parties outside Malaya whose objectives were often entirely opposed to the policy of the Malayan governments or their Education Departments.
Quite apart from the use of education for out and out subversive-
ness, it was clear that the governments could not leave uncontrolled
the system of education turning out boys and girls who were to all
intents and purposes members of a foreign state, owing no duty to
the country they lived in; the teachers were nearly all China born,
recent arrivals in Malaya and often of extremist views. (Purcell
1965:220)

In 1927 the Chinese government established a Bureau of Education and
an Overseas Education Commission. The latter agency sent money and
inspectors to Malaya to oversee the education that Chinese children were
receiving. In 1929 the British banned the Chinese Nationalist Party (KMT)
in Malaya because of its anti-Japanese propaganda and the perceived
threats to British sovereignty in the colonies.

At the close of World War II in Southeast Asia, Chinese money again
flowed to private Chinese-language schools in British territories. This
time, however, the schools became centers of Chinese Communist Party
propaganda (Watson 1973; Chew Kong Huat 1975). Under Japanese occupation, the communists in Malaya succeeded in organizing the only viable
underground resistance. In doing so, they gathered widespread cooperation and support from the Chinese and were thus positioned to gain a
large degree of political control after the war. Initially, the Malaysian
Communist Party (MCP) operated as a parallel government to the British
Military Administration that implemented military rule from September
1945 to March 1946. As British rule became more firmly ensconced, it
took steps to reduce the MCP's power. By 1948 the MCP's position was
deteriorating; police action was destroying the labor movement, and the
MCP had been shut out of the Malayan Union Advisory Councils. Under
an uncompromising secretary-general, Chin Peng, the MCP opted for
armed insurrection (Heng 1988:50). Terming this "The Emergency," the
colonial government, along with conservative elements in the Malaysian
and Chinese communities, set about to consolidate Chinese support for
the anti-insurgency campaign. This was done through education campaigns, detentions, and massive relocation efforts.

The Chinese community was deeply divided; there were substantial
numbers of Chinese who supported the MCP. The Chinese in Malaya had
experienced considerable independence in running their own affairs. The
network of voluntary associations and schools had served as conduits of

Chinese culture. The uncertainty and negotiations leading up to independence threatened to alter these arrangements. Many felt that the MCP
would best promote Chinese rights. It is unknown how many really supported the MCP because there was fear of reprisals if they did not. Some
clearly supported the Nationalist Chinese, and there was also a strata of
British-educated Chinese who looked not to China but to building an
independent Malaysia.[4] The Malayan Chinese Association (MCA), known
as the *Malaysian* Chinese Association after 1963, was formed at this time
as a conservative, business-oriented organization that would work with the
British and Malay elites to redirect Chinese support away from the communists (ibid.:61–65). While the MCP had noteworthy support from large
numbers of Chinese and some Malays, there was also a sizable Chinese
business class in control of vast amounts of capital, and while it is certain
that a significant sum of money went to communist organizations within
the Chinese community, on the surface Chinese business interests were
willing to work with British-educated MCA leaders in order to form a new
state. It was in the economic and political interest of this class to work
against fellow Chinese communists. The negotiations among interethnic
actors in working toward independence would create a pattern of elite
cooperation that would last until 1969.

The concern over non-Malay privilege and ambition (in the form of
Chinese economic dominance) led to the institutionalization of Malay
special rights in the Independence Constitution of 1957. These rights
evolved as part of complex negotiations for multiethnic rule in postcolonial Malaysia. While the Chinese community was dismayed at how
Malay rights were favored by legitimizing the primacy of the Malay identity within the constitution, they were willing to compromise on this in
exchange for concessions on citizenship eligibility and moderate protection of Chinese education (Heng 1988; Kua 1990; Means 1991).[5]

There was a brief window of time during decolonization in 1946–1947
where it seemed that the Chinese might be accorded equal political and
economic rights through the Malayan Union. One plan proposed by the
British was to centralize the three administrative regions: the Straits
Settlements, the Federated Malay States, and the Unfederated Malay
States. There would be common citizenship and equal rights for Malays
and non-Malays. The British were forced to give up the plan because of
"unyielding Malay opposition led by the newly formed United Malays
National Organization (UMNO). The Malayan Union idea was unaccept-
able to Malays, who feared it would enable the Chinese population—
which, with Singapore, exceeded Malays by 2 percent—to dominate the
new nation both politically and economically" (Pan 1999:176). The alter-

native plan proposed by the British was to bring all three areas into a federal system but with guarantees of Malay sovereignty, strict citizenship requirements for non-Malays, and the exclusion of Singapore from the new federation. UMNO clearly favored this arrangement, and decolonization moved forward.

The constitution was drawn up by Malay and non-Malay members of the coalition Alliance Party, where elite bargaining over these issues reflected Britain's goal of crafting a consociational system where leaders negotiated on behalf of their ethnic constituents. The constitution defines a Malay as a Muslim, a Malay speaker, and a follower of Malay custom (*adat*). Non-Malay culture is not defined. The constitution is later pointed to as a justification for pro-Malay politics. As Lee writes, "Thus the legitimation of selected cultural characteristics as ethnic identifiers is an important strategy in fortifying political interests and maintaining ethnic exclusiveness" (Lee, R. 1986:33).

The constitution was drafted as part of a series of conferences in 1956 and 1957. An agreement was reached that Malays would retain their political preeminence while the Chinese's economic position would be undisturbed. Likewise, Chinese and Indians would be permitted to maintain their cultures and traditions. It seemed to be understood at the time that at a later date measures would be enacted to raise the economic level of the Malays and that the national language of Bahasa Malaysia would be accorded a special place in nationalist discourse.

For the first ten years of independence, the ruling Alliance coalition was able to maintain about 60 percent of the votes and keep control both of Parliament and the state governments. In 1969 the system broke down. A riot broke out on May 13th, after general elections in which the Alliance won only 48 percent of the votes, down 10 percent from 1964. They also lost state elections in Penang, Perak, and Trengganu (Vasil 1972). Victory parades were held after the election which were perceived as abusive to Malay sensibilities. Rioting ensued in which thousands (mostly Chinese) were killed, and property was burned and looted. After 1969 a consensus evolved that the disturbance was caused by an economic imbalance between the wealthier Chinese and the less well-off native Malays.[6]

The race riots marked the rise of Malay leadership dedicated to the translation of Malay constitutional privileges into actual policies. This opened the door to a massive shift in economic and social policies to boost the position of Malays within their own country. NEP, or the New Economic Policy, was created. Adopted in 1971, the aim of the policy was to redistribute wealth from the Chinese to the Malays and other indigenous races. A secondary goal was to "eliminate the identification of race with economic function." In other words, it aimed at bringing *bumiputras* (sons of the soil, or ethnic Malays) in to sectors of the economy previously dominated by Chinese. It gave preference to Malays in job allocation, scholarships abroad and university seats, and it required that Malays be given larger ownership stakes in Malaysian companies. In order for this legislation to go forward there needed to be an agreement between Malays and Chinese on the necessity of addressing ethnic income disparity.[7] There was, however, little discussion at the time about the distribution of power within the institutions of power and how NEP would concern various groups in society.

In the years since independence, and especially in the post-1969 transition to NEP and its successors, Chinese Malaysians have been acutely aware that language, education, and employment policies favoring Malays, or *bumiputra,* have impacted Chinese communal political influence and economic opportunities. While policies may not pose direct threats to Chinese lives, there have been occasional outbursts of violence and there is a sense that the Chinese must continually accommodate Malay sensibilities; often this means forgoing economic, and other, opportunities. In the fall of 1987 Malaysia came to the brink of further ethnic violence. In response to Chinese demonstrations against the promotion of non–Mandarin trained education professionals within Chinese schools, discussed later in this chapter, the youth wing of UMNO began holding mass demonstrations calling for greater Malay unity and strength. Fearful of renewed ethnic clashes, Dr. Mahathir declared a state of emergency and arrested more than one hundred political activists from all parties and from nongovernmental organizations (NGOs), Three newspapers were also banned.[8]

Among the policies and practices most often noted as detrimental to Chinese interests the following must be noted: there are sharp limits on educational opportunities for Chinese in Malaysia and preferences in scholarships and college admissions are given to Malays. To cite one example, "nine out of ten students given scholarships to study abroad were Malay" (Ng Beoy Kui 1999:180). Bhasa Malaysia is promoted as the lingua franca, as per the Malayan Federal Constitution of 1957, and there are significant limits on public sector employment for non-Malays.

The results of NEP are hotly contested. Officially, the target of 30 percent Malay corporate ownership by 1990 was not met. Malays own 20.3 percent, whereas Chinese ownership stands at 44.9 percent. Yet some argue that Malay ownership is underestimated, that if you take into account Malay equity held by locally controlled companies (they are counted as non-Malay and Chinese shares) then Malay ownership rises substantially (ibid.). Regardless of the actual percentages of ownership, Chinese business has adapted to NEP and Chinese aggregate incomes have stayed well above that of Malays (see Table 3.1).

When NEP expired in 1990 it was replaced by the National Development Policy (NDP), a ten-year program more concerned with overall economic growth than with ethnic redistribution. While the Chinese were holding their own economically, their political impact as a whole was shrinking. Individual businessmen forged close relationships with Malay elites as a way of prospering under NEP, while associations and political groups that represented community interests more broadly were pushed further to the sidelines. The sections on opposition parties and Chinese education will make this point more specifically.

What is the best way to understand these events and the role of the Chinese in the political process? Three possible frameworks, ethnic, class, and institutional, offer explanations of Chinese political behavior.

COMPETING FRAMEWORKS

CULTURAL EXPLANATIONS

In ethnic or cultural approaches to questions of politicization, it is natural that immigrants organize and articulate political interests along group lines. The traditional argument used is that a group's mode of participation develops from its culture and from its socialization process within the host country. Chinese in Malaysia have maintained a distinctly "Chinese" identity, and there is a wide variety of Chinese associations that exist for community economic, social, and political purposes. One argument for why the Chinese community is less active in politics than the Malay (and less influential) is that the Chinese are socialized to be politically quiescent. If this is

TABLE 3.1 MEAN MONTHLY HOUSEHOLD INCOME		
	1970	1990
Peninsular Malaysia		
Overall	264	1,163
Bumiputra	172	931
Chinese	394	1,582
Indians	304	1,201
Others	813	3,446

(*Source:* Government of Malaysia, Second Outline Perspective Plan, 1991–2000.)

true, then one would need to explain why the Chinese were more active politically in the 1940s and 1950s than they are now. At the time, Chinese schools were hotbeds of Chinese nationalism and political rhetoric. Now Chinese primary schools are funded largely by the government and must follow the national curriculum. On the surface then, cultural socialization may impact political participation and influence.

A more convincing argument about the value of culture in understanding political participation is how culture is used by political elites. Prime Minister Mahathir has conveyed mixed messages about ethnic relations in Malaysia. Formerly an outspoken supporter of Malay dominance, he has more recently made some very public pronouncements about "Malaysian" identity. While he has personally moderated his use of ethnic politicking, he has allowed others in UMNO to insinuate that the Chinese are still outsiders, and he has done much to intimidate and repress any opposition voices in Malaysia.

For its part, leaders of the Malaysian Chinese Association have begun to move away from Chinese exclusivity in membership. In 1994 party rules were changed so that individuals with mixed descent, as long as one parent is Chinese, may become members. Ling Liong Sik, MCA party chief at the time, encouraged Malaysian Chinese to be more multiculturally oriented with the party's "One Heart, One Vision" campaign. He argued that "the different races have not become 'less Malay, or less Indian or less Chinese but all have become more Malaysian'" (Heng 1999:181). To a great extent this image of a multicultural Malaysia has become a reality. Many children, particularly in urban areas, speak two or more languages: Malay and English, Mandarin Chinese and Malay, and sometimes all three, plus another Chinese dialect or two. Some Chinese parents, when asked what languages they and their children speak, answered that they spoke English and a Chinese dialect (Cantonese, Hokkien, etc.) and that their kids spoke "Manglish" (a mix of Malay and English) with their friends from school.

What does greater acculturation, then, mean for political participation? From studies done in the United States one would believe that the more a group is acculturated or assimilated with the dominant population, the higher its participation and influence will be. This has not been the case in Malaysia.

CLASS APPROACHES

Class-based approaches to immigrant political participation take the group's socioeconomic status as the independent variable in determining participation and influence in the political arena. Most classic studies on participation find that social status determines how much an individual will participate politically (Verba and Nie 1972:13–14), and that influence is largely achieved when dominant elites realize that there are economic and/or political gains to be had in fulfilling the interests of a particular constituency. This is more likely to occur when the constituency in question is of a higher social class (Hansen 1991). Likewise, other variables such as levels of education and participation in social networks have been found to correlate with economic status and to facilitate political involvement. Education makes learning about politics easier, and the more knowledgeable someone is about the political process, the more likely they are to participate. Similarly, as discussed in the first two chapters, membership in social or community networks has often coincided with greater political participation. Organizational membership can provide social incentives for civil involvement.

Mean household income for Chinese in peninsular Malaysia is higher than for Malays, levels of education are higher, and there is a wide array of community associations with which to belong. This would imply that Chinese should participate at higher rates than Malays and thus could have correspondingly greater influence. Neither of these is true. In fact, research has shown that rural Malays, who are generally less well-off than urban Malay and Chinese, are the most likely to vote. Likewise, if socioeconomic status or class variables explained political influence, it would be impossible to understand how or why Chinese in Malaysia had considerably more political influence before 1969 than afterward. While the NEP succeeded in creating a Malay middle and upper class, it has not been significantly deleterious to Chinese economic status. Chinese businessmen like Tan Sri Lim Goh Tong, Genting Bhd.'s (corporation) chairman and managing director, have not only continued to do business but have prospered. Genting is a family business; however the management and board of directors are comprised of politically well-connected people. By linking the corporation to Malay elites, the conglomerate has grown exponentially.

On the board of directors are Tan Sri Haji Mohamad Noah bin Omar, the former speaker of the lower house of parliament (he is also the father-in-law of two former prime ministers, the late Tun Razak and Tun Datuk Hussein Onn); Tan Sri Haji Abjul Kadir bin Yusof, a former minister of law and attorney general; Nik Hashim bin Nik Yusof, a prominent lawyer-banker; and Tan Sri Chong Hon Yan, a former minister of health and secretary general of the Malayan Chinese Association. (Sieh Lee 1992:111)

Chinese have become better connected to Malay leaders, yet Chinese political power has shifted and is more circumscribed than prior to 1969. Class analysis alone cannot address this.

CONSOCIATIONALISM

There is another approach that is often used to understand how groups (particularly ethnic groups) interact politically. Through the 1950s and 1960s Malaysian politics are best characterized by what political scientists have termed "consociationalism," or an elite accommodation system. Ideally, this model of power sharing envisions each ethnic group as unified behind leaders who are positioned to bargain for their interests. It assumes that these ethnic elites will negotiate in good faith with their counterparts from other groups, and that once decisions are reached, ethnic constituents will comply with arrangements. Consociationalism seeks to keep ethnic mobilization (and any sort of class-based populism) to a minimum to allow elites to compromise with others and to restrain volatile or extremist elements within each group.9 This is a model of political cooperation that is only quasi-democratic. Its stability comes from the idea that leaders represent ethnic (or religious, or linguistic) groups with the group's interests in mind. While leaders represent their co-ethnics, they also must have enough power to compromise group demands when and if necessary. This sort of model did describe the political landscape in Malaysia before 1969. Malay, Chinese, and Indian leaders in the 1950s and early 1960s were largely British-educated, English-speaking, and fairly Westernized. They shared a vision of an independent Malaya under this sort of political arrangement. The 1969 riots and their aftermath showed the shortcomings in this thinking. Ethnic elites were not necessarily representing the true interests of their constituents. Malaysian Chinese voted for opposition parties in large numbers, and even UMNO seemed to loose political support. As a consequence, Malays took to the street to show their fear and anger at possible increases in Chinese political clout. Politics in Malaysia since 1969 seems focused on preventing a recurrence of this turmoil.

INSTITUTIONAL APPROACHES

The rest of the chapter deals mostly with the various ways that political institutions and leaders of political organizations have shaped the nature and extent of Chinese politicization. There are several approaches that political scientists have used to understand the effect of institutions, or "the rules of the game," on political behavior. Chinese politicization in

Malaysia can be ascribed to the legal conditions and political institutions that both shape and limit their choice possibilities (Katznelson 1973:42). Within an institutional framework it is necessary to understand the links between the institutions: laws, elected officials, the party system, bureaucratic networks, and the members of the Chinese community.

Power in Malaysia has increasingly been centralized in the federal government and particularly in the executive branch with Prime Minister Mahathir himself. While political participation is still largely along the ethnic lines originally crafted, influence is achieved less through officially designated ethnic elites, but through one of two mechanisms: either through the electoral needs of Malay officials pressured by opposition party gains, or through powerful individuals with ties to the regime. Ultimately, what I believe the Malaysia case shows about Chinese political mobilization is that the Chinese community has been targeted either through Chinese opposition party elites or by ruling-party Malays because there are economic and political incentives to be gained in doing so. In contrast, leaders of the Malaysian Chinese Association may be less likely to make strident communal appeals because they are reliant on their Malay counterparts in the multiparty coalition to secure positions within the government. In order to understand this, it is to these institutions that we now turn.

INSTITUTIONS

In all of the major institutions of government the Malay elite has established and preserved dominance. How can one best characterize the Malaysian political system? Is it democratic or authoritarian? There are regularly scheduled, free, and fair elections, and opposition parties contest a large number of seats. However, the major media outlets, particularly the Malay and English newspapers, are owned (in part) by the major political parties. There is also a fair amount of regulation and suppression of NGO activity, and critics and opposition groups suffer close scrutiny by the government. Barraclough (1985) discusses how the most often used method of repression has been the power of detention under Section 8(1) of the Internal Security Act of 1960 and 1972. The state has also used legal means to check political rivals such as the DAP. Leaders such as Lim Kit Siang have frequently been prosecuted for illegal assembly, breaching police permits, and other activities that are deemed to breach civil order.

Anne Munro Kua has called Malaysian politics "authoritarian populist," and it seems like an accurate description. Malaysian democracy exists for those (particularly Malays) who support UMNO and the ruling coalition, and until the political and economic turmoil of 1997–1998 this was probably a significant proportion of the population. But for those whose views are not represented, the playing field is anything but level.

In addition to the repressive characteristics listed above, the organs of the state are stacked in the Malays' favor. The Chinese and the Indians have representation through communal parties in the ruling coalition. This section will discuss the role of the party system, elections, the executive, the bureaucracy, the judiciary, the armed forces, and the monarchy in shaping the nature and effectiveness of Chinese political mobilization. While there are rivalries within or between organizations, these contests do not signal a challenge to Malay hegemony. Malaysia's constitution, discussed earlier, can be pointed to as the first, and perhaps most important, institution in understanding how and why the Chinese are incorporated into the Malaysian polity. Because of who took part and how the negotiations for independence played out, Chinese interests outside of those narrowly defined by business elites will increasingly take a backseat to Malay party leaders. This is because it is the privilege of the ruling coalition to change the constitution at will, and it has done so in order to gerrymander electoral districts in its favor. It is from the constitution that the following institutional arrangements evolved.

THE ELECTORAL SYSTEM

Since independence in 1957 the Malaysian political system has struck a balance between coercion[10] and responsiveness. Since 1957 there have been national elections every five years[11] for the lower house of parliament, the Dewan Rakyat, and for the various state assemblies. In each election the ruling coalition, the National Front or *Barisan Nasional* (BN), has won at least a two-thirds majority, and the conventional wisdom is that if the elections were not so one-sided, then they would not be held.[12] By winning a two-thirds majority in the legislature, the BN is able to change the constitution at will.

The Malaysian parliamentary system combines the British pattern of single-member constituencies with a highly distorted gerrymandering of electoral constituencies both to enhance the representation of (rural) Malay voters, and to give overwhelming leverage to the plurality in each district. Malay voting strength was particularly inflated after the 1984 apportionment. Malays comprise a majority in 70 percent of parliamentary constituencies.

> The disproportion between the largest (mainly Chinese urban) and smallest (Malay rural) constituencies is so great that some non-Malay

majority constituencies have more than three times the population of the smallest Malay-majority constituency. (Heng 1999:179)

This severely disadvantages non-Malay voters and thus serves to minimize their electoral representation while promoting the political fortunes of the BN coalition. After every other election the number of parliamentary constituencies has been increased and the boundaries redrawn, generally to BN's advantage, particularly for the United Malays National Organization (UMNO), the lead party in the coalition. This is perhaps the greatest institutional constraint to Chinese political power. Another limiting factor is that the ruling coalition runs only one candidate from its member parties in each constituency. This effectively minimizes the number of Chinese (MCA or Gerakan) candidates in the political arena. Coupled with the reconfiguration of electoral districts, there is far less need for UMNO or BN in general to be concerned with needs of Chinese voters.

The parliamentary structure has resulted in an overwhelmingly strong prime minister; this is largely due to the strength of Dr. Mahathir bin Mohammed. In office since 1981, Mahathir has been instrumental in developing a political apparatus that favors UMNO power. When he first went into politics he tended toward a militant stance on Malay ethnic issues. One needs only to refer to his book, *The Malay Dilemma*, for examples of this. In the late 1980s and early 1990s he became more of an active advocate of a nationalist ideology which attempts to incorporate the three major ethnic groups within a Malaysian identity. For example, political leaders have attended cultural ceremonies of other groups. Mahathir has attended and participated in a Chinese New Year's celebration and a lion dance; and TV advertisements promote the dual festivities with messages of *"gong xi fa cai"* and *"salam aidilfitri"* (Happy New Year and Aidilfitri, the end of Rahmadan, the Muslim holy month of fasting). This should not, however, be taken as an indication that adat has lost its significance. Chinese and Indian cultures are acknowledged and celebrated, but Islam and Malay status take precedent. While elections serve to constrain Chinese political power, they are a legitimizing force for Mahathir's regime. Elections are seriously contested, and opposition parties not only compete for seats but serve an important role in prompting the National Front parties to appeal to a wider audience. Despite distortions to the openness of the electoral process:

the electoral system has muted ethnic extremism by rewarding pluralities based on multiethnic support. Furthermore, elections have become accepted as the foundation for the Malaysian political system, and as such they have been the prime instrument for preserving and sustaining the democratic component in that system. (Means 1991:296)

VOTING

It is not possible to get a fully accurate picture of non-Malay voting patterns. The proportion of registered non-Malay voters is more or less in line with the population statistics, although the Chinese are slightly overrepresented and the Indians slightly underrepresented (Rachagan 1993:113). Crouch (1996a) speculates that the Chinese are somewhat less likely to exercise their voting rights than Malays, and he uses the following to illustrate the claim:

> In the Federal Territory of Kuala Lumpur, which is entirely urban and predominantly Chinese, the turnout in the 1990 election ranged between 62.1 and 71.3 percent, whereas in predominantly rural and Malay Terengganu, the turnout ranged between 77.67 and 86.79 percent. However, in largely Chinese Penang, where the state government faces a strong Chinese-based opposition, the turnout ranged from 74.33 to 80.76 percent. (p. 128)

The following figures provided even greater indication that there are differences in the degree to which groups in Malaysia participate (Table 3.2).

Table 3.2 illustrates both the differences in voting behavior in Malay- and Chinese-dominated states, and the importance of opposition parties in mobilizing Chinese voters. Voter turnout was consistently higher after the middle of the 1960s in the predominantly Malay state of Terengganu than in Selangor, which is more heavily Chinese. Also, voter turnout rates were significantly higher when the DAP ran a vigorous campaign against

TABLE 3.2 VOTER TURNOUT IN MALAYSIAN ELECTIONS						
PROVINCE	1959	1964	1969	1978	1982	1990[1]
Terengganu	70.3%	77.4%	74.6%	76.2%	80.28%	78–87%
Penang	73.2%	83.5%	77.5%	79.2%	77.27%	74–8%1
Selengor	73.6%	73.6%	65.8%	74.3%	72.8%	62–71%[2]

[1] Voter-turnout statistics after 1982 are difficult to come by. The figures listed for the 1990 election are based on estimations by Harold Crouch (1996a).
[2] These figures are actually for the Federal Territory of Kuala Lumpur, not Selengor Province.

(*Data compiled from:* Vasil 1972, Rachagan 1980, NSTP Research and Information Services 1990, Crouch 1996a.)

BN candidates; in Penang, DAP's stronghold, turnout ranged from 74.33 percent to 80.76 percent versus only 62.1 percent to 71.3 percent in Kuala Lumpur, where BN parties dominate.[13] This certainly seems to support the assumption that targeted mobilization by candidates and elites within the party structures can dramatically affect voter turnout. Likewise, the Semangat '46 and APU coalition that challenged BN in the 1990 election forced BN parties to court Chinese voters. Important, although largely symbolic, overtures were made by UMNO to the Chinese in a series of by-elections leading up to the general elections. UMNO assured the Chinese community of its support for preserving Chinese primary schools, and Tunku Abdul Rahman College, an MCA-sponsored vocational school that will be discussed at length later in the chapter, had several of its certificate courses recognized for purposes of government employment. Dr. Mahathir publicly participated in a lion dance festival, and travel restrictions to the PRC were removed. All of this served as a catalyst for greater Chinese support of the MCA and its coalition partners.

THE POLITICAL PARTY SYSTEM

The Barisan Nasional (BN) is the dominant player in Malaysia politics. Of the parties that comprise the BN, the United Malays National Organization (UMNO) is the leading party. Its major partners include the Malaysian Chinese Association (MCA), Malaysian Indian Congress (MIC), and Gerakan, an ostensibly multiracial party which is by and large Chinese in composition. Each of the major parties on peninsular Malaysia will be briefly discussed.

UMNO was formed during the process of decolonization. British-educated and conservative-leaning Malay aristocrats created it. They believed strongly in winning independence from the British as soon as possible, but not if it meant that Malaysia would be under the control of Chinese parties (conservative, communist, or otherwise). They also felt deep skepticism toward Islamic parties, who were viewed as unable, or unwilling, to modernize and develop the country. Ultimately, UMNO leaders had enough in common personally and enough political and economic incentives in the 1950s to work with their counterparts in MCA and MIC on achieving independence. They also had enough strength to protect Malay dominance in the new constitution and to craft the new government in their favor.

The MCA was first formed in 1949 as a welfare organization led by English-educated Chinese business elites. Although it is still somewhat viewed as a party of *towkays*, Chinese traders, throughout the 1970s and 1980s better-educated professionals have moved into positions of leader-

ship within the party. Some Chinese see the MCA as a channel for bringing demands to the government, others prefer to work through the opposition parties. MCA sees itself as the voice of the Chinese community
within the government. Unlike the DAP and other opposition forces, the
MCA has traditionally avoided confrontation and believes that its constituents' interests are best preserved in negotiating with UMNO as part
of BN.

> As a responsible component party of the Barisan Nasional, MCA has
> taken the positive position that it must convince its partners in gov-
> ernment to focus urgently on issues which negate efforts at build-
> ing a united multiracial society. Any deviation from the spirit and
> intent of NEP would cause increased "racial polarization." (MCA
> 1987:5)

Its willingness to support NEP, and to go along with UMNO goals that
might not be in the interests of the community, opens the MCA up to criticism. A prime consequence of this attitude toward the Malay ruling powers is that the MCA is vulnerable to charges that it has sold out Chinese
interests. After 1969 Chinese power within in the government deteriorated, and the MCA's standing in the Chinese community was also at a low
point. The MCA's position within the Chinese community is not analogous to UMNO's within the Malay population.

One of MCA's main rivals for political representation of the Chinese
community's support is Gerakan. With its stronghold in Penang, Gerakan
was created as a moderate social reform party. It espouses principles of
social justice, human rights, and a more democratic and open political system for Malaysia. Gerakan is more committed than other "Chinese" parties to multiracial integration in Malaysian politics. After the riots in 1969
Gerakan joined the National Front Coalition, challenging MCA's hegemony in claiming to be the voice of the Chinese community within the
ruling coalition. The People's Progressive Party was also brought into the
National Front after 1969. The PPP is a multiracial party based in Perak
which also aims toward ethnic integration and social justice. From outside the ruling coalition the Democratic Action Party (DAP) has (at times)
garnered a fair amount of support from Malaysian Chinese. Estimates
show that about half of Chinese voters support this opposition party. It
may be impossible to know exactly how many registered Chinese actually
vote, but Crouch shows that 20 percent of the peninsula's votes go to the
DAP and 34 to 37 percent of registered voters are Chinese. Assuming that

virtually no Malays supported the DAP, and perhaps one-quarter of Indian voters might have, that indicates that close to half of the Chinese voters supported the DAP (Crouch 1996:71).

The DAP champions non-Malay rights, calling for careful enforcement of all human rights. It is anticorruption, defends Chinese language education and culture, and has been a vocal supporter of Chinese business interests under NEP. The DAP is severely disadvantaged by its lack of access to a patronage network that would allow it to reward supporters with jobs, contracts, or other government-connected benefits.

By 1989, after Tunku Razaleigh challenged Mahathir and the legality of BN, he and his followers were allowed to register a new party: Semangat '46 (spirit of 1946) referring to the year UMNO was established (Jomo 1996:101). This group forged connections with smaller opposition parties such as the Parti Islam Se Malaysia (PAS), a pan-Malaysian Islamic party. In 1989 a formal coalition was formed called Angkatan Perpaduan Ummah (APU), or the Movement of Community Unity, to compete against BN. This offered an unprecedented challenge to BN.

While the DAP and PAS clash over claims to their respective constituents' interests and thus cannot cooperate with each other openly, when APU existed, the DAP, through cooperative working arrangements with Semangat '46, helped lend APU a multiethnic appeal. Multiethnic party coalitions help prevent many, but not all, efforts at strident ethnic politicking by parties. While many politicians still "play the race card," coalition politics tended to mute these appeals. Despite the challenge from APU candidates in the 1990 general election, BN won 127 of 180 seats in Parliament, seven more than necessary to maintain a two-thirds majority (Crouch 1996:125).

In April of 1995 the ninth general election was held. It gave the BN its largest margin of victory since independence in 1957. It won commanding majorities in ten of eleven state assemblies, and the coalition won 65.4 percent of the popular vote and 162 of 192 parliamentary seats. The only state it did not win was Kelantan, where BN lost to APU, the coalition between PAS and Semangat '46. The DAP was decimated, even in its traditional stronghold, Penang, where it lost all but one of its thirteen state seats, this included a loss for former DAP leader Lim Kit Siang.[14] BN's victory seems largely due to Malaysia's booming economy at the time and the sense that life has improved for a broad spectrum of the population.[15] However, the election results should not be taken as an indication that ethnic politics are receding, as the education issues I discuss later should indicate (see Table 3.3).

TABLE 3.3   1995 ELECTION RESULTS FOR SEATS IN THE HOUSE OF REPRESENTATIVES

PARTY	NUMBER OF SEATS WON	CHANGE FROM 1990
National Front (BN)	162	+35
• United Malays National Organization (UMNO)	89	
• Malaysian Chinese Association (MCA)	30	
• Sarawak National Front Parties	27	
• Malaysian Indian Congress	7	
• Gerakan Rakyat Malaysia	7	
• Others	2	
Democratic Action Party (DAP)	9	−11
Sabah United Party	9	−6
Pan-Malaysian Islamic Party	7	
Semangat '46	6	−2
Independents	0	−4
Total Seats	192	+12[1]

[1] The increase of twleve seats from 1990 to 1995 reflects a reapportionment change.

(Results obtained from http://www.ipu.org:80/cgi/multigate.exe/r, an election results website.)

After the Semangat '46 lost two seats in the election and did not seem to be able to offer a counterideology to UMNO and the ruling coalition, members began readopting UMNO party status. By late 1996, Semangat '46 had dissolved and the APU coalition was likewise not a player. Nonetheless, the short period of competing multiethnic coalitions illustrates the important potential of a more competitive system still based along ethnic dimensions.

The original formation of a multiethnic political alliance shows how formal incentives can induce informal arrangements (Horowitz 1989). Both the Chinese and the Malay elites had something to gain in forming a partnership with the other. In 1952, during the communist insurgency, the UMNO-MCA Alliance was created to win local town council elections. The Alliance was a product of a group of Selangor (the territory which includes Kuala Lumpur) UMNO and MCA leaders. Chairman of the Selangor UMNO Election Committee, Datuk Yahaya bin Datuk Abdul Razak, Selangor MCA Chairman H.S. Lee, and Working Committee Members Ong Yoke Lin (a schoolmate of Datuk Yahaya's), and S. M. Yong were able to form an alliance. The partnership evolved due to electoral needs and the personal relationships of the UMNO and MCA elite. The leading party, the IMP (Independence Party of Malaya) was well organized and led by Dato' Onn Jaffar. Onn had resigned from UMNO precisely because it had refused to accept non-Malay members. To compete in urban areas against IMP, the UMNO was forced to form alliances with non-Malay parties. In Kuala Lumpur the local head of the MCA was opposed to MCA national leader Tan Cheng Lock's decision to support IMP in the elections, thus setting the stage for the Alliance partnership. The coalition won in Kuala Lumpur and was then successful as a national multiethnic coalition (Horowitz 1989:27; Heng 1988:156–162). In 1955 most Chinese and Indians in Malaysia had not yet been granted citizenship. The combination of the electoral incentives, the timing of the national elections held after town council elections, and the suspicion of the Muslim-oriented parties such as PAS and of the party leaders provided a favorable response to the constraints that impinged on decision-makers (Heng 1988:188–216).

From 1969 until the 1990s several of these elements changed. Beginning in the late 1960s, MCA lost support from the Chinese community. As NEP increasingly created a wealthy middle class of ethnic Malays, UMNO was less beholden to Chinese economic contributions to the coalition. With each reapportionment, UMNO's position has been strengthened; the results of this can be seen in the 1995 election outcome, listed in Table 3.3. With eighty-nine of 162 coalition seats, UMNO is far more powerful than any of its junior partners (alone or combined). During the fall of 1998 when Anwar was fired and arrested, it looked as if Prime Minister Mahathir's rule might finally be challenged. However, it now seems that he feels confident enough in BN's popularity (and the opposition parties' disorganization) that new general election will take place in November, 1999.

While the electoral institutions alone have served to sideline Malaysian Chinese, the government apparatus itself is also insulated from too much Chinese input.

GOVERNMENT STRUCTURE

UMNO domination of the political system corresponds to their control of the main institutions of the state: the bureaucracy, the armed forces, police, judiciary, and the monarchy. The elites in these positions often came from similar social and economic backgrounds, producing a common outlook on particular features of the political system (Crouch 1996:130). The Malaysian bureaucracy, or civil service (MCS), was closed to Chinese and Indians until the 1950s. After World War II Great Britain added non-Malays to MCS with the stipulation that a minimum of 80 percent of the positions would be reserved for Malays. In the 1970s MCS became known as the Administrative and Diplomatic Service (Perkhidmatan Tadbirdan Diplomatik, or PTD) and expanded rapidly with the task of administering NEP. As the bureaucracy increased in size and responsibility it has assumed a more important role in economic planning and public policy initiatives, and in direct management of significant sectors of the economy. For example, economic planning at both the state and federal level is coordinated by the Economic Planning Unit (EPU), in the Prime Minister's Department. In turn, the EPU reports to the National Development Planning Council. This creates a highly centralized means to oversee economic development planning. Likewise, it concentrates the collection of data and the conducting of research for policy issues in the hands of these few government elites. This makes it vitally important for community and business elites to gain access to these bureaucratic structures for input on decision-making (Means 1991:298).

Most cabinet ministers are Malay. For example, in 1999 there were six Chinese department heads, one Indian, and fifteen Malays; an overwhelming majority of deputies are also Malay. This Malay bias within the bureaucracy makes it somewhat easier to obtain influence in policy implementation, but non-Malay elites do gain access to various advisory bodies. Robert Kuok is a good example of this. After NEP required Chinese family businesses to form partnerships with *bumiputra* and state businesses, the Kuok brothers were able to cultivate highly profitable business networks with UMNO and other state officials (Sieh Lee 1992:110; Heng 1992:132–134). In addition, civil service elites have close ties with UMNO, even though the top level of bureaucrats (A-level civil servants) are forbidden from participating in politics. Lower officials can and do participate vigorously in party activities. In reality the partisan prohibitions are quite lax, and the civil service is a recruiting ground for UMNO (Crouch 1996:133).

THE ARMED FORCES

The military, like the bureaucracy, was formed initially in 1934 under British rule. Known as the Royal Malay Regiment, the armed forces were all Malay. In the 1950s the military established a multiethnic reconnaissance corps, but few were non-Malay. While British officers maintained key positions until the late 1960s, by the mid 1970s the forces were almost fully Malayanized. After the 1969 riot the government expanded the army's role and size as a Malayan force in order to provide backing for the government in the event of further communal conflict. Malays have dominated the officer class of the army and, to a lesser extent, the navy and air force. Malays have also been appointed to the key military command positions: Chief of Defense Forces, Chief of Army, Air Force, and now the Navy. These military officers are linked to the civilian elite by race and through the same small number of families that have overlapping membership in UMNO leadership and the upper echelons of the civil service. As part of this Malay elite, the military leadership has little reason to be ill-disposed toward the Malay-dominated civilian leadership.

THE JUDICIARY

The judiciary, like the military, remained in the hands of British ex-patriots immediately following Independence. Despite the large numbers of non-Malays in the legal profession, the judicial branch of government has been overwhelmingly Malay. Institutionally, judges tend to share in the conservative outlook of their counterparts in the bureaucracy. Courts in Malaysia do not interpret the law in a manner that would restrict the powers of the government or the civil service. This is in part due to the ability of the ruling parties to alter the constitution with a two-thirds majority in both houses of Parliament. Since BN always has this majority, the court has little power to rule something "unconstitutional."

Perhaps it is not surprising then that up until the 1970s there were close relations between the government and the judiciary. Since the 1980s there has been a somewhat more rocky relationship between Mahathir and the courts. The unusual tension stems from a series of judgments made by the courts in 1986 and 1987 that invalidated several government initiatives. Some of the more controversial judgments involved the Minister of Home Affairs, a post which Prime Minister Mahathir held at the time.

One of the most notable conflicts between the executive and the judiciary was the conflict that occurred between the court and UMNO. Opponents within the party challenged Mahathir's reelection as UMNO president in 1987. Renegade UMNO forces were led by Tengku Razaleigh, whose immediate goal was to invalidate the party elections. Party dissidents appealed to the court, and Justice Harun found that the presence of illegal branches within UMNO meant that the party itself was an illegal organization and had to be disbanded. Mahathir established a new party, UMNO Baru (new), with his strongest supporters tightly in control. Razaleigh's forces appealed to the Supreme Court.

The Lord President of the Supreme Court, Tun Salleh Abas, decided to hear the case with a heretofore unheard-of full panel of nine judges. Before the case could be heard, the Yang di-Pertuan Agong (King) suspended Tun Salleh from his position. A hand-picked tribunal concluded that Tun Salleh was guilty of bias against the government and he, along with two other judges, was dismissed (Crouch 1996:140–143; Means 1991:223–227). This had the effect of allowing Mahathir's government to then rid itself of judges who were apt to make rulings unfavorable to the government. As Means notes, "The constitutional mechanisms designed to assure the independence of the judiciary were of little protection in any dispute with the executive" (1991:302). Nonetheless, the judiciary has not lost all independence; since 1988 there have been times when the courts have handed down decisions that are less than favorable to the regime, but the overall tendency of the courts is to lean toward deference for the Malay-dominated status quo.

THE MONARCHY

The oldest political institution in Malaysia is the system of Malay rulers. British colonial rulers transformed the system of ruling families on the Malay peninsula and turned it first into a system of indirect rule, then, using this culturally based institution, they incorporated the Malay monarchy into the blueprints for the independent parliamentary regime. Above the existing nine Malay rulers is the Yang di-Pertuan Agong, the Paramount Ruler, or King. He is elected by the Conference of Rulers from among the nine Malay rulers on the basis of seniority for a single five-year term. His seniority is then not counted for purposes of electing the next king. The king is thus the ruler of the federation as a whole. The monarchy serves primarily two important functions: (1) the rulers provide the parliamentary system with Malay cultural legitimacy, and (2) they have a circumscribed measure of political clout, generally derived from their popularity as an institution that is perceived to be largely above petty politicking. The monarchy reflects the ethnic divide between formal Malay political dominance and the ability of non-Malays to exert some measure of influence, either through negotiated compromise or through personal networks and elite connections.

> Although the Rulers are seen as a bastion of Malay supremacy, non-Malays have increasingly accepted the role of the Rulers, in part because most Rulers have shown themselves to be more moderate and even-handed on contentious ethnic issues than many active Malay politicians. While the Rulers are no longer the primary patronage-givers, they do distribute honour, rank, and public recognition, and their vast personal wealth and investments make them ideal partners for joint ventures, especially for non-Malay partners. (Means 1991:303)

The monarchy may be in an interesting position to be an effective institution to counter executive power. They have a great deal of popular legitimacy and constitutionally they have significant autonomy. Whether they use their position to be complicitous with the executive or independent of it seems to rest with the individual sultan. Means (1991:304) gives as an example of this an incident in 1989, when King Sultan Azlan Shah of Perak did not receive a unanimous election by the Rulers Council and thus refused to be sworn in by Lord President Abdul Hamid Omar, Salleh Abas' replacement. This can be compared to the earlier actions in 1988 of King Sultan Mahmood Iskandar Shah of Johore, when he agreed to impeachment charges against Lord President Salleh Abas and then against five other Supreme Court judges over the UMNO crisis. Recently, however, Mahathir has worked to undermine the power of the monarchy. In 1988 the Prime Minister apparently tried to influence the selection of the next king and, Dr. Mahathir has tried to play the military and the monarchy off each other (Means 1991:300).

The monarchy serves as one more reminder that the Chinese are outsiders in Malaysia. While the sultans do confer honorific titles on prominent Malaysian Chinese, the entire sultanate is meant to reflect Malay traditional leadership. As such it conveys a sense of primacy to ethnic Malays. The legitimacy and support for the monarchy may reflect the fact that is an institution that perpetuates exclusive Malay leadership.

Within this institutional apparatus there are leaders within the Chinese community whose task it is to navigate this structure for either their own or the community's benefit. One of the issues that has been of continued importance to the Chinese in Malaysia is access to education. As illustrated earlier in this chapter, the education movement has been a litmus test of Chinese political power. The next part of this chapter brings the issue up to date. By looking at how the Chinese community has attempted to protect and promote their interests in maintaining Chinese vernacular education, one can better understand how the institutions of power shape and constrain participation and influence.

EDUCATION

Chinese education activists are one set of leaders within the community who have been able to mobilize people in support of particular ethnic interests. They have also formed links to opposition party candidates. This has proved a somewhat successful tactic, not because they have been able to force a change in the power structure, but because it has served as a means of pressuring MCA and UMNO leaders into moderating policies.

Education has been an issue of particular concern to the Chinese in Malaysia, and some of the most outspoken critics of the BN coalition have been leaders from the educationalist movement.

Although Malaysia is a federal system and this presupposes a certain state autonomy, the federal government maintains a preponderance of power over the states. Fiscally, states are heavily dependent on federal grants and budget outlays. In addition, the federal government has the power to suspend state constitutions and impose emergency rule, as well as the power to amend state constitutions virtually at will. The national government can impose its political will on states and municipalities.

> With a fairly centralized national party system extending to all states and the extensive use of federal patronage at the state level, the power and influence of federal authorities have become even more pervasive. (Means 1991:296)

While education policy is decidedly a local issue in the United States, it is a matter of federal policy in Malaysia. Since British colonialism, schooling has also been a communal affair. As part of the negotiations for independence, elites had to decide how to deal with a comprehensive system of vernacular schools which sought government financing and recognition but did not wish simply to be swallowed up by an English or Malay education system. This was only the beginning of what has been a highly politicized, and at times rancorous, series of negotiations over the place and fate of Chinese education in Malaysia.

The first Chinese school on the Malay peninsula is thought to date back to 1815. As sojourner settlements in what is now Malaysia grew, so did Chinese schools. Throughout British colonial rule the Chinese schools were largely independent. Kua (1990) argues that this is because the colonial authorities were "so impressed by the high level of communal organization among Malaysian Chinese that they left them virtually alone to manage their own affairs" (p. 3). Clearly, it is also because neither the colonial government nor the initial indigenous regime was strong enough financially to take over the schools.

> On 31 March 1954, the Chinese student population in Malaya stood at 31 percent (251,174)of the total school enrollment (803,803) in the country. The 250,000-odd Chinese students were enrolled in 1,200 schools, the majority of which received partial financial backing from the government in the form of grants-in-aid. As grants-in-aid per student were lower than grants-in-aid to English, Malay, or

Indian-medium schools, the Chinese schools still depended to a considerable extent upon financial endowments made to them by the *huay kuan* leaders. (Heng 1988:193)

The creation and maintenance of a school system that promoted Chinese language, culture, and high educational standards entailed the mobilization of a cross section of Chinese *huay kuan*, or associations. The Associated Chinese Chambers of Commerce (ACCC) provided much of the funding and leadership, first for the schools themselves, and then for the education movement. As discussed earlier, the post–World War II period was dominated by citizenship, language, and ethnic issues as Malaysia moved toward independence. The question of how to develop a national system of education was intrinsically linked to these debates.

> The Chinese community was told that their vernacular education could not be considered within the National Education System since the Chinese language was not an official language of the country. This, in turn, could only be possible if the Chinese were given citizenship. Consequently, the question of citizenship in the constitutional proposals—the Malayan Union and the Federation of Malaya proposals—concerned the Chinese schools as much as the rest of the community. (Kua 1990:6–7)

The citizenship question succeeded in uniting the disparate Chinese organizations, guilds, and kinship associations; language, status, and education needs cut across clan, dialect, and geographic boundaries. It should be noted that there is no such unifying issue among Chinese in Malaysia today. In the negotiations leading up to the 1957 granting of independence, the leaders of the MCA and MIC negotiated with UMNO to secure expanded citizen rights for these immigrant groups. In exchange they reached an understanding that the Malays would assume a dominant position in the new government (Crouch 1996:157). Through the 1950s the issue of whether to allow vernacular (Chinese and Tamil) schools to continue and if they should receive state funding was part of the negotiations over the constitutional arrangements to be implemented after decolonization. Significantly, Chinese education advocates were willing to compromise some of their school interest in order to achieve wider citizenship allowances for Chinese.

A clear pattern has emerged in vernacular education policy. Every attempt to tamper with these schools has come after a set of elections in which promises to the Chinese and Indian communities about the sanctity of their schools have been made by first the Alliance coalition and then by BN. In 1954, a committee made up of MCA, *Jiao Zong* (the United Chinese School Teachers' Association, UCSTA), and the newly created *Dong Zong* (United Chinese School Committees Association of Malaysia, UCSCA) sent a "Memorandum on Chinese Education" to the colonial government, expressing their dissatisfaction with the way that Chinese schools were treated in the Education Ordinance of 1952. The ordinance prevented Chinese and Tamil schools from taking part in the national system. Mandarin and Tamil would be taught in national schools only if fifteen students per grade requested it. Because of this, the UCSTA came to the forefront as Chinese community associations rallied in opposition to the ordinance (Kua 1990:8) and threatened to derail the decolonization process. At the pre-1955 election meeting with USCTA and UCSCA, MCA and UMNO leaders agreed to safeguard Chinese education and culture, and in exchange Chinese educationalists agreed to postpone their demands for Chinese to be included as an official language of independent Malaysia.

Initially the Chinese education movement was led by businessmen and Chinese schoolteachers who had a vision of a democratic, multiethnic nation where minority languages and cultures were given the right to coexist with that of the Malays' (Tan 1992). *Dongjiaozong* is the Chinese term used to refer to the two organizations above, the *Jiao Zong* and *Dong Zong*, which have worked closely together to articulate Chinese interests and to mobilize support for Chinese education in Malaysia.[16] For a short while Kua Kia Soong played a dominant role, both as a DAP member and as a spokesmen for the educationalists.

The period leading up to the first postcolonial national elections illustrates how the MCA was able to gain support both in the Chinese community and from the UMNO leadership. This was due in large measure to the leadership and commitment of Tan Cheng Lock (first MCA party president) to the cause of Chinese education and his skills at cultivating a personal relationship with UMNO's leader Tunku Abdul Rahman. Tan's support for Chinese culture and education is shown in the following speech given in 1952 to a group of Chinese educationalists:

> While politically the Malayan Chinese must be one and united with the rest of the permanent population of Malaya, culturally they must be independent and must maintain a very strong intellectual and spiritual life of their own.... The Chinese must be brought into harmony with their native Chinese ethos in order that they may preserve their traditions, customs, institutions and manners

and be conversant with the Chinese classics and culture. Thus only can they become good Chinese as well as good Malayans. (Speech delivered by Tan Cheng Lock at the Conference of Chinese School Committees and Teachers on November 9, 1952 in Kuala Lumpur, quoted in Heng 1988:197)

Tan thus received support from the community for his dealings with UMNO, and financial backing from the business elements involved in the *Dongjiaozong*. Likewise, Tunku Abdul Rahman defended the right of different communities to receive vernacular education: "Let the Chinese be taught in their schools, let the Indians be taught in their schools.... Our only concern is that ... Malay must remain an official language of this country" (Heng 1988:204).

Tan Cheng Lock was thus able to work with UMNO behind the scenes to communicate the Chinese community's preferences about preserving Chinese education. However, it is vital to understand that UMNO had significant electoral incentives both to seek and then to maintain the MCA as an ally. As the first municipal, local, and state election results show, the organizational and financial support of MCA contributed toward the overwhelming victories won by the Alliance. In order to comply with British requirements for a multiethnic ruling arrangement, and to defeat the IMP, UMNO leaders found it expedient to pledge to meet Chinese interests. The Alliance party won the 1955 elections in a landslide, gaining fifty-one of fifty-two contested seats and 80 percent of the popular vote (Kua 1990:103).

After the 1955 elections were held, the Alliance took a somewhat more ambiguous stand on Chinese education. The Razak Report of 1956 recommended the following:

> ... a national system of education acceptable to the people of the Federation as a whole which will satisfy their needs to promote their cultural, social, economic and political development as a nation, having no regard to the intention of making Malay the national language of the country whilst preserving and sustaining the growth of the language and culture of other communities living in the country. (Kua 1990:11)

The report goes on to say:

> We believe further that the *ultimate* objective of the education policy in this country must be to bring together the children of all races

under a national education system in which the national language
is the medium of instruction. (Razak Report, Paragraph 12, emphasis added)

The Razak Report incorporated Chinese primary schools into the national
school system that afforded them better funding and official recognition.
However, the position of Chinese secondary schools was not safeguarded;
they were neither recognized nor funded. The Razak Report was legislated
in the 1957 Education Ordinance. The Rahman Talib Review Committee
reviewed this ordinance in 1960, and the ambiguity over Chinese secondary schools left them vulnerable. The Talib Report stated that partial
government aid to these schools would end as of January 1, 1962, and
funding would be accorded only to those schools which switched over to
national-type schooling using English and Malay as the medium of
instruction. In addition, national public exams would be given in English
and Malay only. The crowning blow to the Chinese community came with
the incorporation of the Talib Report into the Education Act of 1961. The
report added another feature: Section 21(2) of the act permits the
government to abolish Chinese primary schools at its discretion (Kua
1990:12).

Resentment toward the MCA and its coalition partners grew during the
1960s, to a large extent because it was perceived as ineffectual at meeting the demands of the community on concerns such as vernacular education (Heng 1988; Kua 1990; Tan 1992). The issue of Chinese education
was, from the start, entwined with that of language. The 1957 federal constitution had stated:

The national language shall be the Malay language ... (but) for a
period of ten years after Merdeka Day and thereafter until
Parliament otherwise provides, the English language may be used
in both Houses of Parliament, in the Legislative Assembly of every
state, and for all other official purposes." (*The Federal Constitution*
Article 152, Clauses 1 and 2)

In 1966, the Alliance government introduced legislation to make Malay
the only official language as of September 1967. Needless to say, this produced considerable alarm in the Chinese community. Protests from the
Chinese guilds and associations persuaded the MCA to push for a moderate compromise when the National Language Bill came to the floor of
Parliament. While Malay (Bahasa Malaysia) was stipulated as the only official language, the government, both federal and state, had the right to use

any translation of official documents in languages deemed necessary to the public interest. The Ministry of Education also announced that students without the Malaysian Certificate of Education or Government's School Certificate, both of which required a credit in Bahasa Malaysia, would not be allowed to go abroad for university studies. This would have prevented Chinese secondary school graduates from going abroad to study or from going to Nanyang University in Singapore, a Chinese university established with funding and support from many Malaysian Chinese before Singapore split from the Federation. Thus in the late 1960s the Chinese community began raising money for Merdeka University, a tertiary institution in Malaysia where Mandarin would be the medium of instruction.

Grassroots support for MU came from all segments of the community. Opposition parties such as the DAP were particularly quick to support the idea of a Chinese university. While the MCA joined the bandwagon of support for MU, it also worked on other, more palatable alternatives. Just prior to the elections of 1969, the MCA announced the creation of Tunku Abdul Rahman College (TARC), an English-language school which would offer engineering and preuniversity courses. There is some speculation that the MCA proposed TARC as a diversion or a wedge issue to stem the flow of Chinese support to opposition parties that endorsed the Merdeka University campaign (Kua 1990:110). While MCA's success at establishing TAR College highlights the ability of the MCA to work through institutionalized channels for moderate goals, something that I will discuss in more detail presently, it was viewed as a poor substitute for a Chinese-language university. Consequently, in 1969 the MCA was handed its worst electoral returns since its inception. In addition, UMNO began to see that the MCA was no longer truly representative of a "unified" Chinese community.

Although the BN coalition retained a plurality of votes, DAP and other opposition party gains were viewed with hostility. Riots broke out that spring in part because Malays feared that the election results indicated growing Chinese political power outside of the multiethnic coalition.

During the State of Emergency that followed the riots, the government implemented policies that changed the whole system of education in Malaysia, and it marked a dramatic shift in the role that the MCA and institutionalized channels of participation would play in affecting influence in Malaysian politics. Education policy would now be made to serve the larger political goals of the New Economic Policy (NEP). In July 1969, Education Minister Datuk Patinggi Haji Abdul Rahman Yaacub stated that English would be replaced by Malay one year at a time starting with the first year of primary school and continuing yearly up to university level. In 1971 the ministry also published the Majid Ismail Report on the development of a quota system for university admission where *bumiputras* would be given priority for places in greater proportions. These pieces of legislation spurred many Chinese to enroll their children in Chinese schools (Kua 1990:115).

The other significant piece of legislation addressing education that came out of NEP was the Universities and University Colleges Act (UUCA), which said that any university or college must have approval of the Yang di-Pertuan Agong and Parliament before it could be established (Kua 1990:134). While not immediately evident, this legislation was later used to justify the High Court ruling in 1981 that Merdeka University was prohibited because it violated this act. The Court came out in support of the government, which had announced in 1979 that it objected to the proposed university on the grounds that:

(i)   the proposed university was contrary to the national education policy since the medium of instruction would be Chinese.

(ii) it would be set up by a private organization.

(iii) it would only be admitting students from the Chinese Independent schools. (Kua 1990:138)

In addition, the Court declared that any university, public or private, in accordance with the 1971 UUCA, is a public authority and as such has to use Bahasa Malaysia for official purposes consistent with the Constitution, Article 152(1).

In 1982 the government introduced a new curriculum stressing the fundamentals: writing, reading, and mathematics. It stipulated that 77 percent of school time was to be devoted to these three subjects. Protests, led by the DAP and *Dongjiaozong*, were held to show their displeasure at the new requirements. The Chinese feared that these guidelines would come at the expense of Chinese-language instruction and that they privileged Malay as the classroom medium for these three areas. There was also a sense that these changes could be a prelude to the conversion of Chinese schools to national-type schools with Malay as the sole language of instruction (*FEER* January 22, 1982:10).

With Mahathir's rise to power in 1981, there was some hope that influence in the political process would be normalized through institutional channels. When the MCA was unable to protect Chinese interests, as the 1982 curriculum shift demonstrates, opposition parties such as the DAP gained support from Chinese constituents.

More recently, prior to the 1986 elections the BN promised that Chinese and Tamil-medium schools would continue in their present form; it further stated that Section 21(2) of the 1961 Education Act would be repealed in the first meeting of Parliament. After its victory in the election, no immediate action was taken (Kua 1992:133). Clearly, education policy was being used for political gain by BN. In 1987 several ethnic issues came to a head. The DAP had done well in the 1986 election; this, combined with financial scandals discrediting several MCA officials (Gomez 1991), left the party defensive and in need of reasserting itself with the Chinese community. UMNO, too, was rife with the factional rivalries that lead to Razaleigh's formation of Semangat '46. Each ethnic group could easily point to the other camp as the source of its difficulties.

Following a controversy at the University of Malaya over the use of Bahasa for optional Chinese and Tamil studies courses, the DAP staged a demonstration which was countered by Malay students. This demonstration was only a minor incident. However, a larger conflict arose when the government appointed more than one hundred Chinese teachers to higher administrative positions within Chinese primary schools. Although Chinese, these teachers did not possess Mandarin Chinese qualifications. To the Chinese community this seemed like yet another move to undermine the Chinese schools. The DAP and *Dongjiaozong* quickly mobilized support for a protest. Fearing that the DAP would garner greater leverage from the event, the MCA also participated in the protest meeting held in Kuala Lumpur on October 11, 1987 (Tan 1992:194; *FEER* October 29, 1987). At the meeting, despite the fact that the government had already decided to reassign the teachers, the leaders agreed to call for a boycott of schools if the appointments were not withdrawn by October 14. The boycott went ahead on October 15.

The Malay response to the DAP/MCA cooperation was dramatic. UMNO's youth wing held a huge rally denouncing the MCA and the Chinese in general. Seemingly unconnected to the political turmoil, a mentally disturbed Malay soldier took a gun and went on a random shooting spree in a crowded area of Kuala Lumpur. Several people were hit, and one Malay was killed. People in the capital feared a repeat of May 13, 1969. Several leaders within UMNO advocated further mass demonstrations. Mahathir put an end to these plans and called for the detainment of activists under the Internal Security Act. Both Chinese and Malay, BN and DAP leaders were arrested, but the UMNO, MCA, and Gerakan members were released fairly quickly; "seven DAP and five Chinese education-movement detainees were among those given two-year detention orders" (Crouch 1991:110).

This incident illustrates two important points. First, feeling pressure from internal and external challenges, both MCA and UMNO were inclined to racialize the issue to mobilize support. Second, although the government may have justly feared renewed communal conflict, it used the crisis to achieve partisan goals. By arresting DAP leaders, the government not only removed the most strenuous backers of Chinese interests but also put an end to criticism from the opposition on other issues, such as questionable patronage ties in the awarding of a large government road-building contract (Crouch 1991:111).

In 1990 a new education bill was drafted but because of the Official Secrets Act it was not made available to the public. Finally, in 1996 the education bill updating the 1961 and 1974 Education Acts was made public. While bringing about some changes in Malaysia's education system, it leaves intact the provision for plural education, where Chinese and Tamil-medium schools coexist with Malay language–based ones. While this protects Chinese education for now, many Malays see this as a continuation of divisive policies: "In this respect, education policy in Malaysia is still hostage to ethnic forces and remains a compromise instrument for fostering national unity" (Jawhar 1996:126–137). Clearly, the issue will be revisited.

While the MCA has tried to accommodate its coalition partners and has not fought enthusiastically for a Chinese university, it has tried to offer an alternative. Tunku Abdul Rahman College is an English-language institute created by the MCA to meet some of the needs of its constituents. The government's reluctance to recognize and accredit the institution illustrates the gap between having a seat at the table and actually being able to deliver what the community needs. In other words, the MCA had the funds and the ability to establish this college but not the political clout or will to fulfill the real aims of the community. While compromise is always a part of the political process, the inability of MCA to get Tunku Abdul Rahman College degrees accredited for so long shows the weakness of the party in relation to UMNO. The establishment and status of the college requires closer investigation.

TAR COLLEGE

Tunku Abdul Rahman College (TAR, or TARC) was created with MCA funding in February of 1969. Half of TARC's funding comes from the government and the rest is made up of donations and money from tuition fees. According to the college's prospectus, as of 1990 TAR was one of only nine universities and colleges to receive government funding. This is significant since there is an acknowledged need for greater access to tertiary education. The creation and funding of TARC is a unique example of cooperation between the government and the private sector and shows the complex relationship between a ruling party, the MCA and members of the Chinese community. It is an English-medium technical school offering courses in business, technical and engineering training, and preuniversity studies. With an initial enrollment of about one thousand students, in 1980 it was up to four thousand students, and several thousand more have been added in the 1990s. In 1994 it added a diploma course in mass communications.

TAR is a college rather than a university because to take on university status would require applying under the UUC Act of 1971. After the Merdeka University controversy there are no plans for TAR to change its status. Students are able to continue their education through twinning programs with schools outside Malaysia (*Star*, July 21, 1994). TAR College has campuses in Kuala Lumpur, Penang, Johor, Perak, Pahang, and Sarawak. For the first twenty years of its existence it was not accorded government recognition for diplomas or certificates (*Star*, October 18, 1988). By the close of 1990 many engineering programs (including material, civil, and mechanical engineering) and computer science certificate courses were recognized by the government, although many saw the timing of the government's decision as being affected by the political necessities of that year's general election rather than as based on academic criteria (*New Straits Times*, October 9, 1990).

Government recognition is important for two reasons: first, this sort of accreditation is necessary if graduates want to be qualified for Malaysian civil service jobs. A more ethnically balanced civil service could help lay the foundation for a more multiethnic public service sector. Second, government certification is important because it symbolizes acceptance. While TAR graduates succeed in getting jobs, recognition has for twenty years been seen as an indication of the MCA's waning position within the ruling coalition, a painful reminder of its lack of influence.

ANALYSIS OF SHIFTS IN COMMUNITY INFLUENCE

The discussion over Chinese education shows is how community influence has shifted. While compromise between Malay and Chinese leaders was possible, and some community interests were achieved from the 1950s up until 1969, since the 1970s Chinese influence in Malaysian politics has been greatly curtailed. Table 3.4 captures this change.

Prior to 1969, politicians of both MCA and UMNO needed Chinese support both for electoral purposes and for funding. Because of the preferences of elites and the need to attract Chinese support, UMNO and MCA

	POLITICIANS	CHINESE BUSINESS ELITES	SOCIAL ACTIVISTS
	TABLE 3.4 POLITICIZATION AND INFLUENCE IN CHINESE COMMUNITIES OVERSEAS: MALAYSIA		
1950–1969	Need Chinese backing for electoral suppport and funding	Willing to work through MCA to fund the coalition Common cause against the communist insurgency	Willing to trade preferred policies for expanded citizenship rights
1970–1998	Less need for Chinese support and funding	Able to work directly with Malay political and economic elite Little need to reach out to the community as a whole	Increasingly centered on "Chinese interests" Now working through NGOs and opposition parties

worked together as part of the Alliance party, thus fulfilling the requirements for a multiethnic ruling structure. Since the Chinese controlled the country's capital, it was doubly important not to alienate Chinese business and kinship networks. Chinese business leaders were willing to work through MCA to support a multiethnic government as part of the condition of independence. Likewise, business leaders had some interest in seeing MCA survive as a counterweight to the communist insurgency. Social activists, in this case Chinese educationalists, were willing in the 1950s to work with MCA to assert their interests. And they were willing to compromise on their preferred treatment of Chinese schools in order to see citizenship criteria expanded to include the maximum possible number of Chinese in the territories.

After the riots in 1969 and the passage of NEP, these incentives for cooperation between political leaders, business elites, and social activists changed. With the creation of a newly rich middle and upper class of Malays, and through the continued gerrymandering of electoral districts, there is less of an electoral incentive for UMNO to cater to Chinese constituents either for funding or for electoral support. MCA, in trying to balance its desire to stay within the ruling coalition with Chinese concerns, has chosen to be a voice *within* the power structure, albeit a somewhat muted voice. Likewise, while Chinese business elites may have actually benefited from NEP, one of the consequences of the economic restructuring has been greater state involvement in the economy. Small family businesses that relied on family or kinship organizations for investment have branched out, sometimes going into joint ventures with other Chinese and non-Chinese businessmen and/or with state governments or foreign groups. Those that have been successful have seen their businesses develop into empires. Under NEP requirements for Malay owner-ship and management positions, Chinese business tycoons such as the Kuok brothers have developed close business and political ties with some of the most influential UMNO leaders. These business-government links have involved both MCA and UMNO elites (Sieh Lee 1992; Gomez 1994), but have served to sever the implicit assumption of earlier consociational arrangements based on ethnic solidarity. Since Chinese business leaders are able to work through UMNO for their own economic benefits, there is little need to reach out to the Chinese community for collective concerns.

Social activists have perhaps been the biggest losers since 1969. The government's concern over maintaining political control has resulted in greater oversight and repression of NGO activity. Since MCA refused to support Merdeka University, education activists have work primarily through the DAP. This almost automatically ensures that few of their demands will be met. While DAP is able to mobilize a great deal of sup-port from the Chinese community, this has not translated into political influence. Likewise, education activists are hampered by collective action problems. Not all Chinese in Malaysia want their children to be educated in Chinese schools, although all would like to see greater access to uni-versity places. Nonetheless, it is harder to unify the Chinese community in Malaysia behind any particular "communal" concern.

CONCLUSION

Prior to 1969 the Chinese community was mobilized to participate in the political process by the MCA. Within the ruling coalition, first the Alliance, then BN, concessions were made to the constituent parties through bar-gaining between like-minded elites. Although Malay interests were priv-ileged, other groups' interests were addressed in significant and tangible ways. The process depended on the personal trust and goodwill built up between Malay and ethnic business elites who represented each com-munity. This accommodation deteriorated after the riots of 1969, but there were still bonds of trust and empathy that facilitated substantial concessions to those parties that had all along remained faithful to the Alliance system of interelite negotiations. For example, the personal ties of trust and support between Tan Siew Sin and Tun Abdul Razak are reported to have altered some of the abrasiveness of government policies toward the Chinese when the thrust of government policy was to give highest priority to the needs and demands of the Malay community (Means 1991:131).

Ultimately, when there are electoral incentives to build coalitions, like the short-lived quasi-alliance between the DAP and PAS within APU, influence may be achieved by posing a challenge to BN. In the late 1980s when BN felt insecure, the Chinese were more broadly targeted than they had been since the 1950s, and the result was greater responsiveness to Chinese interests. While pre-1969 Malaysia was characterized by interelite negotiation or consociationalism, heightened ethnic demands and interethnic tensions after 1969 made the bargaining process more costly. The rise of stronger opposition parties and the less homogenous nature of the second generation of leaders within the coalition made it more difficult to secure constituents' support and less possible to reach accommodation through elite negotiation. Leaders such as Kua Kia Soong benefited from opposing the ruling coalition and gathering support for Chinese-language education.

In many ways the fallout from the riots of 1969, including emergency rule and a series of ordinances giving increased power to the government and the executive, has also, due to NEP's success at building a class of professional Malays, expanded the range of interests clamoring for accommodation. While it seems that the Chinese community in Malaysia has mobilized to participate in the political process when competing parties targeted them for electoral gains, it also appears that most influence has come either through elite negotiation or personal networks forged across ethnic boundaries.

Those who play a role in politics outside the business sector, such as Kua Kia Soong's involvement in the Chinese educationalist movement, show the difficulty in mobilizing Chinese support. Not all Chinese want their children to be educated in Chinese schools, but most do want to maintain fair access to tertiary institutions and the job market after college. The need for collective action to achieve greater influence hinders these types of goals and helps explain the limited support currently for opposition parties. As is the case in Indonesia, the rights of minority "others" may best be protected by institutionalizing more regularized systems of input, but until this evolution takes place, power and influence rely less on community activism than on the initiatives of individuals.

4

Suharto's Indonesia:
Outsiders Tied to the Palace

INTRODUCTION AND RECENT EVENTS

As stated in the introductory chapter, the very different experiences of Chinese in postcolonial Indonesia and Malaysia demonstrate the power of the state in Southeast Asia to impose and condition the opportunities and the manner of elite political strategies. Over time the Chinese in Indonesia have experienced the most varied political conditions under which they organize, identify, and assert themselves. From 1997 to 1999 the Indonesian economy, political arena, and ethnic relations experienced vast upheaval. Indonesian Chinese have been at the core of all three contested realms of life. Sino-Indonesians recently faced physical and economic danger, and Indonesia is currently poised for a (possibly) complete restructuring of political life. The turmoil and dramatic political change illustrate how important political institutions are for shaping the way that Sino-Indonesians are both perceived and treated by other Indonesians and how they are able to organize and mobilize to protect their interests.

Under Suharto's regime Chinese political action could be described mostly as elite networking. Wealthy Chinese businessmen had close personal relationships with Suharto and were able to impact policies that concerned their business interests. There was little collective action by the "community." This all changed in a dramatic and violent series of events in 1997 and 1998. After more than thirty years of restrictions on Chinese communal organizations, in the wake of President Suharto's resignation on May 21, 1998 several groups of Sino-Indonesian intellectuals and activists announced the formation of new political parties. This marked an important departure from a situation where Chinese were limited in the scope of their professional and political activity.

Under Suharto there were no electoral incentives for political leaders to reach out to the Chinese community, nor were there social incentives for community leaders to mobilize Chinese for ethnic interests. There were, however, extensive economic motives for Indonesian political leaders and Chinese businessmen to work together for financial gain. This resulted in a situation where the Chinese as a group were marginalized within Indonesian political and civil life, but where a small number of "tycoons" were closely linked to Suharto and his family; these business-men were successful in influencing policies important to their economic interests.

A minority of Chinese in Indonesia are among the wealthy elite who benefited from Suharto's New Order regime. Of these only a few, however, wield influence in the political process. Despite their relatively small numbers—Chinese are under 3 percent (about five million), of Indonesia's total population of 202 million[1]—state policies have been enacted specif-ically with them in mind. Even with the extensive political changes over the last year, it may be too soon to assert that the old system is dead. Under Suharto's New Order regime a small number of wealthy Sino-Indonesians had considerable influence in very particular areas of economic policy. Nonetheless, it would have been an error to argue that the Chinese com-munity in Indonesia had power as a distinct group. Both under Suharto and currently, the majority of ethnic Chinese are in a precarious political position both within their local communities and in their relationship to national institutions.[2]

This chapter begins with a description of the recent events in Indonesia. After a brief discussion of the historical background, this chapter looks at the institutional structure in Indonesia and how it changed during dif-ferent postcolonial periods. There is a discussion of nongovernmental actors in Indonesia, and the relationship between the government and the economy is examined. The last two sections of the chapter look at the posi-tion of Sino-Indonesians within these institutional features and how their interests were articulated to the state during Suharto's rule.

ECONOMIC CRISIS AND POLITICAL CHANGE

In July of 1997 Southeast Asia's economic boom came to an abrupt halt. Thailand was the first country in the region to be forced to devalue its cur-rency, and other countries in the region quickly suffered the same fate. On July 8, 1997, Indonesia was faced with a rapidly depreciating rupiah. On July 29 Thailand turned to the IMF to shore up its battered financial sys-tem, halting a run on its currency that had shaken markets across three continents. This was a humbling turnaround for what had been one of Asia's most dynamic economies throughout the 1980s. While Thailand's central bankers and finance ministers quickly came to an agreement with the IMF and international lenders, Indonesia's decision-makers and polit-ical leaders were confronted with graver problems. On November 2, 1997, in hopes of encouraging faith in sound financial institutions, Indonesia closed 16 insolvent banks and announced further austerity measures. Instead of bolstering confidence, financial panic ensued and mass demonstrations erupted across Indonesia. Meanwhile, despite an announcement of $33 billion in loans that would be made to revive the Indonesian economy, Suharto was unable to agree to terms of an IMF bailout. On December 13, 1997, Asian currencies again plummeted. In the second week of December 1998 the White House and the IMF launched a joint effort to prevent further economic disaster in Indonesia. In the first few weeks of 1998 Suharto agreed to a package of economic reforms proscribed by the IMF including curbs on official favoritism for companies controlled by his children and his closest allies. Later in January, Suharto announced that he intended to seek a seventh term as president. He hinted in his statement that his choice for vice president would be Technology Minister B.J. Habibie. These pronouncements only served to further skepticism from international investors about Suharto's seriousness in reforming Indonesia's economy.

In February demonstrations increased across Indonesia and on February 14, 1998, protests turned violent. Rioters in Jakarta, Medan, and other cities burned shops, and merchandize was stolen or set ablaze. Churches were ransacked and burnt, and at least one person was killed in some of the worst violence since the outbreak of the economic crisis. On March 10, 1998, Suharto was reelected president by the legislature and was granted sweeping new powers to confront the economic crisis. Thousands of students took to the streets of Jakarta and Yogyakarta in some of the largest and most fiery antigovernment demonstrations seen since Suharto's rule began. Ignoring criticism, Suharto appointed several controversial figures to his new cabinet, including his eldest daughter and Bob Hasan.[3]

May began with violent riots in Medan and other Indonesian cities over price increases. Thousands of students continued their protests, aiming hostility at the government. Some prominent figures began calling for Suharto to step down. Muslim leader Abdurrahman Wahid called for Suharto to resign. He pled with the nation to return to ethnic harmony and to put an end to the invective against the Chinese community and against individual Chinese shop owners for the price increases. Wahid's outspokenness against the government may have given encouragement to the students to continue and to escalate their protests; shortly after his speech, demonstrations spilled over from campuses to the streets. On May 13, 1998, Jakarta police opened fire on thousands of student protestors at Trisakti University. Six were killed and dozens wounded. One day later, on May 14, 1998 riots erupted elsewhere in Jakarta. Young protestors burned and looted hundreds of stores, vehicles, offices, and homes. In addition to immense property damage, hundreds of Chinese women and girls told horror stories of being assaulted, raped, and tortured. Horrible tales of the violence have been widely documented. The following paragraphs provide a brief eye witness account of the atrocities in Jakarta:

> The unidentified men generally began the violence by coming to a street in a truck or a bus and attacking only one house on the street. They encouraged other people in the area to join them in attacking the other Chinese-owned houses in the vicinity and then looted their contents.

> About 10 men came into the house and found three sisters on the third floor. They made the two younger women take off their clothes and told the older sister to stand in a corner, "because you are too old for us." Meanwhile, arsonists entered the lower floors and set fire to the building. After they had raped her two sisters, the two men said to her, "We are finished and we are satisfied and because you are too old and ugly we weren't interested in you." So they took her two sisters and pushed them to the ground floor where there was already fire, and they were killed. (Harsono 1998:1–2)

Panicked Indonesian Chinese fled to neighboring countries that would take them in.

On May 21, 1998, after more than thirty years in power, Suharto resigned as President of Indonesia. While student demonstrators in Jakarta joyously viewed this as the result of their persistent demonstrations, Suharto's resignation seemed to come only once his closest allies urged him that his credibility and effectiveness had been reduced to nothing.[4]

In the aftermath of the riots and following Suharto's resignation, a myriad of new political parties, advocacy groups, and action groups began to spring up. During the second week of June 1998 ethnic Chinese formed two new political parties: the *Partai Reformasi Tionghoa Indonesia* (The Indonesian Chinese Reform party) became the first group to break the long-standing ban on Chinese political activity. The *Partai Pembauran Indonesia*, or *Parpindo* (the Assimilationist party), led by H. Junus Jahja and Jusuf Hamka, also announced its formation on June 10, 1998. *Parpindo*'s founders claim that Golkar thwarted the assimilation process and that while in power it neglected the needs and interest of Sino-Indonesians (*Kompas* 1998). Both *Parpindo* and the Indonesian Chinese Reform Party included in their declarations that ethnic rights and true unity in Indonesia must be achieved.[5] In addition, several advocacy groups were also organized: the Citizens' Forum for Reform, spearheaded by Christianto Wibisono, which seeks to guaranty minority rights, and several legal and human rights forums forged to investigate and document the atrocities committed on May 14th.

Neither of the parties mentioned above competed in the June 7, 1999, parliamentary election. Some of the reasons given for this are that they could not mobilize enough financial or human resources to run candidates in the requisite number of constituencies. One small "Chinese" party did contest the elections: *Partai Bhinneka Tunggal Ika Indonesia* (PBI), headed by Nurdin Purnomo, a Hakka Chinese.[6] Although PBI did not do well in urban areas like Jakarta, it did do well in Kalimantan, and has apparently won three seats in the DPR.[7] According to unofficial estimates of the election results, discussed in greater detail shortly, 75 to 80 percent of ethnic Chinese who voted in the June elections chose to support Megawati's Indonesian Democratic Party in Struggle (PDI-P) rather than the small *Partai Bhinneka Tunggal Ika.*

While the Reform Party and *Parpindo* are still consolidating and expanding their organizations, their future is unclear. If in fact the majority of Sino-Indonesians support Megawati's PDI-P, it would seem to indicate that ethnically centered parties are not the way to encourage participation. Many people seem to believe that PDI-P will be able to grant the ethnic Chinese community equal status and rights if it is in power, and they supported Megawati's bid for the presidency in the 1999 presidential elections. One possible reason that the PDI-P and Megawati Sukarnoputri are so popular among ethnic Chinese is because of the prominence of the economist Kwik Kian Gie (an ethnic Chinese) as her advisor.

The most open and democratic elections since the 1950s were held in Indonesia on June 7, 1999. Forty-eight parties competed for seats in Parliament. In the run-up to the elections, four parties were expected to capture the majority of the votes. The most popular figure going into the elections was Megawati Sukarnoputri, daughter of former President Sukarno and leader of PDI-P, the Indonesian Democratic Party in Struggle. PDI-P had long played a marginalized role as opposition party to Golkar, Suharto's ruling-party apparatus. Five years ago Megawati was elected as PDI-P's leader, but the government feared that she would be able to garner too many votes in the general elections and they engineered her ouster in 1997. In 1999 Megawati campaigned on a platform of peace and tolerance in multiethnic Indonesia. She has been a vocal supporter of "*reformasi*," but also supports keeping rebellious areas within the nation, Aceh, and East Timor for example. Megawati's popularity seems to stem from a resevoir of goodwill and reverence for her father. As the founding president of an independent Indonesia, Sukarno's family name recalls a time of greater equality. Megawati articulated little in the way of concrete proposals on how to govern the world's fourth most populous nation or how to revitalize the country's still-suffering economy.

Other important players in the run-up to parliamentary elections were: Abdurrahman Wahid, leading force behind the National Awakening Party (PKB), and Amien Rais. Wahid, also known as Gus Dur, has long been a leading figure in Indonesian Muslim activities; he heads the largest Muslim organization, *Nahdlatul Ulama,* which claims forty million members. PKB's election platform argued for a more equal distribution of wealth in Indonesia but not at the expense of the private sector. It would reduce the role of the government, save for strategic and infant industries and key sectors like food. Prior to the June election Wahid formed an alliance with Megawati's PDI-P and with the National Mandate Party (PAN).

Another Muslim leader who plays an important role in the contest for power is Amien Rais. He is the former head of Indonesia's second largest Islamic group, *Muhammadiyah,* and is now the leader of PAN. Rais articulated support for federalism as a way of reorganizing political power in Indonesia. He is regarded as a thoughtful academic (he has a doctorate in politics and lectured at Gajah Mada University in Yogyakarta), but has no military background. His lack of ties to the military may be a hindrance when it comes to policy-making in the new Parliament.

Lastly, Golkar, led by President B.J. Habibie, although widely criticized and unpopular in polls prior to the elections, still has the most organized and wide-reaching party apparatus of those groups contesting the election. Although Habibie is thought to lack a power base of his own, he has accomplished more than anyone expected in his fourteen months in office. He offered to let East Timor choose between autonomy and independence. Elections will be held in late summer or early fall, 1999, and he has implemented political reforms, allowing new parties to compete. In addition, he spearheaded changes to limit presidents to two five-year terms and he reduced the political power of the armed forces. Most importantly, he made good on his promise to hold open parliamentary elections.

After a prolonged delay, official results of the June 7, 1999, balloting were announced in the second week of July. Megawati's PDI-P won roughly 34 percent of the popular vote and was believed to be the front-runner for the presidential elections to be held in the fall. PDI-P was awarded 154 seats in Parliament. Golkar came in second with just over 20 percent of the vote. Golkar received 120 deputies due to a complicated system that allocates more seats to outlying islands where the ruling party still enjoys strong support.[8] Both Megawati and Habibie would need coalition partners to secure a majority in the electoral college. The seven-hundred-member body was convened in October to elect the next president of Indonesia.

On October 20, 1999, Abdurrahman Wahid, leader of PKB, was chosen to be Indonesia's next president by the People's Consultative Assembly.[9] This took most Indonesians and Indonesia-watchers by surprise. Throughout the summer of 1999 reports from Indonesia suggested that Megawati Sukarnoputri, whose PDI-D won the largest bloc of seats in the parliamentary elections, would be selected as president. However, by October, Megawati had done little in the way of building up her support base in Parliament. It almost seemed as if she was so confident of being selected that she felt no need to reach out to other parties and power brokers for support. A few hours before the voting on October 20, (former) President Habibie, beleaguered by criticism that he was hindering a full investigation of Suharto's assets, withdrew from the presidential race. This meant that the assembly was faced with a choice between Indonesia's most respected Muslim figure and a secular woman. Muslim parties clearly supported Wahid, and representatives from Golkar also rallied behind Wahid. Megawati had done little to create networks and alliances and so when voting took place that Wednesday in October, Wahid was able to garner the largest number of votes.

In announcing his cabinet a week after taking office, Wahid selected Megawati as his vice president, and other appointments were clearly made to reward supporters from a wide array of parties. In a move to reassure Chinese Indonesians, Megawati's long-time advisor Kwik Kian Gie was named Economic Coordinating Minister.[10] While there was some violence and rioting by Megawati's supporters when she did not get selected as president, it was not aimed at Sino-Indonesians and it was quickly controlled.

Despite violence in several corners of the archipelago (in addition to fighting in Ambon, sucessionist guerrillas continue to wage a low-level war in Aceh), there seems to be a guarded optimism among people in Indonesia right now, and this holds true for Sino-Indonesians as well. Although there is still a great deal of uncertainty about how the political system will be altered and how to revitalize the economy, people seem to view the future with hope. There are no available statistics on how many Chinese left Indonesia for good, or if money has been permanently parked overseas or repatriated. The Indonesian government and scholars of Indonesia are faced with the task of trying to explain the horrific violence of 1998, and to ensure that it does not happen again. One of the keys to carrying this out is to look into Indonesia's recent past to try to understand the nature of the political institutions and how power was distributed among various groups. The task of this chapter is not to give a complete explanation of why the ethnic violence occurred, although possible reasons will be offered. Rather, the aim here is to understand why the Chinese as a group were distinguished from the larger population, and then to understand why new political and social groups formed when they did. Lastly, the chapter tries to unravel the dramatic political shifts that enabled such a radical shift to occur in the nature of ethnic politics in Indonesia after May 21, 1998.

BACKGROUND AND HISTORY

Indonesia is the fourth most populous nation in the world. With 202 million inhabitants, it spans 13,667 islands over 5.1 million square kilometers. Despite the small number of Sino-Indonesians in the population, they have dominated commerce since colonialism and have been the targets of urban unrest. It is often assumed that the Chinese community in Indonesia has been able to maintain a certain invisibility, choosing to withdraw from the conventional political arena. This may help them preserve their economic position in society, but it does not facilitate any long-term solution to the fact that in times of economic and political instability they are subject to harassment and persecution.[11] While there are a few extremely wealthy Indonesian Chinese, their influence on economic decisions is limited to an ability to benefit from particular government contracts and credit allocation; as a group the Chinese have had little input on overall policy decisions (Mackie and Macintyre 1994:32). No group would benefit more from a political system that institutionalized legal processes and procedures that would then protect the rights of minorities.

Political participation can take many forms. One type of participation is obviously voting. Under Suharto there were regular elections in Indonesia, and this chapter will assess what political purpose they served. Although there was little doubt about the outcome of elections under Suharto, it would be a mistake to assume that the elections did not matter. However, as a mechanism for assessing when Chinese communities become active in the political process, and what strategies they use to affect influence, elections from the 1960s until 1999 tell us very little. Likewise, until 1998 it was not fruitful to study Chinese communal organizations in Indonesia since formally there were none. In looking at

Indonesian politics over time it is more useful to understand the institutional incentives and conditions that impact Chinese input into the political arena. At different points in twentieth-century Indonesian history the Chinese community has been presented with various opportunities for politicization. The way in which they have been able to respond has had to do both with the political institutions they confronted as well as internal dynamics of the community itself. The next section of the chapter details some of the history and how Indonesian Chinese have been impacted by the larger political structures of the time.

CHINESE UNDER COLONIALISM

Chinese migration to what is now Indonesia began over four hundred years ago. By the time Europeans made significant note of the Indies in the sixteenth century, substantial settlements of Chinese existed in port cities and even in some rural areas close to the ports.[12] The Chinese came to Java as individuals or small groups. These Chinese became fairly well integrated with the local population and most do not speak a Chinese dialect at home. In West Kalimantan on the island of Borneo, and on the east coast of Sumatra, the Chinese migrated as whole communities to work on plantations and in the mines. Chinese in these regions retained the use of Chinese (Onghokham 1998:1). It was not until the Dutch created a more formal system of colonial rule that the relationship between the Chinese and the *pribumi* (indigenous Indonesians) would be shaped more directly by cultural, economic, and political actions. During colonialism, Dutch authorities worked out a system of indirect rule over Chinese migrants through appointment of a series of Chinese Kapitans charged with accepting or rejecting other potential migrants and with policing their "own" communities. As a gatekeeper, the Kapitan was able to shape the further demographic makeup of the local community. In the colonial plural societies of the Dutch East Indies, the Straits Settlements, and British Malaya, Chinese filled classic middle-man economic roles in a political economy divided by race and class. As traders and moneylenders the Chinese were often in adversarial relationships with indigenous working classes.

Thus since colonialism Sino-Indonesians have been somewhat trapped: neither incorporated as a group within the larger polity, nor assimilated. The central concern of Chinese outside Chinese territory has been their national, political, and cultural identity. Under Dutch rule the Chinese were given a measure of autonomy to live under their own headmen. These officers were chosen by the Dutch authorities and were administratively and politically responsible to them. The officers' role was challenged at the turn of the century by an awakened sense of Chinese nationalism. In addition to Chinese nationalism, there were increasing numbers of Western-educated Chinese who viewed the officers as an anachronism. This diversity of views contributed to the development of Chinese organizations formed to express different needs within the community. These associations, coupled with animosity towards the co-opted officers because of the special privileges accorded to them, served to undermine the Dutch-chosen leaders' political clout (Coppel 1976:24).

There is ample literature on Chinese organizations in Southeast Asia (Freedman 1962a,b; Skinner 1968; Mackie 1976; Suryadinata 1993; Skeldon 1996) and on the divisions between Chinese communities based on regional origins in China, dialect groupings, kinship networks, class, time of migration, and so on. Even at the outset of Chinese associational life, there was little unity among the immigrants. The following are examples of some of the types of associations that were formed to impact the larger political arena. Around the turn of the century the *Tiong Hoa Hwee Koan* (THHK, or the Chinese Organization) was formed as part of a revival in Chinese cultural nationalism. The organization arose out of the conditions in the Indies at the time, as well as taking strength from mounting nationalism in China. The THHK was formed to promote Confucianism and later to create Chinese schools with a modern curriculum (Suryadinata 1997:xiv). In addition to the internal or demographic divisions mentioned above, there were grave differences among Chinese in their political attitudes towards the migrants' host country.

Some favored pan-Asian cooperation with Indonesian nationalists in opposing Western imperialism, some were more oriented toward China, and still others were perceived to ally with the Dutch against Indonesian nationalist movements and worked through Dutch institutions such as the Volksraad to this end. For example, the *Chung Hua Hui* (CHH or Chinese Association) was formed as a political party to represent Chinese interests in the legislature, and it voted with the Dutch in 1935 on a proposal that there should be a majority of indigenous members in the Volksraad (Coppel 1976:33). Unlike other community organizations at the time who were advocating remaining Chinese nationals, for example the *Sin Po* group, the Dutch-educated *peranakan* professionals and businessmen in CHH advocated creating an "Indier" identity. Under this concept the Chinese would be accorded similar legal status as the Dutch and the Japanese but would maintain their own ethnic identity. They did not succeed because the Dutch authorities feared that this arrangement would cause resentment among indigenous Indonesians (Suryadinata 1997:xv).

In 1932, two *peranakan* lawyers, Ko Kwat Tiong and Ko Tjay Sing and a *peranakan* journalist, Liem Koen Hian, formed the *Partai Tionghoa Indonesia* (PTI), the Chinese-Indonesian Party, to challenge CHH directly. PTI urged Chinese in the Indies to support Indonesian nationalism, and seemed to favor political assimilation, arguing that Chinese should adopt Indonesian citizenship when appropriate (ibid.:xvi). As a general rule, Indonesian nationalist parties had no Chinese members.[13] Chinese reluctance to join the mainstream parties was in part due to the institutionally different treatment that Chinese and Indonesian residents received under Dutch law. "The conduct of the colonial administration suggested communal rather than assimilated politics" (Coppel 1976:37). Chinese were segregated from Indonesians in primary schools, in employment opportunities, and in the Volksraad and other political arenas.

Japanese occupation had different effects on Chinese organizations. Independent Chinese media outlets and Chinese political organizations were banned; however, Dutch-language schools were also closed, which had the unintended consequence of re-Sinifying the Dutch-oriented Chinese. Nonpolitical associations were consolidated by the Japanese into one federation, the *Hua Ch'iao Tsung Hui* (HCTH) for the Chinese community's social and economic concerns. Like earlier officers, the elites were appointed by the Japanese military leaders and were responsible to them. Although politically dependent during the occupation, this federation was later transformed into a tool for Chinese cohesiveness. After Japan's defeat in 1945, the HCTH became the *Chung Hua Tsung Hui* (CHTH), which joined the longer-term Sino-Indonesians with the new immigrants. Internal and external factors facilitated this short-lived unity. There was violence against the Chinese in the midst of Indonesian revolutionary fervor, and there was increased Chinese pride at the recognition of China as one of the five great powers victorious in the war. In 1954 *Baperki* (Consultative Body for Indonesian Citizenship) was formed. This subsumed several smaller political organizations, and the new association was more of a mass organization than a political party. *Baperki*'s goal was to promote citizenship and end discrimination among citizens. It gained wide appeal in the *peranakan* community. About 98 percent of its members were of Chinese descent. Neither the consensus within the Chinese community nor the existence of *Baperki* was to last. As part of the crackdown on leftist organizations, *Baperki* was disbanded after the coup attempt in 1965.

Currently, the Chinese in Indonesia are a heterogeneous mix of *peranakan* and *totok*. *Peranakan*[14] Chinese are older settlers who are partially assimilated; they speak Indonesian, many have taken Indonesian names, and a few have become Muslim. *Totoks* are newcomers, usually either first- or second-generation Chinese who may still speak Chinese. Since immigration from mainland China ended in the 1950s, the number of *totoks* is shrinking as their descendants become peranakanized.[15] Most Chinese are Buddhists, Taoists, Confucian, or a mix of the three, but some of the most prominent Chinese have adopted Christianity, and churches are visible distinctions of the boundary between Chinese and *pribumis* (Suryadinata 1998). Yet, despite internal divisions and factional allegiances, most Sino-Indonesians would recognize one another as part of a broader Chinese collectivity, if for no other reason than because they are identified and marginalized by the larger Indonesian society and polity.

POLITICAL INSTITUTIONS IN POST–WORLD WAR II INDONESIA

The first half of the twentieth century dealt Indonesia fifty years of colonialism, occupation, and revolution. These events transformed conceptions of personal identity, altered patterns of social cleavage, and impacted attitudes toward politics and government. William R. Liddle discusses the need for an "integrative revolution," where old loyalties to the village, clan, and kingdom became subordinate to new ties based on common ethnicity, religion, social and economic status, and nationality. He details how secular political parties attempt to build local support by manipulating some combination of these ties (Liddle 1970:98). In order to understand postindependence Indonesia, it helps to describe the relevant institutions and power players in each of four distinct periods: the immediate postwar period, 1950–1955, 1955–1965, and 1965–1998. A section at the end explores the changes that have occurred in the last two years and provides a brief analysis of new forms of Chinese community organization and activism.

THE REVOLUTIONARY PERIOD

At the end of the Pacific war, the Dutch were too weak effectively to resume power. There were indigenous attempts at revolution, but the efforts were loosely organized and there was no one dominant party. Guerrilla fighting against the Dutch in 1948–1949 politicized parts of Indonesia, and there were no elections held during this period (Anderson 1996:27). Sukarno and Vice President Hatta appointed a revolutionary Parliament, the *Komite Nasional Indonesia Pusat* (Central Indonesian National Committee) which was comprised of all major political groups. The Parliament had several Chinese representatives from at least five different parties (Coppel 1976:44). The fledgling government tried to secure the loyalty of as many as possible of the Chinese groups and to incorporate them into Indonesian society (Political Manifesto, 1 November 1945, Suryadinata

1997:223). Between 1946 and 1951 a series of citizenship regulations were passed aimed at the Chinese. The initial policy, Regulation 1946, promulgated at the Round Table Conference, allowed Chinese born in Indonesia to become Indonesian citizens. Yet it was carried out inconsistently by local officials, and steps over the next five years were taken to clarify the act, which allowed *peranakan* Chinese to take Indonesian citizenship, but not the foreign-born, or *totok*, Chinese. At this time debates raged within the Chinese community in Indonesia about identifying with the nationalist versus communist forces on the mainland, and between full support for Indonesian independence and the likelihood of renewed Dutch rule.

PARLIAMENTARY PERIOD: 1950–1958

From 1949 to 1955 there were episodic armed rebellions from forces unwilling to demobilize after independence was achieved. Some armed groups were frustrated over lingering territorial and asset disputes with the Dutch. The 1955 elections were set up in part to channel and contain myriad forces that had fought for independence (ibid.:28). From 1950 to 1955 there was intense intraelite competition for electoral campaigns. The Parliament was a vibrant legislative body which wielded significant power. The other centers of power were the army, political party organizations, and the office of the president. The three strongest parties were the PNI (the Indonesian Nationalist Party), PKI (Indonesian Communist Party), and Nahdlatul Ulama (NU). To illustrate how elections can play a moderating role on party institutions one need only look as far as the example of the PKI. The PKI had steadily increased its recruitment and by 1955 had become the dominant party. In the process, the PKI also became domesticated. In order to accumulate votes at the village level, the party had to appeal to village headmen, thus it needed to accommodate, or at a minimum not threaten, their interests. In addition, PKI leaders pushed to disband communist guerrilla bands in Central Java and worked to reign in trade union leaders and farmer organization leaders whose militancy threatened the party's parliamentary standing. It was through the workings of the legislature that the parties achieved influence in this period (Anderson 1996:29).

GUIDED DEMOCRACY: 1958–1965

Alarmed by PKI's early success, Sukarno and his military supporters quickly brought the period of relatively open political contestation came to a close. Guided democracy was instituted as a way of curtailing party power. Limits were imposed on party organization and a government-sanctioned ideology was propagated throughout the archipelago. In December of 1957 Martial Law was declared. This officially signaled the end of open political participation. Only three political parties were allowed to maintain their organizational apparatus and to participate in elections. Even these three players (PNI, PKI, and NU) were limited in how they could operate. President Sukarno tried to play the army and the parties off one another. Sukarno urged the three consolidated parties to build up their political base through organization-building in order to serve as a counterweight to the army. In reality, Sukarno's gamble would not pay off. By 1962–1963 the parties had adjusted to the government constraints on their activities and their weakened position in government. They even managed to regain some power within the bureaucracy, an area of previous party dominance. Sukarno needed their mass organizations to mobilize support for his projects. As Sukarno and the army increasingly disagreed about the leftness of his policies and rhetoric, Sukarno was forced to turn to the parties for support. Coinciding with this, the PKI and the PNI began to adopt social revolutionary ideology as the basis for their grassroots support (Rocamora 1973:145–150).

In the Chinese community, *Baperki's* (an organization that promoted assimilation with Indonesians) ideology veered leftward toward the PKI, whereas in the late 1950s and early 1960s assimilationists in the Chinese community had looked to the army for support and protection. Since President Sukarno's favor counted most heavily during guided democracy, each faction vied for him to have the other organization dissolved and their ideas condemned.[16]

Several factors led to the violent unrest of 1965, and this treatment of the events will surely not do them adequate justice. Briefly, some of the conditions that led to the coup attempt are as follows: nationalization of Dutch corporations had not provided the economic boost anticipated, and hyperinflation set in, worsening after 1963. In addition, Sukarno's leftist (and antagonistic) foreign policy helped pave the way for anticommunist hysteria from the military. The official version of the events of October 1, 1965, states the following: six leading army generals were killed in an attempted coup led by Lieutenant Colonel Untung. Colonel Untung's forces then took control of the national telecommunications center and the president's palace. The movement quickly collapsed in the face of swift action by the army's strategic reserve, led by Major General Suharto.[17] The military takeover was justified by casting the coup as propagated by communist forces. In the official version of the incident, the PKI had established ties with elements in the military and was trying to consolidate power to take control of the country. Thus when the coup failed, the communists and presumed sympathizers within the military were blamed for the whole affair. The PKI was quashed and *Baperki,* as well as individual Indonesian Chinese, suffered tremendously.

NEW ORDER INDONESIA: 1966 TO 1998

In the aftermath of the abortive coup tens of thousands people were murdered and hundreds of thousands jailed (Anderson 1996:30). The coup attempt radically changed conditions of political activity. It put an end to the PNI's leftist political stance. The PKI's leaders were jailed and the party itself was banned. As Suharto emerged in control of the presidency in the late 1960s, the political parties were left emasculated. The only centers of power were the bureaucracy, controlled by Suharto, and the military, known as *Angkatan Bersenjata Republik Indonesia* (ABRI). Suharto's regime repressed opposition parties and popular participation was mobilized only in so far as it supported his party structure; by the late 1980s his government's legitimacy and stability came to rely on its ability to safeguard continued economic development.

Since 1971 there were a series of elections under Suharto's New Order regime. These events were carefully managed to achieve a two-thirds majority for Golkar, the government's electoral wing, in a passive Parliament without a true representative nature. Suharto skillfully referred to the chaotic past as evidence that the regime's tightly orchestrated system of institutions and beliefs is in the best interest of many Indonesians. Suharto's primary claim to legitimacy is that he promoted the New Order as a developmental regime, the ultimate goal of which was to build a modern industrial economy with higher living standards for all Indonesians. The ideological trio behind New Order's developmentalism was growth, equalization, and stability.[18]

From 1965 to 1989 Chinese associational networks, both for citizen Chinese and noncitizens, were torn apart. Earlier patterns of Chinese participation were largely communally based. "They [the Chinese] have depended for their vigor on a separate press (Chinese or Indonesian), a separate education system (Chinese, Dutch, or Indonesian) and separate associations representing Chinese interests in various fields" (Coppel 1976:65). These all required government tolerance, which did not exist under Suharto today. While the community was encouraged to participate through these designated institutions, input needed to come through informal channels.

GOVERNMENT STRUCTURE

From the 1965 coup attempt to 1998, there were five parliamentary elections. These elections sent representatives to the *Dewan Perwakilan Rakyat*

(DPR) or the People's Representative Council, four hundred of the five hundred seats are elected; one hundred[19] of the seats were reserved for military appointees. The DPR meets annually and approves legislation and the budget. There is also a superparliament, the *Majelis Permusyawaratan Rakyata* (MPR) or the People's Consultative Assembly. The MPR consists of all DPR members plus five hundred additional appointees. It meets once every five years to elect the president and vice president, as well as setting the basic outline of state policy for the next term. The concept of *Pancasila*, although mixing Western and traditional elements, is intended to indigenize the institutional basis; thus it justifies departures from Western concepts of democracy (Liddle 1996:43). Reliance on this ideology provides for stable institutions and aims to divide resources more or less fairly. Conflict over the distribution of spoils is resolved in such a way that winners and losers are able to try again; for example, there is electoral contestation, and there are mechanisms in place to redress grievances through bureaucratic, legislative, provincial, district, and village means. Often small measures are taken to show flexibility in the system (ibid.:57–58). Three political parties were allowed to compete: Golkar (*Golongan Karya*, or functional groups), the *Partai Demokrasi Indonesia* or Indonesian Democratic Party (PDI), and *Partai Persatuan Pembangunan* or Development Unity Party (PPP). In every election Golkar won more than 60 percent of the vote. Golkar was not a party in the conventional, or Western, sense. Instead it really served as the electoral component of the military and the bureaucracy. The PDI and PPP were fusions of nine other parties and their leaders were handpicked or approved by government officials (Ibid.:45). In the run-up to parliamentary elections, mass rallies were held to promote visible support for Golkar.[20] The Chinese were not distinctly mobilized or targeted by candidates or political parties for electoral support. In part this is because elections were used almost symbolically, as a tool to illustrate popular support for the regime; in this sense there was no need to distinguish Sino-Indonesians from the rest of the population. Also, the Chinese are a small enough percentage of the population that there was little urgency for Golkar to worry about their electoral support. Toward the end of his rule, Suharto paid more attention to Islam, and the Chinese suffered from a backlash against earlier associations with the Katholic Parti and other non-Islamic groups. More on this split will be discussed shortly.

THE ROLE OF ELECTIONS

There is an assumption that although there are elections in the authoritarian regimes of Southeast Asia, because they do not fit the criteria of "open and fully contested," somehow they do not matter. The following are some conventional views on the role of elections: Western ideals posit elections as legitimizing acts. The role of elections, in theory, is to choose leaders to represent and rule in the name of the population. At the time of decolonization in Southeast Asia and elsewhere, elections were a precondition of self-rule set by the withdrawing powers. The people often base nationalist movements on the idea that independence means self-government, or self-rule. Lastly, in democratic theory elections are a way of allowing expressions of diversity—a preservation of minority rights (Taylor 1996:3–5). Although elections in Indonesia did not fulfill the functions stated within democratic theory, they were taken very seriously by officials, and thus merit a closer look here. While elections under Suharto in some sense may have legitimized the regime, they also served to reinforce a sense of powerlessness of the electorate, that is elections were depoliticizing, limiting political possibilities to mere formalized campaigns between narrow choices (ibid.:9). Elections can encourage change in social attitudes by destroying patterns of deference and forcing elites to recognize the legitimacy of "loyal" opposition. Elections can atomize people's identity and/or cause affirmation of an identity only marginally felt. New social groups can use opportunities that elections provide for organization and discussion even if these actions are constrained, either by law or by practice, to further rights for themselves. Elections serve all these functions in Indonesia, but until this year, they were primarily an instrument for mass mobilization in support of the regime. To this extent, Chinese were not targeted any differently from other groups in society. The significance of this is explained later.

Since both stability and rapid economic development disappeared in 1997 and 1998, the new government will have to earn legitimacy through a complete overhaul of the political apparatus, and the new regime will have to do so while also improving the economic situation. There are high expectations of Wahid to reform the system and to get economic growth back on track.

NONGOVERNMENTAL ORGANIZATIONS

There are other groups in society that play a role in the transmission of demands and supports to the ruling apparatus. Nongovernmental Organizations (NGOs), exist in Indonesia and could be viewed as occupying a semi-autonomous position. There are thousands of these working in areas such as consumer rights, environmental issues, health care, and so on. Perhaps the most prominent of these is the Indonesian Association of Muslim

Intellectuals (ICMI) an Islamic organization that had Suharto's acceptance, despite being an alternate source of power. The ICMI is a network of Muslim bureaucrats, intellectuals, and businessmen. They were led in 1990 by Habibie, and Suharto tolerated them in hopes that he could co-opt this potential group of dissidents. In general the NGOs are important as sources of values; although politically quiescent (until 1998), they could take on more importance in post-Suharto Indonesia.

ISLAM AND CHRISTIANITY

Many of the direct attacks on ethnic Chinese from the 1950s to the present have been carried out by Muslim organizations or in the name of Islam. This antagonism is economic, political, and cultural.[21] Many Chinese converted to Christianity after 1965 as insurance against suspicion of communist sympathies.[22] In 1971, some Catholic Chinese who favored assimilation joined forces with Indonesian army intelligence, led by Ali Moertopo and Soedjono Hoemardani, allies of Suharto, to establish the think tank CSIS, Center for Strategic and International Studies, now headed by Jusuf Wanandi. While CSIS focused on political and economic research, it was also *perceived*[23] to be connected to Moertopo's involvement in covert operations, such as the invasion of East Timor, and the creation of the Komando Jihad in 1977. Komando Jihad was Moertopo's effort to persuade Muslim activists to instigate demands for the creation of an Islamic state. This was done to discredit the Muslim political party, PPP, at a time when it seemed poised to challenge Golkar. This provided Suharto with an excuse for arresting Islamic activists. General Benny Moerdani, commander of the armed forces from 1983 to 1988, succeeded Moertopo as CSIS's government link.

> In some Muslim circles, the CSIS is responsible for fomenting the bad blood between the military and Islam in the 1970s and 1980s, through its association with Benny Moerdani, a former intelligence chief who was forced into retirement in 1993. (Cohen 1998:17)

General Moerdani was in charge of troops who were sent in 1984 into Tanjung Priok, portside Jakarta, to put down Muslim demonstrators. The soldiers opened fire and dozens of people were killed.[24] These two events, Komando Jihad and the killings at Tanjung Priok, along with the links between Moerdani, Moertopo, and CSIS, convinced many Muslims of a Chinese-Christian-military conspiracy to keep Islam weak. Through the 1980s CSIS was well positioned to influence government policy—Jusuf Wanandi was instrumental in crafting Suharto's New Order ideology—but it has fallen out of favor and has been removed from the corridors of power since Islam and ICMI have gained prominence.

In the first few months of 1998 Jusuf Wanandi and his brother Sofyan (a wealthy businessman), as well as CSIS and its enemies were again in the news. In mid-February 1998, as price-related (and anti-Chinese) riots spread through several Javanese towns, a mob demonstrated outside CSIS chanting anti-Chinese slogans and condemning the Wanandis. Suharto replaced armed forces commander General Feisal Tanjung with a long-time Suharto loyalist, General Wiranto. Wiranto has sought to cool the anti-Chinese demonstrations and the campaign that has discouraged businessmen from repatriating possibly billions of dollars sent overseas. He publicly warned against provoking anti-Chinese sentiments: "If this happens, it's wrong. We have to fight against it and neutralize it" (McBeth 1998:15). This attitude may clash with some sectors of the armed forces. Feisal and other military leaders have been outspoken in their attacks against Jusuf and Sofyan Wanandi (ibid.:15), triggering their detention and questioning in regard to a bombing in Jakarta late in 1997.

STATE AND ECONOMIC LINKS

There is a powerful predisposition in Indonesian political culture to favor state intervention and oppose private capitalism, of either the domestic or foreign variety. Since the domestic business community is largely Sino-Indonesian, this leaves them vulnerable to state whim. Opponents of neo-classical growth who favor greater egalitarianism include middle-class indigenous (*pribumi*) who see their path to greater economic power blocked by Chinese dominance of the business class. The most important statist supporter is B. J. Habibie, Minister of Research and Technology, under Suharto and president from May 1998 to Fall of 1999. Currently, there are a number of officials in the bureaucracy and *pribumi* elite who favor greater protectionism and have tried to achieve their goals by working through the bureaucracy rather than through the executive (Liddle 1996:39–42). Other forces that oppose neoclassical growth models, and who favor increased state efforts at egalitarianism include the indigenous middle class. They see their path to greater economic power blocked by Sino-Indonesians' dominance of the business class. This group would largely favor protectionism and they have tried to achieve their goals through the bureaucracy.

Because of Indonesia's economic success under Suharto, the social structure has changed. There is now an Indonesian middle class, in addition to the Chinese business leaders who have moved from a middle-class position under colonialism to more of an upper class in New Order

Indonesia. Anderson asks if this might lead to democratization, as many modernization theorists predict (1996:31–33). The answer seems to be: not necessarily. Colonialism left the country racially polarized and bureaucratically weak, and even with Suharto's economic success, these conditions have not changed. The current economic crisis has illustrated the dangers of economic development based on interconnected business and government links.

Economically, Suharto in the mid-1990s begun to favor free trade. At the APEC meeting in Bogor in November 1994, he pushed for greater openness between Asian nations. In spite of close family and personal ties, he rejected a 40 percent tariff protection request from Chandra Asri consortium, a $1.2 billion olefin project partially owned by one of his sons and Prajogo Pangestu, a favored Sino-Indonesian businessman. However, the overall structure of protections for pet projects remains safeguarded from drastic liberalization (Mallarangeng and Liddle 1996).

Key shifts in the top military officers, ensuring that the military will not be completely hostile to Islamic forces, plus the continued strength of the ICMI signaled an increasingly "green," or Islamic, tint to Suharto's regime. Although the opposition parties NU and PDI suffered some harassment in 1995, at the time they were no more than symbolic threats to Suharto's established power. The most powerful alternative source of political strength comes from ICMI, which was among Suharto's strongest supporters. At ICMI's second national congress in December of 1994, Habibie was reelected for a second five-year term as the movement's leader, and Adi Sasono was elected as the secretary general. The new secretary general was a longtime activist and proponent of dependency theory; he believes in "*ekonomi kerakyatan*" or people's economy, a phrase that reflects pre-Suharto Indonesia's socialist version of nationalism. This ideology reflects popular hostility at economic injustice and increasing inequalities in wealth, and it particularly targets Sino-Indonesian "conglomerates" (Mallarangeng and Liddle 1996:114–115).

LINKS TO SUHARTO

As in the past, Suharto has used divide-and-rule tactics to weaken the ranks of the military, and it has increasingly become clear that through the 1990s, Suharto was Indonesia's most significant power source. His political power base relied on the vast business networks assembled by his six children. They were aided by eager-to-please tycoons who control the most lucrative areas of the economy. "The web of profitable enterprises woven around his family and their mainly Chinese business associates is one source of Suharto's strength"; with two to three billion dollars in assets,

Suharto can count on unlimited funds for political purposes (Vatikiotis 1993:6). Suharto's ties with the Chinese business community stem, in part, from his position in 1957 as Central Java's military commander. In Java in the 1950s links developed between Indonesian army units and Chinese businessman. Military units required supplies and Chinese traders were able to meet their quartermastering needs. This is how Suharto met Liem Sioe Liong who, with other Chinese merchants, helped finance his procurement needs. Another such individual is Kian Siang (Bob Hasan),[25] who had such influence with Suharto that he was able virtually to write government legislation favorable to his financial interests: rattan and timber.[26] After 1965, indigenous businesses were left financially weak or politically discredited. Likewise, Indonesian Chinese felt vulnerable after the invective and persecution of the 1965–1966 period; thus they were in the position of being able to trade their capital for protection from the new regime. They have benefited from this relationship, so much so that Suharto at the end of his rule had to distance himself from the community. Presidential decision no. 10 decreed that a proportion of government contacts over two hundred million rupiah had to be approved by the State Secretariat. This is a departure from the process of going through the military that generally relied on Chinese contractors. The purpose of the act was to ensure that contracts were awarded to non-Chinese. Secretary of State Sudharmono has used this to steer business to his cronies, and this has been at the expense of Sino-Indonesian interests (ibid.:50–53).

Nonetheless, several of Suharto's reforms bolstered the positions of Chinese business interests in Indonesia. In 1988 reform efforts included the banking liberalization which opened up banking to private interests—previously it had been controlled by the state. Not only did this give private and foreign banks room to operate, but it boosted business confidence and spurred domestic investment. By 1990 over forty new banks had licenses; many of these went to large Sino-Indonesian business groups who then, with the help of Suharto's children, established questionable savings schemes. In addition, Sino-Indonesian business profits were also reinvested in Indonesia instead of being sent abroad to Singapore, Hong Kong, or North America. This served a useful domestic political purpose for Suharto by helping fuel the economy. On the whole, the business community was pleased with the reforms of the late 1980s, first because they were already in a position to benefit from liberalization, and second, because powerful economic players have always been consulted by relevant economic ministries before the reforms actually went public.[27] Vatikiotis speculates that this was one way to secure the requisite public support because the financial interests lie behind the minister's political power. Perhaps to appease opponents of liberalization, the economic reforms have no legal standing in law; most have been enacted by presidential decree and are thus subject to be reversed at whim.

As of the late 1980s, Suharto moved ideologically closer to the Muslim community. In 1989 a new education law placed greater emphasis on the role of religion in schooling and offered greater security to private religious schools. In 1990 the former religious affairs minister Alamsjah Ratu Perwiranegara collected signatures of Ulama in East Java calling for Suharto's reelection in 1993 for five more years. In the same year, Suharto allowed the ICMI to form, then, six months later, a group of *pribumi* businessmen formed their own organization to promote a greater role for Indonesians in business (somewhat similar to Malaysians' role as NEP beneficiaries). While it would be threatening enough to Sino-Indonesians to promote Islam as doctrine, other occurrences were perhaps more disturbing to the Chinese community at this time. In March of 1990 Suharto approached his Chinese business connections and demanded that they share their wealth more equitably. On state TV he called on them to promote social equity by selling up to 25 percent of the equity in their firms to cooperatives. This had two significant consequences. First, it legitimized attacks on Chinese wealth and privilege. This resulted in rumors that Sino-Indonesians moved as much as US$26 billion of private capital overseas to Singapore and elsewhere. Second, Suharto's moves toward Islam, and against his Chinese allies, seem to reflect concern over succession (Vatikiotis 1993:157–67).

Again in fall of 1996, Suharto's regime called on wealthy business owners to pay a 10 percent tax to alleviate poverty. By the 1990s, questions of equity in Indonesia were enmeshed in the delicate issue of race and ethnicity. Although Suharto won reelection in 1993 quite handily, even those who prospered at the end of Suharto's rule wonder what is in store for Indonesia economically and politically. There was fear that once Suharto was gone, the balance between ABRI and the Muslims would escalate into further conflict. While the events of 1997–1999 unfolded differently than predicted, it is still unclear what forces will dominate Indonesian politics. While private interests are less dependent on the state's largess and patronage for financial success than twenty years ago, and infrastructure and telecommunications improvements have facilitated national integration, Sino-Indonesians may see their position become more tenuous.

OTHER MEANS OF INTEREST ARTICULATION

While most analysts of Indonesian politics, and particularly those who study the links between the Chinese and Suharto's inner circle, view

Chinese actions as evolving out of a patron-client type model (Crouch 1986, 1988). In a larger sense, in studying Indonesian politics, there is a predominant focus on the power of the state. Yet there are important cases of interest articulation that are done neither through formal bureaucratic politicking or military connections (iron triangle-like relations), nor through patron-client ties. Macintyre (1990) shows how various industry groups have mobilized themselves, outside of designated corporatist organizations, to achieve measured influence on matters of concern to their industry. This extrastate influence is complex precisely because (a) Indonesia is usually perceived as state-centric, and (b) because the business class is dominated by Chinese elites and since they are an unpopular minority, their position has often been viewed as a hindrance to the capacity of the business community to project collective political interests in any direct or organized manner (Macintyre 1990:3). In part because of the downturn in the economy in the mid-1980s with the collapse of oil prices, Indonesian business has developed new independent political capabilities. The established network of corporatist representative associations which have dominated the economic policy scene is being challenged by new patterns of coalition-building within and outside the official state apparatus. Chinese business leaders, while not necessarily representing the Chinese community, are pressing for benefits for a different set of constituents: their industry cohorts.

Under Suharto, Golkar was the umbrella over all corporatist networks. Ostensibly, the New Order's establishment of these functional groups was to provide channels for interest articulation; in actuality, these networks served to eliminate nonstate-controlled avenues of input. For example, there are professional organizations such as Indonesia's Chamber of Commerce and Industry (KADIN) and a myriad of regional and subregional branches of KADIN. Reestablished in 1968, KADIN is seen by business leaders as a tool of the government. Few of the major Chinese businesses bother to join, partially because a small number of the top leaders had their own patron-client links to key government officials. At Suharto's request, Liem Sioe Liong subsidized KADIN's operating expenses; while Liem got little direct benefit from this, he does expect that in exchange the *pribumi*-dominated organization will not interfere with his business activities (ibid.:43). Other industry groups, however, do have influence in policy-making and their behavior is not just clientalistic. Groups such as the Spinning Industry Joint Secretariat (SEKBERTAL) and the Pharmaceutical Association (GPF) have to some extent been able to use the corporatist structures for their benefit, instead of serving as a tool of the state. To briefly illustrate, Macintyre's (1990:142–201) study of the pharmaceutical industry shows how Chinese industrial leaders are able to forge coalitions within economic sectors and with elites in the government, and have successfully used the press to further their aims vis-à-vis the "official" corporatist body. The pharmaceutical industry is overwhelming controlled by Sino-Indonesians. This would only seem to heighten the difficulties in attempting to exert extrastatal pressure on the regime. Eddie Lembong, a Chinese Indonesian, was head of GPF in the mid-1980s when a conflict developed over drug prices. The Ministry of Health, which overseas this industrial sector, had a deep interest in seeing the price of drugs come down, while the manufactures represented by GPF were concerned with their profitability.

Negotiations between GPF and the Minister of Heath, Midian Sirait, produced a cooperative venture that would make particular classes of drugs cheaper and more readily available. In reality it was more of a political "quick fix" that the industry realized would have only a limited impact on the overall price of drugs.

> One notable feature of GPF's operations were the "behind the scenes" personal links between Eddie Lembong and Midian Sirait. However, to present this case as just another example of patrimonialism would be to abuse an otherwise valuable concept. Their relationship was not patrimonial: the two men had roughly equal standing. More generally, one of the most important aspects of GPF's behavior is that, as with SEKBERTAL, it was group-based. It was an organization striving for collective rather than particularistic benefits. (Macintyre 1990:191)

SINO-INDONESIANS

As this chapter has repeatedly said, political vulnerability as an unpopular minority leaves Sino-Indonesians in a politically sensitive position. Economic wealth is not allowed to transfer into wider political influence. The Chinese community cannot act collectively as an ethnic group, nor do they form any sort of viable "social class," whereas an Indonesian middle class might increasingly play a role in developing wider policy preference or in affecting the ideology of the country (Mackie and Macintyre 1994:33).

Coppel (1976) develops a typology, or set of patterns, to describe the methods of political involvement by the Chinese in Indonesia at different times and in response to different historical circumstances:

- The traditional officer system: used under Japanese occupation and again after 1965;
- The nationalist pattern: where political activity is an extension of Chinese politics;
- The integrationist pattern: in local politics particular parties represent the interests of the Chinese community;
- The assimilationist pattern: where Chinese began to act as individuals rather than as a unified group;
- The assimilated pattern: Chinese political activists operate as individuals, not as representatives of an ethnic minority;
- The "cukong" influence: Chinese businessmen exercise informal political influence over Indonesia's power holders through business or personal connections.

Coppel's chapter on patterns of Chinese political activity has provided us with an invaluable history of Chinese political participation in Indonesia. His empirical analysis is perhaps the best tool for moving past "internal" or cultural explanations for political mobilization. Each manifestation of Chinese political organization is directly tied to the larger institutional changes and the elites who control them. That is, each of Coppel's characterizations takes place within the context of particular events and political structures, something he pointedly emphasizes (Coppel 1976:20–21). Yet he does not use his own material to draw the same conclusions put forth here.

It should be noted that the different ways that Chinese have participated in the political arena in Indonesia throughout the years is dependent on the pivotal connection between how the Chinese have organized and how they have been courted or constrained by the political institutions of Indonesia. In each period there were systematic differences underpinning the patterns of participation. These differences pertain to the political conditions and the institutional payoffs to participation. For example, under colonial occupation the conditions existed where ethnic insularity and organization were not only possible but necessary.[28] The Japanese reinforced earlier efforts at achieving a distinct Chinese identity. Of course there were internal reasons for the Japanese to do so—by separating groups it was easier to maintain control over the various groups. Indonesian political parties were unwilling to accept Chinese as full members so the costs to participating were prohibitively high. Under Suharto's regime there were significant economic rewards and incentives to work on the individual level for political connections and government largess.

Ultimately there needs to be a combination of electoral, economic, and social incentives in order to affect participation in the political process. As the explanation of the political institutions and economic networks illustrates, there are few political or electoral incentives to mobilize Chinese for participation in this manner, while there were economic incentives for business leaders to link themselves to President Suharto. But what about social incentives to protect Chinese identity and culture?

Official Indonesian state ideology, enshrined in *Pancasila* (five principles), designates Bahasa Indonesia as the national language and, as part of the continuing goal of national integration, requires citizens to be supraethnic in their orientation. The national slogan of the postcolonial Indonesian state, *Bhinneka Tunggal Ika*, unity in diversity, promotes assimilation and neopatrimonial political involvement, especially toward non-Malay minorities. In this endeavor, the Chinese feel themselves to be provisional members of the national community (Dusenbery 1996:10). There are seven specific policies or issue areas that directly impact how Chinese interact and are identified vis-à-vis the Indonesian state.

1. In keeping with the *Pancasila* belief in "one God," the state officially recognizes five world religions: Islam, Protestantism, Catholicism, Buddhism, and Hinduism. All Indonesians must identify themselves with one of these faiths. Thus, the Chinese must accept categorization and treatment as a member of one of these religious groups. While all five of these religions are officially sanctioned by the state, Islam is unquestioningly the dominant force. Political groups such as NU and the prominent NGO ICMI have established places in the polity and society that are unmatched by the other four religious organizations.

2. One of the primary means of forging national unity has been through education. To this end Regulation 158 from the Ministry of Education calls for the nationalization of private schools. Bahasa Indonesia is mandated as the medium of instruction in school, and restrictions have been placed on Indonesian nationals attending local international schools. The most dramatic effect of these policies has been the destruction of Chinese-language schools. Without access to Chinese-medium schools it is difficult to teach children Chinese, particularly Mandarin, which is increasingly the most common language of Chinese trading networks. Most Sino-Indonesians send their children to state-run schools or Christian schools where the national curriculum is taught in Bahasa Indonesia. In order to teach their children Chinese, or even English (desirable for international commerce), tutors are hired or children are sent overseas (Taiwan, Australia, or the United States) for part of their education.

3. Under SARA [sensitive issues concerning ethnic (*suku*), religious (*agama*), and racial (*ras*) harmony] materials deemed offensive to another

religion or group were suppressed. Thus any Chinese language material was subject to banning on the grounds that it is ethnic chauvinism.

4. There are immigration restrictions on the entry of foreign religious teachers. This makes it difficult, if not impossible, to attract Buddhist teachers, and it has severely curtailed the propagation of various Christian faiths and traditions.

5. There are also immigration restrictions on foreign spouses. This forces Chinese to find mates within the Sino-Indonesian community, move abroad if a foreign spouse is found, or marry a non-Chinese Indonesian. This last option, although increasingly common,[29] is still problematic. Muslim women in Indonesia are forbidden to marry out-side the Islamic faith, and for men that marry out, there is the issue of dietary laws. Muslims do not eat pork, a food often central in Chinese cooking.

6. Under Suharto, civil society played a backseat role to instruments of the state. As David Brown writes; there was neopatrimonial involvement of instruments of the state in civil society. Brown pointedly emphasizes that: "the inherent fragilitys of the neo-patrimonial state generate the development and politicization of communalism . . . in the form of inte-grative communal patronage networks" (1994:112). While Indonesia under Suharto was capitalist, there was significant state involvement and guidance in economic planning. Close links developed between military leaders, the bureaucracy, and private businessmen. Sino-Indonesians have been seen as the greatest beneficiaries of these arrangements. A result of this is that Chinese business elites and their allies in the Indonesian mil-itary, police, national security agency, and various government depart-ments have fueled the cynicism that community "leaders" owe their position to state connections rather than because of popular will.

7. There were restrictions on freedom of speech and assembly, and still all Indonesians must follow an ideology of noninvolvement in the internal politics of a foreign state. Although not specifically worded as such, this regulation is clearly aimed at ethnic Chinese. Chinese alle-giance to Beijing or Taipei has long been suspect in Indonesia, and these restriction are a way to monitor and check Chinese loyalties.

In place of an ethnic focus, the Chinese, like all Indonesians, are forced to identify themselves within one of these frameworks.[30] Religiously, most Chinese identify themselves for these purposes as Buddhist or Christian (either Catholic or Protestant). Each recognized religion is accorded a net-work of state actors. As Dusenbery shows in his work on the Sikhs and the state in Southeast Asia, ethnic group interests in Indonesia are often articulated through this mechanism. Like the Sikhs, the Chinese have an interest in two major policy areas: business and education. While Sino-Indonesians might have wanted to develop and maintain a network of Chinese schools like those in Malaysia, after 1965 this was completely impossible. Instead, the educational issue that concerns the Chinese is access to universities (particularly the University of Indonesia where there were widely perceived quotas on the number of Sino-Indonesians enrolled), to English-language courses, and to business-management training courses. In this respect they are more likely to organize not on ethnic-communal lines, but according to areas of interest.

Since Suharto resigned in May of 1989, Habibie has promised to do away with ethnic coding of identification cards and to forbid the "unofficial" quotas on Chinese admission to universities and applications to study abroad.

CONCLUSION

What does the case of Indonesia under Suharto tell us about the political strategies of Chinese minorities? Since Indonesia had a relatively closed political system, one where elections mattered for regime legitimacy but not for deciding among different sets of interests, electoral channels of political participation were less critical for evaluating political influence than were other methods of interest articulation. There were few social or economic rewards for championing ethnic group rights in Indonesia. Sino-Indonesians can perhaps be better understood as two (at a minimum) communities. There are the small number of very well-off businessmen who may be able to achieve influence either through personal ties or through industry representation, and there are the rest of the Chinese who are scattered in local communities throughout the nation. The wealthy Chinese seem to exemplify the stereotype of *guanxi* capitalism, developing ties to Suharto that facilitated their enrichment and personal influence. However, this opportunism should not be interpreted as one-sided. It is not surprising that Suharto chose to build business empires connected to the Chinese minority. Developing a strong class of Indonesian economic elites might have threatened his power if this group attempted to acquire a certain autonomy. Wealthy Chinese, however, had little chance of developing a constituency or support network outside of Suharto and a few key loyalists.

More formally, until now, host-society institutions have not provided a framework for the Chinese to choose an ethnic-group strategy for political mobilization. One possible means of group representation could be through accepted state religious organizations. However, unlike other minority communities like the Sikhs, the Chinese are not all represented by the same religious umbrella. Participation through industry groups, as the example of GPF illustrates, is possible but it contributes to the perception of the Chinese as a privileged set of businessmen and does little to mitigate the hostility felt toward the larger community.

Ultimately, the tension between Sino-Indonesian and *pribumi* stems from two sets of perceptions: that the "Chinese" are suspect as citizens, and that they have gained disproportionately from economic development and favoritism from Suharto. Quoting a young Muslim activist, Margot Cohen of *Far Eastern Economic Review* writes:

> . . . there is no real difference between ethnic-Chinese conglomerates and small shopkeepers. "They will follow what the conglomerates say, both in their political and economic stance," he asserts. (Cohen 1998:17)

A quote from the National Committee for Formulating a Policy for Solving the Chinese Problem in 1967 still seems relevant over thirty years later:

> First of all we are aware that the historical background and development in the political, economic, and sociocultural process of the two groups [Chinese and *pribumi*] have caused Indonesians to be suspicious of the Chinese population in general. (Taken from Suryadinata 1997:234)

Conversely, a majority of Sino-Indonesians feel persecuted for huge gains that they themselves have not reaped. They feel that they are discriminated against even though they have Indonesian citizenship and have chosen the country as their homeland. There is a sense that the opportunities of an elite few have jeopardized the middle and lower classes' safety. Under Suharto, the lack of institutional arrangements for open participation, coupled with the economic and political benefits gained from personal or quasi-corporatist links to the regime, shaped how and to what extent "Chinese interests" were articulated. Now, with the explosion of new political parties and new civic organizations created after Suharto stepped down, there is a chance that Sino-Indonesians could become more fully integrated into all facets of political life in Indonesia. From these early attempts at communal organization, it seems as though a small number of ethnic Chinese are opting for separate, ethnically based associations, while the majority of Sino-Indonesians want to support parties and groups that stand for a more encompassing, multiethnic vision of Indonesia.

5

Chinese in the United States

There are important similarities and differences between Chinese communities in the United States and those in Southeast Asia. Certainly, there are far fewer Chinese in North America than there are in Southeast Asia, and Chinese Americans are a smaller percentage of the population than they are in Indonesia or Malaysia. Outside of the broad demographic differences in both parts of the world, Chinese on both sides of the Pacific Ocean have confronted discrimination and institutional impediments to political incorporation. Chinese immigration to the United States has occured during two distinct waves: first between the late 1840s to the 1880s, and second from 1965 to the present.

BACKGROUND

The first significant number of Chinese to immigrate to the United States came in the 1840s and 1850s to work as laborers. Immigration was prompted by the discovery of gold in California and by the need for cheap labor in the rapidly developing Western United States (Chan 1991). There were three significant ways that male Chinese migrated. They could pay their own way or they could come on the credit-ticket system. Using the second method, the credit-ticket system, they could borrow the money for travel from a family or clan member, from a Chinese broker, or from an established Chinese immigrant already in the United States. The loan would be repaid with interest after arrival. The third way that Chinese migrated from their homeland was through contracts to plantations or mines. This was a system of indentured servitude that bound thousands of Chinese to years of labor in Cuba, Peru, and the West Indies (Pan 1999:61). Chinese were brought to America either through the credit-ticket system and/or on contracts from railroad or mining companies. By 1851 there were 25,000 Chinese in California (Kwong 1996:12). After the gold rush peaked, additional numbers of Chinese were brought into work on the transcontinental railroad. By 1875 Chinese workers on the West

Coast had reached 105,000 strong (ibid.). Workers departed from Guangdong and Fukien provinces in China in part because population growth outpaced agricultural development of the region. In addition, political turmoil in China as a result of the Opium Wars prompted some to leave, as did a weakening of Qing penalties for emigration; and lastly, there was chaos surrounding the Tai Ping Rebellion of 1850–1964, which made emigration seem like a worthwhile risk.

CHINESE EXCLUSION

By the mid to late 1800s there was a backlash against the Chinese immigrants. The Chinese Exclusion Act of 1882 barred the entrance of Chinese workers to America for ten years. It was extended for an additional ten years in 1892 and then indefinitely in 1902 (Fong 1994:28). Despite the passage of the Chinese Exclusion Acts, allowances were made for wealthy Chinese intellectuals to come to the United States to study or for short visits. Sun Yat Sen and other Chinese nationalists were energetic fundraisers throughout the United States. These well-to-do Chinese had little contact with their counterparts in Chinatown; instead they raised money from American businessmen, intellectuals, and religious charities. U.S. money and ideas of self-determination may have had a profound impact on twentieth-century Chinese politics.

The issue of Chinese migration provides evidence of America's ambivalence towards immigration. Enactment of the legislation against the Chinese bears analysis here because the institutionalization of policies that prohibited Chinese from participating in political and civil life in the United States began with the Exclusion Acts and continues to influence the manner and extent of Chinese politicization today. With the completion of the transcontinental railroad and the recession in the late 1870s, increasing numbers of white workers made their way out West and competed with Chinese for jobs. The Chinese were often hired at lower wages, prompting extreme antipathy from white workers and the early labor activists, who saw the Chinese as cooperators with large capitalists. In the post–Civil War political landscape, the Democratic party attempted (successfully) to gain support in California and elsewhere in the West by shifting from proslavery rhetoric to nativist appeals. Thus a coalition of politicians from Western states, allied with Southerners, was able to pass the Chinese Exclusion Act in Congress in 1882. It was the only federal legislation that would ever single out a particular nationality for exclusion.

The Chinese already in this country became greater targets of abuse and violence. Most were driven out of the small towns and rural areas where they lived and worked, and took refuge in larger cities. This was the beginning of the formation of Chinatowns, first on the West Coast, San Francisco and Los Angeles, then in New York, Boston, Chicago, and other cities. In 1880 83 percent of Chinese lived on the Pacific Coast. In 1920 that figure was down to 55 percent (Kwong 1979). This urbanization was neither voluntary nor temporary. Although most of the Chinese migrants intended to make some money and then return to China, many of these sojourners, although unwelcome, stayed.[1]

When faced with the Exclusion Act, the Chinese were not passive victims. Chinese in the United States at the time attempted legal recourse. In response to the 1892 Geary Act, requiring Chinese to register with local authorities for identification or face imprisonment and deportation, Chinese leaders advised noncompliance with the law and contested it legally. The Supreme Court ruled that the Geary Act was legal and compliance necessary. In *Fong Yue-ting* v. *The United States of America*, the Chinese again tried to protect their right not to be deported as punishment for legal offenses. The Supreme Court's decision stated that deportation was not merely a just punishment for criminal behavior, but it could also be used as an administrative procedure to return "undesirable aliens" to their home countries (Kwong 1979:36). Threatened with deportation for agitation, the Chinese became reluctant to engage in open or active political participation in U.S. affairs.

Through this legislation early immigrants were politically disenfranchised and excluded from participating in American political, economic, and social processes. The most crucial court case to affect the institutionalization of discrimination came with the outcome of *Ozawa* v. *United States* (1922). The decision forbade Asian immigrants from becoming naturalized citizens. This legal barrier prevented early Chinese immigrants from any form of electoral politics in the United States (Nakanishi 1990:15–16). Both the immigrants themselves and U.S. legal institutions viewed Chinese labor in California as temporary. California courts considered the Chinese inassimilable aliens; they had no legal rights and were subject to racially discriminatory ordinances and taxation.

Prior to World War II, the history of Chinese in America is clearly one of economic discrimination, legal segregation, social ostracism, and political disenfranchisement (because *Ozawa* v. *United States* deprived Chinese of the opportunity to become U.S. citizens, they were also unable to vote). Until the 1960s two strategies emerged for fighting discrimination: communities appealed to their homeland government for protection (in this case, to mainland China and after 1949 to Taiwan) and some tried to fight discrimination through the U.S. judicial system, as the earlier court case illustrates (Wang 1991:47). This history sends a message as to what sort of institutional or legal protections Asians, and Chinese in particular, could expect from the United States political process. However, even given this history, it does not mean that there was little political activity going on *within* the Chinese communities. In fact, the opposite is true. From the 1880s until the present, Chinese communities have had vibrant and influential communal organizations that have impacted the Chinatown power structure and the economic and social life of local residents, as well as political events back in China. In most of the Chinese communities in the United States there were a number of associations which governed the internal workings of Chinatowns as well as serving as business, cultural, or welfare organizations. More information on these associations will be provided in the sections on Monterey Park and New York City.

POST-1965 CHANGES

The 1965 Immigration Act ended the discriminatory practice of admitting immigrants based on national-origin quotas. Quotas had been established in 1924 and they were meant to preserve the racial and ethnic makeup of the country. As a result, between 1924 and 1960, 79 percent of immigration slots were assigned to people from Europe and North America (Nakanishi 1990:17). The 1965 legislation replaced these preferential set-asides for a flat number: 20,000 immigrants were allowed from every country outside the Western Hemisphere. Changes in immigration law were made possible, in part, because of the heightened awareness within the United States of race relations and issues of equality. Coalition-building between groups such as Poles, Italians, Greeks, and Jews contributed to the political clout behind the fight for the new immigration provision. Following the Civil Rights Act of 1964, the Immigration Act was aimed at redressing racial discrimination. Currently the greatest beneficiaries of the act are Asians and Latin Americans. By the 1980s legal immigration from Europe had shrunk to 12 percent of the overall total.

Two very different groups of Chinese benefited from the new immigration standards. Under the specific provisions of the legislation, preference is given to uniting families of American citizens and to those with professional skills. Since the first waves of Chinese immigrants had come from economically disadvantaged, mainly rural and southern mainlanders, the family unification provision allowed thousands of Chinese to reinvigorate urban Chinatowns. The other group of ethnic Chinese who would take advantage of the more open immigration policies would be a large cadre of professionals from Hong Kong and Taiwan. This group is better educated, wealthier, and theoretically more readily able to contribute to and assimilate with the larger American society.

STRATEGIES AND IMPEDIMENTS TO POLITICAL PARTICIPATION

LEGAL CHANNELS

Clearly, prior to the 1950s, Chinese Americans were severely limited in how they could access the United States political system. Discriminatory immigration and naturalization laws and other legal restraints at the federal, state, and local level resulted in little or no political participation through the ballot box or other electorally centered activities. Chinese were also prevented from holding government jobs. "In California, between 1879 and 1952, the state constitution prohibited employment of the Chinese by any government entity or corporation in the state. Earlier, between 1854 and 1872, a Chinese individual could not testify against whites" (Lien 1997:35). The only means to protest the system was through legal challenges in the courts.

One of the reasons that voting is such a crucial marker of political participation is that it serves as an indicator of the overall satisfaction of the public. It also provides equity among citizens. Each person gets one and only one vote. There are several barriers to political participation in the American democratic process. The first and most debilitating for the Chinese stems from the disenfranchisement through discriminatory law that denied citizenship to Chinese immigrants. Since the removal of these barriers, Chinese have had some of the highest rates of naturalization, yet many communities are still comprised of permanent residents who are not yet eligible to vote. Since many Chinese are foreign-born, they are less likely to be fully proficient in English. While immigrants must demonstrate a basic understanding of English to meet citizenship requirements, this level of proficiency may not be adequate for understanding complex electoral procedures, propositions, or referenda. In other words:

> there is an additional "cost" to this most common form of participation—the acquisition of citizenship, which is itself a process most likely to be influenced by proximity to the mother country, fear of officials from Immigration and Naturalization Service, lack of information and knowledge, difficulty in meeting language and civics requirements, and a general lack of a sense of political efficacy and trust rooted in the political institutions of the mother country where socialization was initiated. (Lien 1997:27–28)

Once naturalized, Chinese Americans still must register to vote. Today, voter registration seems comparatively easy. The forms are short and widely available, due to the Motor Voter Act. However, registration may be somewhat more of a challenge for Chinese immigrants. Since a significant proportion of Chinese Americans live in urban areas where there is less of a need for a car, knowing where to go to register may still be somewhat of a mystery to those without a need for a driver's license. In addition, the thirty-day residency requirements and the need to reregister after moving may prevent some people from registering.

Lastly, electoral districts have often fragmented Chinese communities, diluting and inhibiting Chinese Americans' ability to organize and develop political cohesiveness. If Chinese Americans live in a particular part of a city or county and the electoral boundaries do not coincide with the parameters of where Chinese Americans live, then their input or influence on elected officials is diluted. Thus the minority community can become an even smaller minority of an election district. In return, if a politician or official can maintain his or her position without the support of a small group, there is less of a motivation for that official to reach out to Chinese Americans or to mobilize them for support.

All three of these barriers have been formally addressed through legal channels. The Voting Rights Act of 1965 is generally pointed to as the key instrument in protecting the voting rights of minorities. The act states that no group shall be prevented from voter registration or from voting, and that no one's vote should count more than another person's. In 1982, after the decision in *City of Mobile* v. *Bolden*, (U.S. 55 1980), Congress amended Section 2 of the Voting Rights Act with the specific purpose of eliminating the requirement of providing discriminatory intent. A "results" test was substituted, so that any voting law or procedure "imposed or applied by any state or political subdivision on a manner which results in a denial or abridgment of the right of any citizen of the United States to vote on account of race or color (or language status)" (Tamayo, Kwoh, and Tomo 1991:7) is prohibited. Thus a violation of the Voting Rights Act occurs if Chinese-American voters are shown to "have less opportunity than other members of the electorate to participate in the political process and elect representatives of their choice"(ibid.). In the "effects" test of *Thornburgh* v. *Gingles*, three criteria must be met to prove a Section 2 violation when there is no intent to discriminate.

The minority group must show:

1. it is sufficiently large and geographically compact enough to constitute a majority in a single-member district;

2. it is politically cohesive; and

3. the majority votes sufficiently as a bloc to defeat minority candidates (ibid.:7–8).

This legislation has opened the door to increased political activity in Chinese communities. It has given incentive to community leaders, working with elected officials, to attend to how election districts are drawn and how minority groups are enumerated. One other important factor in providing an incentive for activism by leaders in the Chinese community is that in 1977 the U.S. Office of Management and Budget began using the designation "Asian Pacific Islander" in compiling federal statistics. This simple act of naming the group provided institutional recognition to Asian communities as a distinct group, and the designation began to be used by all agencies—the Department of Education, Health and Human Services, HUD, and so on. It is also used for EEOC purposes and other service and evaluative efforts (Lott 1991:60–61). Without recognition of a distinct group, it is difficult for social service agencies to demonstrate "need" for underserved populations and it is impossible accurately to target the community for political mobilization. Thus simply acquiring this category has helped empower community activists. The metropolitan Los Angeles area is the best place to study the nature and effects of these incentives.

DEMOGRAPHICS

Chinese Americans, in the aggregate, are newer to the United States than their counterparts are to Southeast Asia. The Chinese-American population rose from 806,027 in 1980 to 1,645,472 in 1990, an increase of 104 percent. About 33 percent of this growth came from immigration. The rate of increase of Chinese Americans is among the fastest of major groups in the United States. This rate is about twice that of Latinos, six times that of African Americans, and twenty times that of (nonHispanic) whites (figures are compiled from the Statistical Yearbook of the Immigration and Naturalization Service, various years, and from U.S. Bureau of the Census 1993b). Some population estimates show that given the current rate of growth, a reasonable assumption if there are few changes in immigration policy, Chinese and other Asian Americans will comprise one-tenth of the American population by 2050 (Lien 1997). In addition, the remarkable growth of the Chinese population in the United States is coupled with fairly high levels of socioeconomic achievement. Chinese Americans also tend to live in states with large populations. The ten states with the largest Chinese populations are: California, New York, Hawaii, Texas, New Jersey, Massachusetts, Illinois, Washington, Maryland, and Florida (Pan 1999:269). This is significant because many on this list are states with electoral college importance: California, New York, and Texas in particular.

Like in Southeast Asia, Chinese in the United States have had their loyalty questioned, and larger international politics or foreign policy concerns have affected how U.S. political institutions and laws have treated the Chinese. While there has been nothing in the United States comparable to Malaysia's "Emergency" period or the suspicion after 1965 of Sino-Indonesians' communist leanings, the United States' foreign policy tensions with China are placing Chinese Americans in an awkward position. Just as Sino-Indonesians have been in the news because they are the targets of rioting and political and economic rage over the last two years, so have Chinese Americans been brought to national attention.

RECENT BUT UNWELCOME ATTENTION
TO CHINESE-AMERICAN POLITICAL ACTIVITY
SECURITY QUESTIONS AND ESPIONAGE

In March of 1999 a Taiwanese American, Wen Ho Lee, was accused of passing classified computer files about nuclear weapons testing to China. Lee had worked on computers and other high-tech equipment to simulate nuclear explosions. The goal of such work is to model nuclear explosions in order to maintain the reliability and safety of nuclear weapons without having to test them. The "legacy codes" that he supposedly gave to China contain complex mathematical formulas and computer programs which would enable the Chinese to build and test smaller and more accurate warheads. The United States Federal Bureau of Investigation claimed that Lee had been under surveillance since 1996, and despite the fact that Lee admitted being approached by Chinese intelligence agents while on a trip to Beijing in 1988, the FBI has not been able to mount a case against him. In an interesting twist, both Wen Ho and his wife Sylvia provided the FBI with information about other possible security breaches at U.S. laboratories and about scientific conferences they attended in Beijing during the 1980s (Drogin 1999:A1). Although he has yet to be charged formally with any crime, he has been fired from his job at Los Alamos, and other Chinese-American scientists are coming forward with stories of job discrimination and suspicion because of their ethnicity. The espionage charge comes on the heels of another political controversy in which Chinese Americans (as well as Southeast Asian Chinese and Chinese nationals) also figure prominently.

CAMPAIGN FINANCE SCANDAL

In the months leading up to the 1996 presidential election, William Safire wrote an op-ed piece in the *New York Times* stating that illegal campaign contributions from Chinese and other Asian sources had been given to

President Clinton and to Democratic party coffers. Only U.S. citizens or legal residents of the United States may donate money to political campaigns. While many of the individuals implicated in the fund-raising scandals are legally eligible to donate money, an investigation by the Democratic party and by the *Los Angeles Times* found that much of the money may have only been funneled through these players from sources outside the United States. Likewise, some of the people who appeared closely connected to President Clinton at fund-raising events were ineligible to donate because they were Indonesian or Chinese citizens.

> One of the foreign guests seated with Clinton at the head table was Ted Sioeng, an Indonesian businessman with close ties to the People's Republic of China whose family publishes a pro-Beijing, Chinese-language newspaper in Monterey Park, CA. Sioeng, who does not speak English, also sat next to Clinton at subsequent Huang-orchestrated events in Washington and Los Angeles. Sioeng flew in from Asia for each event. Veteran fund-raisers say a place at the president's side is a badge of honor reserved—in advance, with Clinton's knowledge—for the major underwriters of the event or someone whose generosity is being recognized. "That is a prized seat," a Clinton advisor said. "Why would you give it to a guy who can't write a check at a DNC fund-raiser?" (Willman, Miller, and Bunting 1997:A1)

One of those who would come to figure prominently in the campaign finance scandals was John Huang. John Huang, on President Clinton's recommendation, was hired as a fund-raiser for the Democratic party. Huang, it seems, solicited more than half of the $3 million that the party later returned as illegal or suspect. Huang had started out in Washington D.C. in July of 1994 as a Deputy Assistant Secretary in the Commerce Department. Huang left Commerce in December of 1995 and moved to the Democratic National Committee. Huang was only one part of what seemed to be a concerted effort by both parties to increase donations from Asian Americans.

John Huang was brought into the Democratic fold in the middle of the 1980s in California. Huang was the senior U.S. representative for the Lippo Group, as well as serving on the board of the Lippo Bank. The Lippo Group, an Indonesian conglomerate run by the Riady family, had begun forming ties with Clinton in his first term as governor of Arkansas in 1979. John Huang was introduced to Clinton in the early 1980s through James Riady. In the late 1980s Huang, living in Glendale, California, teamed up with other politically ambitious Chinese Americans like

Maria Hsia, an immigration counselor, and in 1988 formed the Pacific Leadership Council. The Pacific Leadership Council was created to involve Asian Americans in the political process and to increase the community's political standing. Leo McCarthy, speaker of the California Assembly from 1974 to 1980, and lieutenant governor from 1982 to 1984, encouraged the group's activities. In his position as lieutenant governor he directed the state's trade development office. McCarthy met John Huang through various trade missions to Asia when Huang worked with Lippo Group.

In 1988 Huang, Hsia, and others donated money to the Democratic Senate Campaign Committee to help elect Leo McCarthy. They became increasingly active and generous in their contributions and they became correspondingly well known within Democratic National Committee circles. In exchange for their efforts, the group met with various senators active on issues with which they were concerned; immigration law, for example. An essay in the *New Yorker* from April of 1997 reports on some of the origins of the fund raising scandals:

> In 1989, [for instance] Huang and Hsia were going on a trip to Taiwan, which would be paid for by the Taiwan-based Fo Kwang Shan Buddhist group. McCarthy, who had lost his Senate race, was also going along, and Huang and Hsia requested that an important senator make the trip as well. Wanting to please them, the Democrats asked Al Gore to go, and he did.
>
> Last April (1996), the Fo Kwang Shan group offered its Los Angeles temple as the site for a DNC fund-raiser organized by Hsia and Huang. The event was attended by Gore, and, of course, became a major embarrassment to him. (Boyer 1997:52)

The press would later ridicule Gore and the entire event.

> Accepting thousands of dollars from nuns and monks sworn to poverty was hardly a desirable campaign story, and Gore made things worse by saying at first that he had had no idea the event was a fund-raiser and later admitting that he knew it was "finance-related." (ibid.:52)

Asian American involvement in American presidential politics came just as the need to raise monstrous amount of money to contest elections became paramount. Ron Brown took over as head of the Democratic National Committee in 1989 and he focused on bringing new money and new groups to the party. Nora and Eugene Lum, political facilitators from

Hawaii, Johnny Chien Chua Chung, Charlie Yah-lin Trie, John Huang, Maria Hsia, and Melinda Yee were just some of the Asian and Chinese Americans who, through Ron Brown, became active in the Democratic National Committee and in political organization within the Chinese-American community. These activities began in the early 1990s, continued with the election of President Clinton in 1992 and culminated in the effort to reelect the president in 1996. These players were useful primarily because of the amount of contributions that they were able to solicit from friends, family, and business acquaintances. The Huang-Riady relationship from the Lippo Group was one example.

> Following Clinton's victory in 1992, Riady hastened to fortify his relationship with the president-elect. He traveled to Little Rock to participate in an economic conference organized by Clinton. Riady and Huang contributed $100,000 to help defray expenses related to Clinton's inauguration, and Riady was on hand when the new president took the oath of office. (Willman, Miller, and Bunting 1997:A1)

Ultimately Huang was fired by the DNC just weeks before the November 1996 election. Yah Lin "Charlie" Trie, the owner of a popular Chinese restaurant in Little Rock frequented by Clinton when he was governor, was indicted as a result of a Justice Department investigation of Chinese contributions in U.S. elections. In 1996 alone, the DNC returned $645,000 in donations contributed or solicited by Trie (ibid.). In February of 1998 Maria Hsia was indicted on charges of using a false cover to channel illegal funds to election campaigns. And, in July 1998 Thai businesswomen Pauline Kanchanalak was charged with conspiring to give illegal contributions to President Clinton's reelection campaign.

POLITICAL PARTICIPATION: VOTES VERSUS CONTRIBUTIONS

In 1980s politicians realized that Asian Americans donate a disproportionate amount of money to political campaigns relative to the size of the community:

> Whereas Asian Americans constitute no more than one-tenth of the population in California, they often contribute 20–30 percent of the total campaign funds collected by a supported candidate. . . . Because of this demonstrated strength in campaign finance, both Asian and nonAsian political candidates now make special efforts to campaign in Asian American neighborhoods while highlighting Asian American concerns. Beyond state or local politics, Asian

contributions made to national campaigns have been remarkable as well. Nakanishi (1997) reports that in the 1988 and 1992 national elections, Democratic and Republican presidential candidates shared about equally in the over $10 million dollars contributed by Asians. This makes the Asian American community second only to the American Jewish community in terms of the amount of campaign money raised by an ethnic minority group. (Lien 1997:5)

Erie and Brackman note: "Asian American politics has remained to an unusual degree 'politics by other means,' i.e., not direct electoral representation but indirect access through campaign contributions, lobbying, litigation, and protest (1993:47)." A *Los Angeles Times* poll taken in May of 1997 shows that 15 percent of Chinese American respondents reported making campaign contributions.[2] This compares favorable to rates that white Americans donate to campaigns. Yet, if one were to study rates of voter turnout among white and Chinese Americans, the figures are vastly disparate. Why would Chinese Americans, whose rates of voter turnout are notably lower than white Americans' (see Table 5.1), contribute to political campaigns in rough parity with white Americans?

Despite a political system that is open to contestation through the holding of free elections, why does Chinese-American political participation seem (on the surface) to sound like the personal networking that occurred between President Suharto and Sino-Indonesian businessmen? And does this sort of networking result in significant political influence for Chinese Americans?

TABLE 5.1 VOTING AND REGISTRATION BY RACE IN THE 1994 AND 1996 ELECTIONS			
NOVEMBER 1994 ELECTION	**CHINESE**	**WHITE**	**LATINO**
Citizenship	50%	98%	59%
Registration	23%(46%[1])	68%(69%)	31%(53%)
Voting	16% (32%)	50%(51%)	20%(34%)
• among Registered Voters	70%	74%	64%
NOVEMBER 1996 ELECTION	**CHINESE**	**WHITE**	**LATINO**
Citizenship	53%	98%	61%
Registration	30%(56%)	72%(73%)	36%(59%)
Voting	23%(43%)	60%(61%)	27%(44%)
• among Registered Voters	76%	83%	75%

[1] Percentages in parentheses represent the proportion of citizens registered or voting.

(*Source:* U.S. Department of Commerce, Bureau of the Census. Current Population Survey: Voter Supplement File, 1994, 1996 (computer files). ICPSR version. Distributor: Ann Arbor, MI: Interuniversity Consortium for Political and Social Research.)

SOME MACRO ANSWERS

Following the arguments laid out in the first two chapters, one reason for this type of political behavior could be that Chinese cultural legacies impede voting while facilitating contributions to campaigns. Some argue that the Buddhist-Confucian norms of a respect for hierarchy, reverence for authority, resignation, and passivity discourage Chinese Americans from civic actions such as voting. However, such an argument still cannot explain why Chinese Americans do engage to a greater degree in some types of political participation while lagging far behind white Americans in other means of participating.

The short answer is that Chinese Americans make campaign contributions and develop networking alliances because they have the resources, incentives, and opportunities to do so. This answer couples both a socioeconomic and an institutional approach.

Research on political participation in the United States has consistently found that the higher the socioeconomic status one is, the more likely one is to be politically active (Verba and Nie 1972; Rosenstone and Hansen 1993; Verba, Schlozman, and Brady 1995). Refinements in this basic argument add that participation is the result of a conjoining of several factors: mobilization by elites, incentives (economic or social) to participate, and having the resources to participate (Rosenstone and Hansen 1993; Verba, Schlozman, and Brady 1995).

Taeku Lee, in a paper presented to the American Political Science Association meeting in Boston (Lee 1998), runs a statistical analysis of the American National Election Studies participation measures and finds that voting and registering to vote are statistically independent of other participation actions, such as contacting officials, donating to campaigns, attending meetings, or actively campaigning. Of the various forms of participation listed, the one for which financial standing matters most is making contributions to campaigns and causes (Verba, Schlozman, and Brady 1995:28). If this research holds true for Chinese Americans, then one explanation for why they give campaign contributions is that it is a result of their socioeconomic success. However, this is not what current analysis shows. As Lee's presentation at the American Political Science Association highlights, and Lien (1994, 1997) shows, socioeconomic factors seem *not* to impact Chinese-American participation in the same manner that they do for other Americans. Lien (1994, 1997) finds that none of the standard measures of socioeconomic status—income, education, or occupation—show a significant effect on participatory actions. Again, one must ask why.

One answer is that the conventional models of political participation assume a particular civil socialization. As people grow up they learn about the larger political culture around them and they form views about which ideologies, parties, and causes matter to them. This process may well be substantially different and produce different opinions about strategies for immigrant communities and for those who are native-born. Wendy Tam Cho (1999) and Taeku Lee (1998) argue that socialization matters and that it impacts how Chinese Americans participate, or why they may *not* participate. Cho writes: "the socialization process is the mechanism that determines which elements are prominent in the cost/benefit analysis preceding participation," and she uses two variables to indicate that socialization processes will differ: whether one is foreign-born (versus American born), and degree of English proficiency.

Lee adds other crucial indicators (generation and tenure in the United States, degree of economic investment in either the United States or in the immigrant's country of origin, and activism within the Chinese-American community) of differences in socialization between Chinese Americans and white Americans, for example. Lee finds that while socioeconomic status, as measured by income and education, does impact whether an individual donates money to political campaigns, it is less significant a factor than how long an individual has lived in the United States. This is somewhat curious: the longer one is in the United States, the more likely one is to donate money. This would seem to indicate that it is not a participatory behavior that is learned in the immigrant's country of origin. Rather, as Cho finds, it maybe that certain aspects of Chinese Americans' socialization in the United States leads them to believe that donating money to campaigns is the way to effect the political process. Lastly, Lee finds that those who had economic investments in either the United States or in their native country (China, Taiwan, Hong Kong, or elsewhere in Southeast Asia) were significantly more likely to make contributions.

Lee also finds that while turning out to vote in elections does not influence contributions, community activism does predict the giving of campaign contributions. This suggests that communal activism can serve as an important locus of political mobilization. Finally, individuals who believe that Chinese-American political participation is an important goal are more likely to contribute than those who do not think that group mobilization matters. These findings may be interpreted to mean that contributions reflect a desire to advance communal interests rather than simply individuals seeking personal gain through political connections (Lee 1998).

STRATEGIC QUESTIONS AND THE ROLE OF ELITES

Fundamentally, whether one is asking about Indonesia, Malaysia, or the United States, the strategic questions remain the same. Chinese community leaders face uncertainty in the political climate of their adopted countries. Will the Chinese be persecuted or discriminated against, or will they be accorded the same rights and status as other citizens? In seeking to protect the rights and interests of the community, they will adopt strategies that they think will best work. Likewise, community leaders want to maintain their own standing as figures of prominence and respectability within the community. Politically minded elites face competition from within the community from those who believe that the Chinese are better off staying removed from or outside the host society and polity. These inward-looking leaders are part of an older sojourner diaspora who looked toward Taiwan or mainland China as "home," or as a place they intended to return to, whereas the new generation of elites aims to secure benefits for the community by tapping into U.S. government resources. This new cadre of leaders needs to receive these benefits in order to develop or win the support of the community. This is how they will be able to provide for their constituents' needs.

To explain this more fully, in the United States Chinese leadership is split into two distinguishable groups: social service elites and business leaders. Business leaders are better positioned to effect influence in the political process, but this does not necessarily result in greater political participation from the community as a group. Social service elites' position rests with meeting the needs of the community through the provision of social benefits and services; this gives them a basis (and often a mandate) for facilitating politicization of Chinese Americans. Yet this mobilization does not necessarily lead to influence. Because not-for-profit agencies receiving government money are required to be nonpartisan, there are severe limits to the types of political behavior that they can sponsor. For example, social service agencies can hold candidate forums but not endorse any particular party or candidate. These limitations impact the degree of influence they can effect, despite attempts at increasing community politicization. These divergent outcomes can be explained in two ways: the first emphasizes the role and motivations of elites, while the other points to consequences of political institutions on their actions.

There are very few Asian or Chinese Americans found in national- or state-level electoral positions. As of 1999 there were two Japanese-American U.S. Senators, both representing Hawaii; one Chinese-American governor, Gary Locke in Washington; six Asian-American

Representatives in the House, of whom one is Taiwanese American, David Wu (Democrat from Oregon), two from California, and one each from Guam, Samoa, and Hawaii. In California, Matthew Fong, when he served as State Treasurer, was the highest Chinese-American elected official. No Chinese Americans hold statewide office in New York. Despite these statistics, Asian Pacific Americans,[3] the nation's fastest growing immigrant group, have, due to John Huang and the Democratic National Committee fund-raising problems, become increasingly visible and potentially influential actors in American politics. Although the media attention, stereotyping, and innuendo over illegal campaign contributions are resented, Asian Americans, and particularly Chinese Americans, are beginning to demonstrate that they have the will, organizational apparatus, and fiscal resources to advance their concerns in the political arena.

NATIONAL ADVOCACY

There are several organizations that are active in raising the national profile of Chinese Americans in a political context. The Committee of 100 was founded in 1990 by a group of concerned Chinese Americans who are pioneers or leaders in their fields. Their goal was to form a body that could educate and advise political leaders, interest groups, and the corporate sector on matters of concern to the Chinese community. It is a national, nonpartisan-aligned organization of Chinese Americans. The group makes recommendations on both foreign policy questions (U.S. policy toward China, Taiwan, and Hong Kong) as well as on domestic issues of concern to Chinese Americans. Its members derive their insight on the U.S.-China relationship based on their bicultural background. They believe a constructive relationship between the peoples of the two countries is crucial to peace and prosperity for the two major powers in the world. Committee members included architect I. M. Pei, author Amy Tan, cellist Yo Yo Ma, educator Chang-Lin Tien, scientist David Ho, sculptor and architect Maya Lin, and Washington State governor Gary Locke. At their 1999 national meeting, Energy Secretary Bill Richardson spoke to those gathered about accusations of espionage against Wen Ho Lee and reassured the group that the current case would not become a larger witchhunt against Chinese-American scientists. The Committee of 100 also sent a letter to President Clinton stating their dissatisfaction with how the security concerns at Los Alamos were handled and their fears of increased racism stemming from the incident.

A second advocacy group is the Organization of Chinese Americans (OCA). OCA is a national civil rights organization with over forty chapters and twenty-three college affiliates across the United States. Founded in

1973 to ensure the civil rights of Chinese and other Asian Americans, it educates Chinese Americans on legislative issues that might impact the community. It makes policy recommendations and suggestions to Congress and to executive agencies. OCA organizes outreach programs and conferences to involve students in community activism. It is a nonpartisan organization, which means that it cannot endorse or support particular political candidates. As a nonpartisan association, the group may be limited as to the extent it influences the political process. This limitation will be discussed at greater length in the chapters on Monterey Park and New York City.

The next two sections of the book look at two specific Chinese-American communities: those in Monterey Park, California, and New York City's Chinatown. The two locales differ in their demographics, socioeconomic statistics, in rates of political participation, and in the communities' relationship to local political institutions. What will be particularly highlighted is the shift in community leadership, from business or economic elites to social service elites. The transition that has taken place in Monterey Park, while in New York there is a greater division between these two sets of players, and it is unclear if economic leaders will remain dominant or whether social service elites will usurp the old guard's power.

6

Suburbanization:
Chinese in Monterey Park,
California

INTRODUCTION

As Chapters One and Five point out, there is important variation in the nature and political involvement of Chinese communities in the United States. Monterey Park is a city within Los Angeles County. It lies about twenty minutes east of downtown Los Angeles and has a population of 61,854.[1] What makes Monterey Park unique is that the majority of the population is of Asian descent. Coupled with the surrounding towns of the San Gabriel Valley and with Los Angeles's Chinatown, this area of Southern California is an important place to study in order to understand ethnic politics.

This chapter shows that the Chinese community in the Los Angeles area is better-off economically than the one in New York, and that they have organized to participate in the political arena in somewhat more effective ways. Yet they have enjoyed only moderate levels of success in increasing rates of participation and influence. Since Chinese Americans by themselves are minorities in all but the most local electoral districts, they either need to form coalitions with other groups or provide non-electorally based incentives to officials with which to influence the political process. In Monterey Park, California, Chinese have been able to form working relationships with other groups. They have also cultivated their own social networks which serve to facilitate political participation. However, it is unclear at this time how successful these networks are at either increasing political participation or achieving influence.

Why is it that in places with closed political systems, like Indonesia, the Chinese seem to exert a great deal of influence, while in places where there is open contestation, as in the United States, they participate at lower rates than others and have only modest influence in the political process? The Los Angeles area is an important case with which to answer this question. More than in New York or San Francisco, the Chinese-American community in the greater Los Angeles area has led the way in building networks and political coalitions with other Asian groups and with Latinos. This is a new image of ethnic politics in the United States; it is neither the "melting pot" of old nor is it an example of ethnic special interests clamoring for individual gains, a sort of "balkanized" view of ethnic politics. Fong (1994) calls the community leaders who have been instrumental in building these links a "social service elite" because of their ties to not-for-profit agencies. This chapter will show that these elites have succeeded in increasing politicization among Chinese in suburban Los Angeles and the neighboring San Gabriel Valley, but it is less clear that they have been able to exert influence on the issues that most concern the community: access to education, immigration legislation, and a climate favorable to Chinese-owned business. Map 6.1 shows Monterey Park within the context of greater Los Angeles and the San Gabriel Valley.

The figures in Table 6.1 clearly show the demographic and political differences between Monterey Park and New York City's Chinatown. Household income is higher in Monterey Park and voter turnout is also somewhat higher than in Chinatown. As earlier discussions suggest, there are several possible explanations for this. There could be cultural differences between the two populations of Chinese Americans, there is clearly variation in the socioeconomic standing of the two communities, and communal organizations and leadership differ. We will look at each of these factors in turn.

COMPETING APPROACHES

CULTURE

Prior studies of Chinatowns in the United States have looked at the influence of Chinese culture on patterns of social organization and behavior. Heyer (1953) and Cattell (1962) saw the community as a closed enclave independent of the larger society's influence. These studies emphasize how the population characteristics—economic resources, leadership, cultural aspects, social issues, and so on—impact the role of voluntary associations in promoting social change within Chinatown. The assumption is that the Chinese immigrants' identity as a distinct ethnic group is of fundamental importance to understanding their role in the political process. In fact, much of the literature on immigrants and American politics points to particular traits of a group as the defining characteristics that explain their behavior in the political arena (Glazer and Moynihan 1963; Jalali and Lipset 1992/93).

Certainly race and the organization of communal interests have long been important in American politics. For European Americans this was manifest in machine politics (Erie 1988; Banfield and Wilson 1962), and

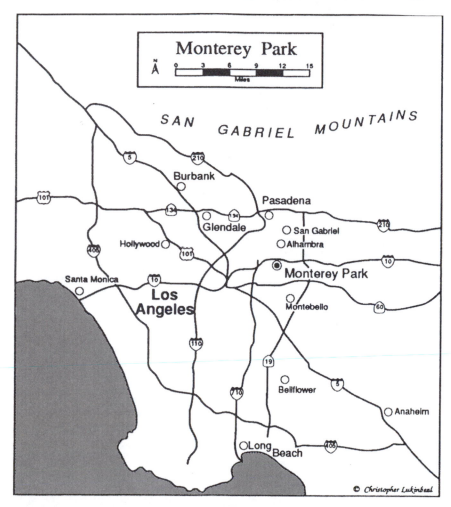

MAP 6.1 MONTEREY PARK, CALIFORNIA   (*Source:* Fong 1994.)

for African Americans mobilization evolved out of a history of slavery and a civil rights movement that targeted their empowerment. The Asian-American experience is quite different from these models. Chinese and other Asian immigrants were denied de jure and de facto political and civil rights in the United States until the late 1960s (L. Wang 1991:43). This fact, as much as cultural attributes, shapes their political involvement today.

Cultural explanations cannot account for differences within the same ethnic group in different settings. Chinese in Monterey Park,

TABLE 6.1 OVERVIEW OF CHINESE IN MONTEREY PARK AND NEW YORK CITY

	MONTEREY PARK	NEW YORK CITY CHINATOWN
Percent of Population	40%	28%
Naturalization Rate	59%[1]	na
Percent Registered to Vote	35.5%[2] / 69%[3]	38%[4]
Percent Voting	32%	27%
Household Income	$37,256	$21,345

[1] This figure represents the naturalization rate of Chinese in the areas of Southern California covered by the 1997 *Los Angeles Times* survey, Kang 1997:A1.

[2] This figure represents Chinese in all of Los Angeles county (Muratsuchi 1991:24).

[3] Sixty-nine percent of Chinese-American citizens in the Los Angeles vicinity are registered to vote.

[4] This figure, taken from the Voter Assistance Commission 1994 Annual Report of the New York City Voter Assistance Commission, Appendix K, pp. 71–72, represents the percent of those registered who are eligible to do so. To illustrate the difficulty in assessing data for Chinese Americans, the Annual Report cited above finds that voter turnout for all eligible Asians in the 62nd Manhattan Assembly district, which encompasses Chinatown and where Asians (most of whom are Chinese) are 36 percent of all eligible voters, is only 16 percent. Forty percent of Asians who are registered turned out to vote.

(Data taken from New York City Voter Assistance Commission; Ong and Azores 1994:106; *Los Angeles Times* Survey #331, 350, 370, 1992, and #336, 1997; and Muratsuchi 1991:24.)

California, are accessing the political system in very different ways from those in New York City. In Monterey Park, as this chapter will show, Chinese Americans are using multiethnic coalitions and creating their own political party clubs to advance their interests in the greater Los Angeles area. In New York, these developments have not occurred. One of the reasons that cultural explanations are so unsatisfactory is that they often become deceptive stereotypes. For example, Asian Americans are often touted as the "model minority" in U.S. society. Part of the "model minority" myth about Asian Americans is that they are more interested in prospering economically in order to send their children on to higher education than they are in pursuing influence in the political arena. Asian Americans, particularly Chinese, are often touted by the media as exemplary immigrants because they have overcome poverty and early discrimination to achieve educational and economic success. Pundits point to Asian students at elite academic institutions (Stuyvesant and Bronx Science High Schools in New York City, Harvard, Princeton, Yale, and MIT) and argue that their representation at such schools is far greater than their proportion of the general population. Hence the belief that Asian Americans tend to be bright and high achievers.[2] This label of a "model minority" simplistically implies that other minority groups can rise above discriminatory barriers to likewise achieve the American dream. The stereotype of the hard-working, studious, and successful Asian American hides the fact that many Asians have not succeeded economically or educationally. Likewise, it implies that concern over their political marginalization is unnecessary. Ethnic or cultural explanations cannot explain why Chinese communities in various places behave and affect politics in differing ways.

CLASS

As explained in greater detail in the next chapter, Peter Kwong (1979, 1996) portrays Chinatowns as places of class privilege. He argues that the Chinese are prevented from greater participation because the economic elite in Chinatown maintains a monopoly on interaction with host-society institutions and elites, thus most Chinese are marginalized because of the power of their own community leaders. While this may offer a useful portrayal of traditional leadership structures within Chinatowns, it does not explain the shift in the nature of elites within the community and why new elites might have different incentives for political organization. Likewise, there is ample work in American politics on who participates in politics and why. Early literature on voter turnout and political participation found that socioeconomic status and education were positively correlated with voter turnout (Verba and Nie 1972). Later work has shown that although economic status is an important predictor of an individual's likelihood of voting, there are other mobilizing factors to consider. These factors include the way that political institutions shape the nature and extent of immigrant politicization, and the ability and likelihood of elected officials and community leaders to mobilize constituents for greater political participation (Rosenstone and Hansen 1993).

At first glance, it seems that class analysis might explain some of the differences between Chinese communities in the United States. Chinese in Monterey Park are wealthier and different demographically from their co-ethnics in New York City. This might help account for the variation in organization and rates of politicization, yet, as the Southeast Asia cases show, socioeconomic status alone cannot address the complex reasons for ethnic politicization and community influence. As the next two chapters will show, the Chinese-American communities in Monterey Park and New York City differ: more Chinese in Monterey Park migrated from Taiwan rather than the People's Republic of China, and family income is higher in Monterey Park than in New York's Chinatown. In both places Chinese Americans vote at lower rates than do white Americans. While culture and class do matter, they are not the only answers to why levels of participation are low.

INSTITUTIONAL

There are political circumstances that may induce participation. Membership in a social network can create selective rewards and thus help overcome the "rational ignorance" that accompanies nonparticipation. These social networks can be mobilized for political advantage, and mobilization is the process through which people are induced to participate (Rosenstone and Hansen 1993:25). For politicians, parties, interest groups, and activists, access to social networks makes mobilization possible.[3] Without the selective benefits offered by membership in such groups, politicians have only collective returns to reward those who participate. For candidates there is no need to target all people, all the time; thus the strategic calculation of whom to target can influence and possibly help determine who participates and when (ibid.:33–35).[4] Leaders of these social networks obviously play a key role in passing on the information and overall direction to the groups' members. Much of this chapter looks at these elites within the Chinese community and examines their incentives in either pursuing a participatory strategy with the larger society or maintaining an ethnic insularity. While understanding the role of community elites and political leaders may help explain the nature and extent of political participation, can it also address the issue of influence in the political process?

If the Chinese are too small a percentage of the population to be the target of political party mobilization, then any efficacy at influencing political outcomes would have to be through either personal connections or interest-group activity (Hansen 1991:225–227). Traditional works by Schattschneider (1935) and Truman (1971) found that influence in the political process is achieved by powerful groups that have large memberships, are well endowed financially, and are well organized. These interest groups are seen as favored while others risk being ignored. If, according to Hansen, a smaller group enjoys comparative advantage over rivals in meeting reelection needs, and if legislators expect the issues and circumstances that created the comparative advantage to recur, then the group may wield some influence (Hansen 1992:5).

In looking specifically at Chinatowns, Nee and Nee (1986), Wong (1988), Weiss (1974), and Kuo (1977) do point out the important influence of national and local policies on the community, but they do not capture the important role that community leaders play, and the relationship between the host society's politics and institutions, and the corresponding participation and influence from the Chinese community.

Some do not see any reason to point to cultural, class, or ethnic features when discussing a group's politicization. In looking specifically at questions of ethnic group politics in the United States, Robert Lane argues that race, religion, immigrant status, and other cultural markers do not affect political participation (1969:85). He writes: "once the minimum legal period has been achieved and citizenship won, the immigrant votes now, as he did thirty years ago, fully and as frequently as the nonimmigrant." Nor does generation time in this country affect frequency of participation—at least not in a systematic way, Lane argues. He goes on to say that: "persons of ethnic backgrounds are interested in politics for the same reasons as the rest of the population: they have occupational interests which may be affected by tariffs or regulation, they are subject to local and national taxation, they have personal preferences among candidates and parties" (ibid.:86–87).

What Lane does not take into account is the way that a group may access the political system, and the impact that local elites within and outside the community have in choosing to focus the groups' energy and attention. Parenti finds that party leaders, precinct workers, and candidates rely on ethnic strategies as mobilizers of minority symbols and interests (1969: 268). Likewise, Bucuvalas (1978) looks at cultural differences in political participation and finds a persistence of cultural differentiation between ethnic groups on the basis of their political participation. This questions unitary models of behavior for predicting where differences between ethnic groups' participation will occur. No one approach to understanding this question is sufficient, and most studies on immigrants or ethnic groups focus on the cultural and class dimensions without looking at institutional factors and the motivations of elites to act as they do.

Cultural explanations are particularly relevant in understanding processes of socialization. In both Monterey Park and in New York's Chinatown, there are a myriad of Chinese-language newspapers and cable TV stations. Some are pro-Beijing, some pro-Taiwan, and some are neutral on the question of Chinese politics; however, all offer a perspective different from mainstream American news outlets. Bilingual or Chinese-speaking Chinese Americans are able to receive information about the United States and about international affairs through channels not used by other (non-Chinese-speaking) Americans. Similarly, many Chinese send their children to "Chinese school" after the regular schoolday is finished. At Chinese school, children learn to write Chinese characters, read

Chinese stories, and learn a variety of Chinese cultural arts, calligraphy, dance, and martial arts, to name a few. The effect of acquiring information in this manner, coupled with the way that American political institutions impact immigrant politicization, may account for some of the differences in rates of participation in Chinese American communities.

While the different demographics in Los Angeles do play a role in accounting for the higher rates of participation and influence, the comparison also shows how vital elite activity is in mobilizing this community. The chapters on Monterey Park and New York City examine the relevant community organizations and at how well each community has built coalitions with other groups. The importance of coalition-building is demonstrated by looking at the Chinese community's efforts to influence the reapportionment of voting districts in 1991.

COMMUNAL ASSOCIATIONS

Chinatowns have been known for the complex (especially to outsiders) network of communal associations that once served as the unofficial government of the Chinese in the United States. As is true for other ethnic communities, Chinese associations have provided cultural, economic, and political support to fellow immigrants far from home. Chinese organizations have been based on family and kinship networks, and on district or language groupings. While the leaders of these associations often presided over economic and social matters within the community, they also exercised a great deal of political control over Chinese within Chinatowns. This was true in the Los Angeles Chinatown, as well as in the larger Chinatowns of San Francisco and New York City. Since the focus of this chapter is more on Monterey Park than on Los Angeles's older, inner-city Chinatown, a more extensive examination of the internal community structure of Chinese associations is deferred until the next chapter.

The San Gabriel Valley in Los Angeles County is composed of several small cities with high numbers of Asian immigrants. Monterey Park is the only city in California with a population majority of Asian Pacific Americans (58%), with Chinese alone numbering more than 37 percent of Monterey Park's population (Ong and Azores 1994:12).[5] Of this, only 41 percent are registered to vote (as compared to 60 percent of Americans as a whole).[6] Despite the low rates of registration, what is interesting about this figure is that Nakanishi (1990:20) found that Chinese Americans in Los Angeles as a whole had voter registration rates of 35.5 percent, about 6 percent lower than in Monterey Park where Chinese are a significant proportion of the population and where Chinese political outreach is at its highest and community leaders are most visible. These are the issues to which we will now turn.

While New York adheres to older patterns of immigration, with new-comers filling jobs within the ethnic enclave and living with the city boundaries, Los Angeles offers a different pattern. First, instead of con-verging on Los Angeles's historic Chinatown, recent immigrants head outside the city to near by suburbs. "In 1990, when 245,033 Chinese lived in Los Angeles County, only 4 percent made their homes in the tradi-tional Chinatown" (Waldinger and Tseng 1992:98). The primary target for Chinese settlement has been Monterey Park and other cities in the San Gabriel Valley. "Monterey Park contains four census tracts in which more than half of the population is Chinese; another eight tracts in Monterey Park and Alhambra are more than one-third Chinese" (ibid.:99).

Chinese immigrants to Los Angeles first flocked to their co-ethnics' areas of economic activity. Where once the restaurant, gift, and garment trades dominated Chinese employment, there are now emerging busi-nesses and professional activities that include an expanded import and export trade,7 physicians and health care services, insurance and finan-cial expertise, real estate, and hotels. These sectors require higher skills and represent a shift in traditional immigrant employment opportunities. Like the divergent patterns of settlement and economics, politicization and influence of Chinese in New York and Los Angeles vary. Since the Chinese in Los Angeles have moved away from the urban core, they are somewhat removed from the high level of ethnic segmentation found in cities like New York. In Monterey Park, Chinese newcomers faced monoethnic dominance from longtime white residents. But in converging on a city with a population of less than a hundred thousand, the Chinese were able to make an immediate impact on local politics.

LOS ANGELES AND MONTEREY PARK

There have been several significant studies done on Monterey Park's trans-formation from a quiet suburb of Los Angeles to a vibrant multiethnic city (Horton 1992; Lamphere 1992; Fong 1994; Saito and Horton 1994). Each documents the conflict between long-standing white residents and the Asian newcomers over business development and zoning and the use of Chinese-language signs. These studies carefully illustrate the reluctance of established centers of power to adapt to changing realities. These pro-jects do not emphasize how particular community leaders in Monterey Park have successfully reached out to the Chinese for political and eco-nomic purposes. In order for whites or Latinos to continue to win politi-cal office, they clearly needed to reach out to the growing Asian-American

TABLE 6.2 ASIANS AND CHINESE IN MONTEREY PARK, CALIFORNIA

YEAR	NO. ASIAN AMERICANS[1]	NO. OF CHINESE	TOTAL CITY POP.
1960	1,113 (2.9%)	NA	37,821
1970	7,540 (15.3%)	2,202 (4.4%)	49,166
1980	18,890 (34.8%)	7,735 (14.2%)	54,338
1990	34,898 (57.5%)	21,971 (36.2%)	60,738

[1] Asian American here includes those of Korean, Japanese, Filipino, Indian and Southeast Asian ancestry, as well as Chinese from the PRC, Hong Kong, Taiwan, and elsewhere.

(*Sources:* Saito and Horton 1994:236–237; U.S. Census Bureau 1983, 1991.)

population. Table 6.2 shows the population increases of Asian Americans and Chinese in Monterey Park from 1960 to 1990.

The enormous increases in Chinese immigration were spurred by several factors. First were the changes in the immigration laws, discussed earlier. Second, the normalization of relations between the United States and the Peoples' Republic of China made Taiwanese and Hong Kong Chinese uneasy about their future in relation to the People's Republic of China. Without U.S. official recognition, many in Hong Kong and Taiwan feared an invasion from China. This prompted more people to think about immigrating. More specific to Monterey Park, Frederic Hsieh, a real estate investor, bought up large tracks of property in Monterey Park and began advertising the area in Chinese-language newspapers in Taiwan and Hong Kong as the "Chinese Beverly Hills" (Fong 1994:26).[8] This direct marketing overseas in the late 1970s and into the 1980s capitalized on the fact that many of the Chinese immigrating from Hong Kong and Taiwan came to the United States with education, professional skills, and middle-to-upper-class ambitions. "Hsieh knew that the crowded and unattractive Los Angeles Chinatown would not suit these affluent newcomers: There's no place to live. By word of mouth they came to Monterey Park. We did some promotion, such as advertisement in the magazines [and] in the newspapers over there in Hong Kong and Taiwan to encourage people to come and invest and patronize our (real estate) company" (Fong 1994:31).

To walk or drive around certain parts of Monterey Park in the late 1990s is to feel as though one is in Asia.[9] Many signs are in Chinese, and the library has Chinese-language books and periodicals as well as bilingual librarians. Brightly colored neon signs advertise a myriad of Chinese and Asian restaurants, health clinics, and shopping complexes. While the purchasing of Chinese-language books and periodicals for the library was contentious in the 1980s, they are now an accepted part of the library's collection. Likewise, in the 1980s, racial tension developed between long-time (white) residents and the new immigrants. One of the most contentious issues was a dispute over a law requiring English on business signs, and attempts to make English the city's official language caused a campaign to mounted in order to recall three City Council members. By the late 1990s most of the controversy had died down and Monterey Park, by many people's accounts, has become a peaceful, multiethnic suburban community.

Chinese may be the largest single ethnic group in Monterey Park and they are part of a larger trend in Southern California. Many cities and towns throughout the state are seeing increased growth of Asian Americans in the population. Chinese political activity has come, in part, as a result of the shift in residence from ethnic enclaves such as Chinatown, Koreatown, and little Tokyo to the more multiethnic suburbs such as Monterey Park. Politicization is facilitated by a more accessible set of political institutions in the suburbs. For the pioneering Asian Americans who were first elected to Monterey Park's City Council, the mainstream political and social networks served as the conduits to political office. This route to office began to change with the election of Lily Lee Chen in 1982.

Even though there have been significant changes in residence patterns, where Chinese in Los Angeles are settling away from the urban Chinatown, most Asian Americans involved in the political arena have rediscovered the symbolic and monetary importance of maintaining ties to the enclave communities. This was not the case for the first Asian-American candidates for political office in Monterey Park. Alfred Song was a Korean American elected to the City Council in Monterey Park in 1960. His election was followed by George Ige's (1970) and G. Monty Manibog's (1976) elections to the city council. Song recounts that he worked primarily through the established political channels—the party clubs—in this case the Monterey Park Democratic Club and the Lions and Kiwanis clubs that were managed by the predominantly white power structure. He is quoted as saying:

> In all of the years that I have campaigned for elective office, I have never had the help, financial or otherwise, of any organized Oriental group whatever their origin may be, Korean, Japanese, Chinese, Filipino or any others. . . . In twenty years, I think I could count the individual Asians who have come to my assistance on one hand and still have fingers left over. (Song 1980:16 quoted in Saito and Horton 1994:242)

In 1982 Lily Lee Chen was elected to the City Council. Her campaign, to a greater extent than Song's and the others', relied on a network of Asian and Chinese-American organizations and fund-raising. For example: a mailer was sent out endorsing Chen's candidacy. The mailer was paid for in part by Gold Star Investment Company of Monterey Park and America Tsui of Mandarin Realty, among others. These are subsidiaries of Taiwanese firms who supported progrowth policies and less restrictive development in Monterey Park. Investors saw Monterey Park as a community with potential for economic development. The economic growth potential, coupled with a more accessible set of political institutions, opened the door to Chinese developers. They became important players in local politics, and Lily Chen benefited from this. She was able in turn to campaign on a platform of greater ethnic tolerance and mobilize many Chinese to support her campaign (Fong 1994:92–95).

Judy Chu began her political career in 1985 by getting elected to the School Board. In 1988 she ran for City Council. She ran at a time of extreme racial tension, and her opponent was Barry Hatch, a longtime Monterey Park resident who was at the forefront of several contentious campaigns for "English only" ordinances. Chu ran as part of a moderate, multiethnic coalition. She reached out to a broad spectrum of Democratic voters in Monterey Park and had the backing of the Monterey Park Democratic Club. Traditionally, presidents of the Monterey Park Democratic Club became candidates for City Council. George Ige, Al Song, and other club activists had been instrumental in assisting Lily Chen with her successful bid for City Council in 1982.

In yet another departure from tradition, Chinese candidates have now formed their own networks for political success. For example, the Asian Pacific Democratic Club was formed in 1986 to mobilize Asian-American voters. In 1988 they became involved in Judy Chu's campaign. The club canvassed neighborhoods and worked to get out the vote.[10] They also worked on local, state, and federal issues of interest to the Asian-American community. For instance, they worked to expand immigration under the fifth preference category, family sponsorship, and developed good working relations with other immigrant community leaders with whom they had common cause.[11]

Judy Chu followed Chen's pattern of campaigning for multiethnic support from a Chinese base, and she is still in office. In meetings and conversations with Judy Chu in the summer of 1997, it was clear that she uses a multitude of networks to increase political awareness and activity in the Chinese and Asian communities. She participates in a variety of not-for-profit events and conferences designed to reach out to Chinese in

Monterey Park and neighboring areas for voter registration and fund-raising, and to increase general awareness of issues that concern the community. One such concern is the upcoming census in 2000 and possible reapportionment efforts after the census is complete.

The latest City Council election in Monterey Park was held in the spring of 1999. Three seats were up for grabs. Four Chinese Americans contested the elections; none won. The top three vote-getters were Frank Venti, Francisco Alonso (an incumbent), and Fred Balderrama. The combined votes for the four Chinese-American candidates (David Lau, Anthony Wong, Lisa Yang, and Margaret To) equaled 32 percent of the total vote, far surpassing the leader's (Frank Venti) total of 13 percent. While each candidate may have had different policy ideas and may have attracted votes from certain segments of the population, one wonders if it would be more fruitful for the community to urge candidates to cooperate with one another rather than to compete against each other.[12]

COALITION-BUILDING

One example of the type of events that Judy Chu and other community leaders are involved in is the following: in July of 1997, AP3CON, the Asian Pacific Policy and Planning Council, held an agenda-setting conference in Monterey Park. The purpose was "to develop a proactive strategic plan that will address the ongoing and emerging issues and concerns of the APA community" (AP3CON conference material, July 25 and 26, 1997). Founded in 1976, AP3CON is one of the largest federations of social service agencies—more than forty are represented. Its focus ranges from political advocacy issues to social justice concerns. Judy spoke at the 1997 conference's opening sessions about the community's efforts to have a say in the wording and choices on the census 2000. The fear is that if people identify themselves as "multiracial" on the census, then this may dilute the numbers of "Asian Pacific Islanders" in a particular geographic area. This would impact how political districts are drawn under the Voting Rights Act of 1965, and what sort of funding local agencies receive for their client services.

Organizations represented by AP3CON, such as the Chinatown Service Center and the Asian Pacific American Legal Center, are almost entirely social service agencies bound by 501(c)3 status, which forbids not-for-profits from engaging in partisan activity. AP3CON is not restricted by this, so there was much discussion about the possibility of cultivating or endorsing political candidates, activities that go beyond what most agencies have done in the past. To this end, AP3CON has been instrumental in mobilizing Chinese and Asian Americans in the past for political issues.

AP3CON helped organize a demonstration in September 1996 on the steps of Los Angeles City Hall to criticize the Welfare Reform Bill of 1996 for reductions in funding to immigrants, and it opposed California's anti–affirmative action measure, Proposition 209.

Outside of these service-based agencies and coalitions, traditional Chinatown organizations have also played a limited role in the political fortunes of Chinese-American activists. Judy Chu has maintained a good relationship with her family association in Chinatown, which shows that despite the waning power of the traditional modes of elite dominance in Chinatown, there has not been complete abandonment of these kinship organizations. These organizations are particularly useful for fund-raising purposes. Councilwoman Chu said that it certainly helped her to have Chinese businessmen hold a dinner for her reelection campaign.[13] Again, there are important differences between the traditional Chinatown organizations and the newer social service agencies that play a role in the social, economic, and political life of Chinese Americans. The traditional Chinatown organizations are not bound by not-for-profit status and so can raise money and endorse candidates.[14]

While both types of structures can provide economic benefits to their constituents, there are pronounced differences in the nature of their orientation and in how they are able to operate in the political arena. The traditional hui guan are characterized by their inward focus and their concern for maintaining traditional Chinese cultural institutions. So, for instance, the Chinese Consolidated Benevolent Association (CCBA) might help fund Chinese language and art classes for children, but it would not necessarily get involved in designing and working with the Board of Education to create a bilingual, bicultural school, as one new organization has done in New York City. The social service agencies that evolved out of the expansion of the welfare state in the 1970s are often staffed by second- and third-generation Chinese who have high levels of education and professionalism. These agencies rely on a great deal of local, state, and federal funding that necessitates greater contact with government institutions and elected officials. Since a condition of their not-for-profit status is nonpartisanship, these agencies are able to carry out voter registration drives, candidate forums, and educational programs for the community, but they cannot endorse office-seekers, nor can they cultivate and groom prospective candidates. This means that even while developing dense networks within the Chinese community, they are limited in the degree of influence they can exact on the political process. In part, this helps explain why Chinese political participation in California, particularly in Monterey Park, while higher than in New York, is also still lower than for white Americans.

It also helps explain why influence is still largely circumscribed despite an open political system that allows for access in a number of ways.

REAPPORTIONMENT OF 1991

The other advantage Los Angeles has over New York is the coalition-building that has occurred both between Chinese and other Asian groups, as AP3CON shows, and between Asian and Latino groups. The most illustrative example of this is in the redistricting efforts in the San Gabriel Valley in 1991. After each census, state political districts (assembly, senate, and congressional) are redrawn to reflect changes in population. Reapportionment—how the districts are drawn—is vital for ethnic politics because it can dilute or enhance a group's proportion of the district, depending on how the boundaries are delineated. The Voting Rights Act of 1965 and later amendments in 1975 and 1982 prohibit minority vote dilution by fragmenting communities. Thus after every census, activists in minority communities and both incumbent and hopeful politicians brood over demographic profiles and census tapes to design political districts that will support either their constituents or their chance of re-election. In 1991 there was a concerted and well-documented effort by Asian-American groups to rectify the dilution of their communal impact. Judy Chu spoke on behalf of the San Gabriel Coalition of Asian Pacific Americans for Fair Reapportionment:

> Our votes are fractionalized. The cities [in the West San Gabriel Valley] . . . are divided into two supervisorial districts, three assembly districts, three senatorial districts, and three congressional districts. (Judy Chu, March 9, 1991, Testimony delivered in Los Angeles to the California Senate Committee on Elections and Reapportionment)

Most of the members of the coalition were Chinese American, with a few Japanese Americans also involved, reflecting the demographic mix of the area. As Saito notes, those who were most active in the coalition were community leaders who already had developed skills and networks with the requisite government institutions and officials (Saito 1993:59). These were highly educated professionals, who, as consociationalism describes, were able to cooperate with Latino leaders representing an even larger minority in the same geographic area, and ultimately decide on a plan for redistricting that met some of each of their needs.[15]

What the two groups decided upon is as follows: using the 59th State Assembly district's basic boundaries, they redrew the district to include Rosemead and San Gabriel to keep the four cities, Monterey Park, and

Alhambra with the largest Asian-American population together. Latino groups agreed to this plan because, although it created a district where approximately 35 percent of the population is Asian American, Latinos and Democrats still were well over 50 percent of the population, giving the Latino incumbent a viable base from which to run again should he decide to seek reelection. On August 30, 1991, the San Gabriel Valley Latino and Asian-American groups held a press conference in Monterey Park's City Hall to present their plan for reapportionment. In September, a group of these leaders went to Sacramento to meet with elected officials and to lobby for their joint plan. Although Governor Wilson vetoed the plans presented by the state legislature, the state Supreme Court took over the redistricting task and appointed a "special masters" committee to create a new plan. The Asian and Latino groups both testified to their support for this reworked district. On January 27, 1992, the Supreme Court adopted the new plan, which created a new assembly district, 49, in line with the recommendations of the San Gabriel Valley groups (Saito 1993:64–65). Maps 6.2 and 6.3 show the district before and after reapportionment.

COMMUNAL DIVERSITY

Clearly one of the other significant impediments to greater political influence is that the Chinese community is divided on many issues. In Monterey Park, as elsewhere, there is disagreement among the Chinese. There is no consensus over issues such as business development and zoning within the city boundaries. Crucially, the Chinese are split between registered Democrats, Republicans, and independents. On education, there is dissent over the scope and nature of bilingual education. By far the most contentious issue has been over the pace and rights of business growth in Monterey Park. Chinese and Chinese-American investors have built large shopping complexes and townhouse developments. Developers and businessmen generally promote fewer restrictions on zoning and permit issues, while other community members want to limit the pace and scope of economic growth.

NETWORKING

In addition to party channels, Chinese Political Action Committee (C-PAC) is also a player in Monterey Park and San Gabriel Valley politics. C-PAC was headed in 1990 by Lily Lee Chen and Mike Eng and has supported candidates of either party. For example, it ran a major fundraiser for Sam Kiang, a republican, in 1990. It has been active in issues that concern the pace and nature of business development in Monterey Park. C-PAC is mostly first-generation Chinese and professionally

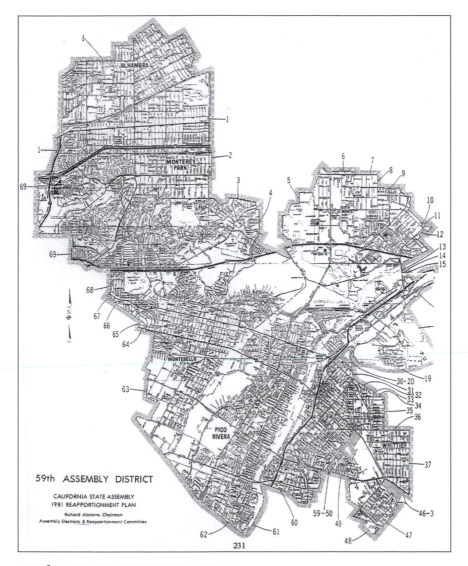

MAP 6.2 ASSEMBLY DISTRICT PRIOR TO 1991

(probusiness) oriented. This is somewhat different from the social service professionals who have become involved in Democratic party politics and who have become leaders of the community agencies that operate in Los Angeles and the San Gabriel area. These service-oriented elites are mostly second- and third-generation Chinese Americans and are more likely to support Democratic candidates and policies and to favor slower growth in the area. Due to both the constraints of their agencies' 501(c)3 status, and

MAP 6.3 REAPPORTIONED DISTRICT 49

because they have been educated in the United States, many of these elites were involved with the movement in the 1970s on University of California campuses for Asian-American empowerment and civil rights.[16] They have been inculcated with an activism and a sense that their actions need to benefit the larger community, not just them personally or their "business."

Where C-PAC can directly influence electoral campaigns with its donations, it professes to work for a particular set of interests, not the group as a whole. Its actions have little to do with increasing politicization from the community. This phenomena is somewhat similar to that of wealthy individual Chinese and Asians who have donated to political campaigns. Some view campaign contributions as a method of participating in the political process and an attempt to gain recognition as a political community for either immediate or potential influence on later issues. Nakanishi (1990) estimates that in the 1984 presidential election Asian Pacific Americans contributed over $10 million to the Bush or Dukakis election efforts, a figure that was second only to campaign money raised by the American Jewish population (p. 16). In the 1992 election, *A. Magazine* stated, the largest single donor of "soft" money to the Bush campaign was an Asian American (*A. Magazine* Oct./Nov. 1996:74). Similarly, in the 1996 election Asian Americans were reported to have donated more than $10 million to presidential campaigns (*A Magazine* Oct./Nov. 1996:82).[17] "Unfortunately, those contributions are seldom focused on any political agenda, or specific issues" (Bau 1995:23). As the fund-raising scandal illustrates, many players claiming to represent the Asian-American or Chinese-American community seem to donate to political campaigns to facilitate their own businesses and to acquire a photo of themselves with important political players. Those who seem to concentrate on building networks and grassroots activity and support in the community are constrained by the very organizational status necessary to do their work.

REFUTING *"GUANXI"* POLITICS

It has often been argued (and this book tries to explain why) that Chinese, and Asian Americans in general, participate politically by making campaign donations. The exit poll conducted in 1996 by the Asian Pacific American Legal Center of Southern California found that Asian Pacific American voters participate in a wide range of political activities, and what is more notable is that many newly naturalized and first-time voters were involved in political behaviors.

Some of the reasons offered for this activity are as follows: proposed cuts to legal immigration and legislation aimed at ending government benefits for legal, noncitizen immigrants mobilized some previously inactive Chinese Americans. Likewise, many nonpartisan community and grassroots organizations launched massive outreach campaigns to educate and involve their communities about the issues and candidates. Extensive coverage by Chinese media outlets also reached potential voters and helped mobilize the community.

Campaign contributions have been one such method of both participating in the political process and represent an attempt to gain recognition as a political community for either immediate or potential influence on issues. After the last twelve months of invective and innuendo about supposed Chinese influence-buying in the 1996 reelection of President Clinton, leaders in the Chinese community have said that they need to reassess how and why they donate to political campaigns.

The recent political scandals of "Asian" gift-giving to the Democratic National Committee appear to support the stereotype that Asians work through personal connections and "back doors" (*guanxi*) to achieve political influence in politics. This is certainly the spin that is placed on the events surrounding President Clinton's 1996 reelection campaign. However, what is often neglected in this view of events is how leaders within the Democratic Party such as Ron Brown and others sought out Asian donors *in particular* and used these individuals to further networks within the Chinese and Asian-American community to pump others for more money.[18]

CONCLUSION

Chinese communities in the United States face very different challenges and institutional constraints from their counterparts in Southeast Asia. In the United States, where pluralism is the ideal and conflict is institutionalized, Chinese associations can be seen as adaptive mechanisms to the policies of the state. One of the major points that this work hopes to convey in comparing Chinese communities in Southeast Asia and the United States is the direct relationship between the nature of government policies and institutions and the way in which the communal interests are expressed and organized, particularly the actions of community leaders. The Los Angeles Monterey Park area shows that where social service elites are at the forefront, political participation from the group as a whole may be higher, but it is less clear that influence will result from these actions, in part because not-for-profit agencies are restricted in ways that they can affect the political process. When the Chinese community has built networks with other groups, they have had greater success in achieving political goals. For example, Stewart Kwoh and the Asian Pacific American Legal Center have worked to build bridges with all Asian communities, and with African-American and Latino groups. Speaking of Kwoh's efforts, Xavier Becerra, a Latino congressman whose district includes parts of Chinatown, states: "the work he does can be felt here in Washington, D.C. I call Stewart a master bridgebuilder" (Saito 1997:139; *Los Angeles Times:* Kang 1995). It may be only a matter of time before the increased attention will result in greater impact as well.

7

New York:
The City of Ethnic Politics

INTRODUCTION

The newspaper headline "City Minorities May Now Be Majority" from the *New York Times* on October 24, 1989, did not refer to European immigrants but to the combined force of blacks, Asians, and Latinos, which by 1990 made up approximately 54 percent of the city's population. The percentage is presumably higher today. While ethnic politics is not new in New York City, the Chinese community is emblematic of a new importance placed on the diversity of ethnic groups in New York City politics. The idea of America as a vast "melting pot" that would Americanize all newcomers has been scrapped and replaced by "cultural pluralism," where the retention of cultural differences is accepted and valued.

If cultural maintenance is desirable, how well do different ethnic groups become incorporated into New York City political institutions? New York City's Chinatown evolved toward the end of the nineteenth century and in several ways it, more than any other Chinese community in the United States, continues to resemble the ethnic enclave it originated as. While the tremendous influx of new immigrants after 1965 has changed the overall landscape of immigrant and ethnic politics in New York City, and while satellite "Chinatowns" have developed in Sunset Park, Brooklyn, Upper Manhattan; and Flushing, Queens, Chinatown remains a vibrant and important center for first- and second-generation Chinese in the United States.

COMPARISON OF NEW YORK AND MONTEREY PARK

While the New York and Los Angeles Chinese communities began as demographically similar, the two have been transformed by increased Chinese immigration in very diverse ways. By 1980, Los Angeles's Chinese population was buoyed by newcomers from Taiwan, many of whom came with higher levels of education, professional status, and entrepreneurial experience. While the People's Republic of China was mired in the chaos of the Cultural Revolution during the 1960s and 1970s, Taiwan's economy was beginning to grow. Although they may have flourished economically in Taiwan, immigrants who came to the United States from Taiwan during this period were often seeking greater political freedoms. Many came to the United States for graduate study and were able to secure employment in the United States upon finishing their degree. In contrast, Chinese immigrants to New York hailed largely from the People's Republic of China (PRC) and Hong Kong. Immigrants from the PRC and from Hong Kong were often those seeking greater economic opportunities. Many are from rural areas and have little education or capital to contribute with which they might improve their lot at home. Educated and wealthy Chinese from Hong Kong have tended to immigrate to Britain or Canada, rather than to New York's Chinatown. These disparate origins yielded divergent class characteristics and ways of interacting with the existing community and political institutions.

Like the Chinese in peninsular Malaysia and in Monterey Park, California, Chinese in Manhattan make up approximately 30 percent of the local electoral district. There are a number of ways in which Chinese might participate in and affect local politics. Two ways of interacting with political institutions will be discussed in this chapter: local elections and voter turnout; and coalition-building and social service activity. While Chinese Americans have been elected to local political office in Monterey Park, California, and have successfully networked with other minority groups in the county, there are few examples of either behavior to be found in Chinatown, New York. New York City's Chinatown illustrates how the combination of divisions within the community and institutional constraints on their power to bring about political change have resulted in continued political marginalization despite a long presence in the city.

TABLE 7.1 PLACE OF ORIGIN OF CHINESE IMMIGRANTS TO NEW YORK AND LOS ANGELES, 1990

	PRC	TAIWAN
	%	%
Admitted by Occupation:	17	42
Intended Residency:		
Los Angeles	11	22
New York	28	9
Preimmigration Occupation:		
Blue collar, Farmer, Service	60	15
Professional, Managerial	30	66

(*Source:* Waldinger and Tseng 1992:94, taken from 1990 INS Annual Report.)

New York City politics has often hastened to integrate immigrants into the polity. As Waldinger notes:

> In New York, politics has been a vehicle for the expression of ethnic interests and a means for the organization of ethnic conflict, ever since the mass arrival of the Irish in the 19th Century. The pattern of ethnic group incorporation is linked to basic patterns of political conflict, in which the succession of one migrant wave after another has ensured a continuing competitive conflict over political influence. (Waldinger 1995:6)

Waldinger sees this tradition as alive and well in New York, as Mayor Giuliani sought to balance his 1993 ticket with Susan Alter (Jewish), and Herman Badillo (Puerto Rican). He remarks that the city's diversity puts a premium on building and maintaining ethnic coalitions. It is significant to understand that the Chinese on the Lower East Side have not been as successful as Latino groups in New York at appearing on the political map, nor have the Chinese in New York been as successful as their co-ethnics on the West Coast in developing the political and social networks necessary to maximize the community's role in politics.

CHAPTER OVERVIEW

This chapter begins by examining different perspectives on the organization and politicization of New York's Chinatown and examines community demographics. The second part of the chapter analyzes the shift in leadership in Chinatown from an inwardly focused business elite to a more acculturated social service elite that seeks greater input on local and national politics. The third part of the chapter looks at the institutional incentives and constraints to participation and influence of the Chinese in New York City. Lastly, several case studies are examined: the election of judges Doris Ling-Cohan and Dorothy Chin-Brandt, and the failed election challenge to City Councilwoman Kathryn Freed by Jenny Lim; the creation of a bilingual, bicultural school; and the issue of district reapportionment after the 1990 census.

BACKGROUND

Despite the image of Chinese Americans as uninterested in politics and as "model minorities" who work hard and achieve success through an emphasis on higher education and professional achievement for their children, Chinatown remains one of the poorest areas of Manhattan. Heated battles have been waged between community members on a

number of political issues (workers' rights in restaurants and garment factories, City Council and congressional election districts, etc.). Although
they make up more than a third of the 1st City Council district, no
Chinese-American candidate has ever been elected to the Council or to the
State Assembly or Senate. Po-Ling Ng has served on the local school board
for sixteen years and is often held up as one of the few Chinese Americans
to win electoral office in New York City. Several Chinese Americans have
won election to serve as Civil Court judges.

Peter Kwong is one of the most prominent scholars of Chinatown. In
his 1979 and 1996 works he develops the argument that Chinese in New
York are a dynamic and politically vibrant community but that they are
internally focused as a product of a class struggle between a merchant
elite, supported by foreign capital, and a larger number of working-class
immigrants. He attributes this inward focus to two significant and interconnected causes: legal and institutional discrimination against the
Chinese in the United States, and the creation of an unofficial governing
structure within Chinatown by the merchant elites. How and why did this
inward focus evolve?

HISTORY

As Chapter 5 explains, the Chinese began migrating to the United States
in large numbers as laborers between 1847 and 1860. Arriving first on the
West Coast to mine gold and build the railroads, the Chinese suffered
from the turmoil and scapegoating coming out of growing unionization
in the United States during the mid-1800s. The combination of legal and
economic persecution prompted Chinese in California to begin migrating to the Eastern United States around the turn of the century.

From the 1950s on, Chinatown steadily outgrew its original boundaries
within a single census tract.[1] In 1970, seven of eight continuous tracts,
including the original Chinatown, were over one-quarter Chinese and

TABLE 7.2 CHINESE POPULATION OF NEW YORK CITY	
YEAR	POPULATION SIZE
1880	800
1900	6,321
1940	40,000
1960	33,000
1980	124,260
1990	238,795

(Statistics compiled from Kwong 1979:38; U.S. Census of Population for 1980 and 1990.)

three were over half Chinese; a decade later, all eight tracts were over one-quarter Chinese and four were over half Chinese; by 1990, seven of the eight were over half Chinese, and one was more than 30 percent Chinese (Waldinger and Tseng 1992:97).

COMMUNAL ORGANIZATION

The dense web of ethnic associations that have been identified as active in the internal politics of U.S. Chinatowns are a direct manifestation of two situations. First, benevolent societies were created by immigrants to help each other and to assist newcomers. Second, in the middle of the twentieth century, "overseas Chinese" in the United States developed close ties to the Nationalist Party, *Kuomintang* (KMT), on the mainland of China, and some of the leaders and Chinatown organizations remained tied to the KMT once its members fled to Taiwan after 1949. Like many other immigrant organizations, Chinese associations have provided cultural, economic, and political support to fellow ethnics far from home. An individual might belong simultaneously to several organizations to which he is eligible. For instance, a person might belong to his family name association, a business group, and perhaps a cultural or social organization. The interlocking or crosscutting group affiliation of so many individuals and so many organizations meant that community leaders were often those that held leadership positions in several associations.

The smallest unit of traditional organization in Chinese communities has been the *fong*, or family grouping. *Fongs* are generally made up of people from the same village or kin group in China. The associations, like other immigrants' mutual aid societies, provided economic assistance to members. The next level of organization is the *hui guan*, or the district or language groupings. *Hui guan* would represent communities such as the Hakka or Toishan speakers from the Canton region of southern China. Larger associations might own their own headquarters as well as other buildings used for schools or cultural and business activities. Leaders of the district associations often also play an active role in the *tongs*, or business associations. The *tongs* are economic alliances and serve as arbitrators within the Chinatown communities. Leaders are generally the economic elite. *Tongs*, or triads, are often spoken of as the "secret societies" of Chinatowns the world over. In reality, these organizations did not form in secret and they served as brotherhoods for a wide range of activities, from martial arts to political societies.

Rivalries between family and economic associations sometimes resulted in violence, and the political structures outside of the community wanted a way to understand, interact with, and oversee the community.

To minimize rivalries between groups, an umbrella organization, the Chinese Consolidated Benevolent Association, or CCBA,[2] was formed in New York in the late nineteenth century.[3] A mediator for intra-associational conflict, this CCBA also become the external representation for all of Chinatown with the larger host society. Usually a combination of communal and external factors necessitated the creation of an overarching association like the CCBA. Another key purpose of these organization was to create a "Chinese identity out of various sub-regional identities" (Chan 1991:78). Even though a large number of Chinese immigrants came from southern China, not all of the dialects they spoke—Cantonese, Toishanese, Hokkien, and so on—were mutually intelligible. Having an umbrella organization facilitated interaction between groups and a greater sense of common solidarity and identity among the diverse immigrants.

The CCBA originated in San Francisco in the early 1850s. The six most powerful Chinese businesses came together and formed one organization, known as the Six Companies, to oversee all immigrant activities and to respond to anti-Chinese incidents. With the passage of the Chinese exclusion acts of 1882, the organization was transformed to an internal government of Chinatown. The Chinese Consulate recognized the Six Companies as the leading body of Chinatown (Nee and Nee 1976), and U.S. officials were largely relieved to allow the community to mediate and police themselves. The Six Companies registered with the U.S. government as the CCBA, and the New York and Los Angeles organizations were modeled on San Francisco's (Kuo 1977:36).

Mutual aid organizations and internal governing structures evolved and acted where the power of the host society's government was weak or nonexistent in the Chinese communities. However, the focus of these groups was internal, within the Chinese community.[4] Figure 7.1 shows the organizational hierarchy of Chinatown organizations.

Family, district, and merchant associations are all members of the CCBA, but it is the *tongs* that dominate both the business organizations and the executive leadership of the CCBA. The CCBA itself is organized and run like a government. There is a constitution which states that the CCBA is the "supreme organ of all Chinese in New York and the neighboring states" (CCBA 1949 Constitution). It has an executive board and a representative body of all member organizations. Voting is weighted depending on the influence and affluence of the association. For example, the Ning Young and Lian Chen Associations are the only two district associations from which the "mayor of Chinatown" is chosen (Kwong 1996:91). It is also interesting to note that the constitution urges that disputes be settled outside of U.S. political institutions. The constitu-

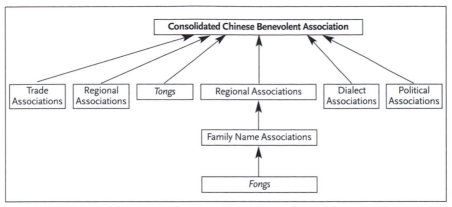

FIGURE 7.1 CHINATOWN'S COMMUNITY STRUCTURE (*Source:* Wong 1988:78.)

tion stresses that settlement of Chinatown issues should be kept out of U.S. courts.

So while the CCBA played the ultimate brokerage/patronage role in Chinatown, overseeing disputes within the community and regulating almost all of the business and cultural activity that occurred, it also served to keep Chinatown inwardly focused. It was not until the recent evolution of social service agencies funded by government and private (non–Chinatown based) grants that Chinese leaders began to learn how to navigate the complex set of U.S. political and service institutions that govern and provide programs and benefits to different constituents (Skinner 1958; Kuo 1977; Kwong 1979:38–45; Wong 1988:Ch. 3).

After World War II the nature of communal organizations shifted somewhat. Since immigration from China was slight, Chinese in New York were increasingly locally born. Labor unions and other progress political organizations were attacked by conservative, pro-KMT (the Nationalist Party fighting a civil war against the Communist party in China) forces within the Chinese community. Chinatown, until the middle of the 1970s, was overseen by a small merchant elite, and only with new immigration and the acculturation of second- and third-generation Chinese Americans did leadership evolve from other sources.

During the first half of the twentieth century, New York City's Chinatown, as well as other Chinatowns in American cities, could be described as an enclave. With the maintainenance of rigid boundaries between communal life and processes and the larger society, there was little possibility that there would be political incorporation of Chinese with the host polity. This segregation served as yet another institutional factor constraining political participation and influence on local government.

Perhaps one of the most illustrative accounts of this world-within-a-world is found in Paul C.P. Siu's 1987 work *The Chinese Laundryman*. Told through narrative accounts and based on a lifetime of work as both a laundryman and a scholar, Siu describes Chinatown life in Chicago and Boston as only an insider can. The following example shows the connection between Chinese immigrants in the United States during the 1930s and political events occurring in China at the time; it also illustrates how decisions were made by community leaders and exacted on merchants by volition or force. This demonstrates the personal conflicts both within the Chinese community and between Chinese laundrymen and their American clients:

> Those who refuse to contribute to the war fund ought to be punished. I have just paid my bi-monthy dues last week. I paid eighteen-fifty. According to my business, I would not have to pay so much. What of it? If we should lose to the Japs, what good is the money? So I decided to do my best. Some are beaten for refusal to pay the war fund. I think they deserve it. (Sui 1987:225)

In this case, the community agency in Chicago that collected contributions for the war was the National Salvation Fund. The fund operated in most urban Chinatowns and was run by patriotic business leaders within the community. This story illustrates the internal conflicts among the Chinese. The internal focus and the sojourner mentality would continue within the U.S. Chinese community until the repeal of the Chinese Exclusion acts in 1943 and the lifting of the racial restrictions from the "War Brides Act" of 1945. It was at this juncture that many Chinese in the United States decided to bring over their families and apply for citizenship. Additionally, when the communists won control of China in 1949, many immigrants who dreamed of returning home decided to remain in the United States. This shift in focus from sojourner to settler gradually began to have an effect on the political and social organization within Chinese communities.

After 1965 new migrants began coming to Chinatown again in large numbers. While Chinese immigration to the United States in the nineteenth century was predominately from the southern provinces of China, and those who arrived in the United States entered the economy on the lowest rungs of the ladder, it is currently of a more varied nature. Since 1965, Chinese immigrants have continued to arrive from southern China, but they have also come from elsewhere on the mainland and from Hong Kong, Taiwan, and Southeast Asia. Likewise, not all immigrants are penniless and unskilled. Distinct origins and class status have greatly impacted the nature of Chinese communities and their internal organizations. This, in turn, affects how they interact with the larger host society and institutions. One of the most obvious political divisions in any Chinatown can be characterized as a split between those who look upon Taiwan and the Nationalist regime as a "homeland" identifier, and those whose sentiments are more oriented toward the mainland. While this affiliation has political elements, it also reflects language, status, and familial components. The same division spills over and affects the contest over leadership within Chinatown. Older immigrants, whose focus has been on Chinese Nationalist politics, have traditionally headed the CCBA and family associations, whereas younger social activists are more progressive in their political outlook and they tend to look to American political issues as the mobilizing forces rather than China/Taiwan issues.

Since the shift in immigration law in the 1960s and the passage of civil rights and antipoverty legislation in the mid- and late 1960s, the CCBA's power within China has steadily eroded. The second half of the chapter will detail how social service agencies and other activists have contributed to the Chinese community's increasing politicization.

The CCBA's hold over Chinatowns was challenged as the community began to grow and change after World War II. The Chinese Exclusion Act was repealed in 1943. The United States was allied with China against Japan, and immigration policies reflect this. Chinese were once again allowed to enter the United States, although the yearly quota was only 105 persons. Many of those who came to the United States between 1945 and 1947 were women allowed in because they were wives of American citizens, or war brides to those in the armed forces. As the sex ratio became more balanced and more families were allowed into the country, Chinese orientation toward China began to shift; of those who had come as sojourners, many were settling down permanently. The Immigration Act of 1965 changed the nature of Chinese immigration even more substantially.

SHIFT FROM CCBA DOMINANCE TO SOCIAL SERVICE INVOLVEMENT

Following the tradition of the civil rights movement of the 1960s, Chinese immigrant groups and Chinese Americans began asserting themselves and pushing for expanded legislation addressing a century of discrimination and disenfranchisement. These groups were more than just brokers between the host society and the Chinese community, they were prepared to advocate on the community's behalf and they aimed to get a larger share of allotted benefits then ever before. While Chia-ling Kuo (1977) views these social service agencies as forerunners of political pressure groups, and Wong (1988) sees them as competition for the old economic elite, each of these analyses seems only partially correct. Social service organizations and their leaders are better skilled at navigating government bureaucracies and at building coalitions with other groups, yet they are significantly hampered by prohibitions against partisan political activity. In order to qualify for 501(c)3 status as a not-for-profit, agencies are limited to running candidate forums and voter registration drives. They cannot endorse a particular candidate. Clearly this prohibition may serve as a substantial hindrance in mobilizing the community behind one candidate. While both sets of groups (the benevolent associations and service agencies) would like to claim to represent the community as a whole, and both assume important positions of leadership, the two types of organizations actually serve different functions. If the old guard stuck with representing business interests, the social service agencies could focus on serving the social welfare needs of the community. Where they clash is over political representation and political power.

As somewhat of an alternative to these two types of groups, pressure groups have developed in the Chinese community, such as the Organization of Chinese Americans (OCA).[5] OCA has both regional and national offices and does serve to advocate for Chinese interests in the political arena. While the local New York OCA chapter head, Josephine Chung, has assisted (in a personal capacity) recent Chinese candidates for political office, such as Jenny Lim, Doris Ling-Cohan, and Dorothy Chin Brandt, without a corresponding political action committee, Chung and OCA are hampered by nonpartisan status. Its other constraint is a self-imposed one: OCA, like other ethnic organizations wants to be seen as inclusive of the whole community, but in officially endorsing candidates it may alienate some segments of the community. OCA has primarily run get-out-the-vote activities to register Chinese-American voters and has canvassed Chinatown neighborhoods to educate people about the importance of electoral activity. Also, OCA has been active in responding to the Democratic National Committee's backlash against donors with Asian surnames.

The shift from the old (economic) elite dominance, derived from the leadership of lineage associations, to a professional social service elite looks more like a rivalry than a transition process. Peter Kwong describes the split between an older elite entrenched in the kinship-oriented CCBA hierarchy and a new core of social service professionals and illustrates the schism by looking at labor disputes at the Silver Palace Restaurant in 1980 and at Jing Fong Restaurant in 1995. The restaurant disputes pit Chinese labor against Chinese owners, just one of many divisions within the community. In 1995 a waiter, Sheng Gang Deng, complained to managers that busboys and waiters were paid as little as $65 to $100 a week for working sixty hours or more, a workweek that should have earned them $213 a week at the minimum wage, plus tips and overtime. When Sheng Gang Deng complained he was fired. In January of 1997 the attorney general's office filed a lawsuit charging:

> the restaurant with cheating workers out of more than $1.5 million in tips and wages since 1993 by illegally controlling the distribution of tips and withholding some of them. The Asian American Legal Defense and Education Fund had filed a lawsuit against Jing Fong in U.S. District Court seeking $500,000 on behalf of workers who said the restaurant had failed to pay overtime and violated minimum-wage laws. (Chen 1997:1)

A settlement was announced in October of 1997 saying that owners are responsible for paying fifty-eight workers $1.1 million in installments over the next thirty-two months. Waiters will be in control of the collection and distribution of tips, and Deng will be rehired (ibid.). The owners of the restaurant, speaking through their attorney, said that they would have rather worked through a court of law than through the attorney general's office. The owners hailed from the class of economic elite that Kwong sees as representative of the traditional kinship associations, where as agencies such as the Asian American Legal Defense and Education Fund are emblematic of "social service" type groups proving alternative leadership within Chinatown.

There are times, however, that the CCBA and the kinship associations have been better positioned than the social service agencies to promote politicization. For instance, family associations are able to make financial donations to political candidates. Jenny Lim's family association hosted a fund-raising dinner at a large restaurant in Chinatown for her several weeks before the primary. Speeches were made in Cantonese and Toishanese praising the candidate and wishing her luck in the election. So, while the social service networks are embedded in the community, trying to raise awareness and get out the vote, the traditional associations are in a better position to back those wishing to run for office.

"MODEL MINORITY MYTH" REVISITED

Ethnicity and the organization of communal interests have long been important in American politics. For European Americans this was manifest in machine politics (Erie 1988; Banfield and Wilson 1962), and for African Americans mobilization evolved out of a history of slavery and a civil rights movement that targeted their empowerment. The Asian-American experience is quite different from these models. Chinese and other Asian immigrants were denied political and civil rights in the United States until the late 1960s (L. Wang 1991:43). Part of the "model minority" myth about Asian Americans is that they are more interested in prospering economically than in becoming involved in the political arena. Asian Americans, particularly Chinese, are often touted by the media as exemplary immigrants because they have supposedly overcome early discrimination to achieve educational and economic success. This label of a "model minority" simplistically implies that other minority groups can rise above discriminatory barriers likewise to achieve the American dream. The stereotype of the hard-working, studious, and successful Asian American hides the fact that many Asians have not succeeded economically or educationally. For example, Asian-American children do flounder in school. At a minimum, the New York City dropout rate for Asian Americans is 10.5 percent; only 2 percent of guidance counselors in public schools are Asian American. Finally, the suicide rate for Asian youth is reported to be one third to one half higher than the general population (*New York Newsday* March 14, 1997:G8).

NEW YORK CITY POLITICAL INSTITUTIONS

Sayre's and Kaufman's (1959, 1965) landmark studies of New York politics painted a positive view of how the city was governed. These early studies saw the city as open to competing groups and ideas in society. New York City was seen as a pluralist system where issues were addressed through negotiation between new participants and more entrenched coalitions. Likewise, Robert Dahl's was a leading scholar whose work, *Who Governs?* (1961, Yale University Press) reflected this sort of optimism. Sayre and Kaufman (1960) argued that groups would be formed when individuals joined with other like-minded people and that their views would be heard and reflected in policy decisions. "Anyone who feels strongly enough," they argued, "can form an organization and compete in city politics."

By 1970 this picture urgently needed to be rethought. New York as a pluralist democracy seemed increasingly inaccurate. The civil rights movement highlighted the inequalities of America's democracy, and urban politics was not immune from reexamination. Critics came to view New York City politics as elite dominated; while policies might have been decided upon in an open and transparent manner, the agenda was set by a handful of powerful leaders. Many groups, notably African Americans and Latinos, were far removed from the process. The civil rights move-ment also stimulated different actors and methods of advocacy. The bat-tle over New York City's school decentralization illustrates how great the conflict could be. Community groups were at odds with traditional cen-ters of power, such as the teachers' unions and the central administration (Bellush 1990; Rogers 1990).

One institutional impediment to all non-English-speaking immigrant groups is language. There were no bilingual ballots (English-Chinese) until 1994, which seriously hampered naturalized citizens' ability fully to participate in electoral politics. Even if an immigrant learns enough English to qualify for citizenship, navigating and understanding election procedures and referendum is more difficult than just knowing enough English to pass the citizenship test. For Chinese Americans this is a sub-stantial barrier. "It is estimated that 65 percent of Chinese Americans working in New York City's Chinatown do not speak English well or at all" (Asian American Almanac 1995:351). From discussions with community leaders, it seems that bilingual ballots have increased political participa-tion in Chinatown, but there are as yet no statistics which compare turnout data before and after 1994.

Regardless of pluralist theories about how policy was made in New York, agenda-setting power and budgets for city agencies were largely the province of only two players. Until 1989 New York City politics was dom-inated by the mayor and the Board of Estimate.

THE MAYOR

The mayor is the most visible symbol of New York City politics. During the 1960s and 1970s, political scientists hailed the end of the urban polit-ical machine. True, local politics became less dominated by party leaders, but they were replaced by charismatic mayoral figures promoted by the media. The mayor's executive power is granted by the city charter. Mayors have significant control over the day-to-day operations of the city, and their staff has increased in number and purpose over time.

The party primary system in New York is an important step for candi-dates, mayoral, council, and otherwise. Third parties and fusion candidates give voters a myriad of options on primary and final election day. Third parties such as the Liberal party have given candidates the opportunity to participate in the general election even if they have not been successful in the Democratic or Republican primary. For example, in 1969 Mayor Lindsay was defeated in the Republican primary by State Senator John Marchi. He ran on the Liberal ticket in the general election and was able to defeat Democratic candidate Mario Proccacino (Eichenthal 1990:77). Over time there has been a proliferation of candidates who contest the primaries; thus these runoff elections have become an important weeding-out process for candidates with minor public experience or exposure.

The two-party system poses challenges for the Chinese-American community, not just in New York but wherever that partisan primaries are held. Chinese Americans' party affiliation is split among Democrats, Republicans, and independents. In 1996, approximately 48 percent of Chinese were registered Democrats, 20 percent Republican, and 29 percent independent (Asian American Legal Defense and Education Fund, *Outlook* Winter 1997). Since you must be registered as a Democrat or Republican to vote in the primaries, almost 30 percent of the already small community is ineligible to vote in this crucial stage of the electoral process. Also, since the community's party affiliation is split, there is less of an electoral incentive for candidates to target the community for support and political mobilization. The mayor, like a president or prime minister, has considerable power in setting the agenda for the city. Mayors have extensive powers of appointment, and they serve to set the tone for the city's political discourse. The mayor's actions and words can temper or inflame ethnic conflict, or they can be proactive in facilitating ethnic incorporation. If the Chinese are not viewed as a necessary constituency for a mayoral candidate's election or reelection, then their views and needs are more likely to get muted within the city's larger ethnic mosaic.

In fact, the Chinatown community often feels as if their interests are ignored. The Chinese Lunar New Year celebrations were strikingly quiet in 1997, 1998, and 1999. For the third year in a row the mayor forbid the use of fireworks or firecrackers as part of the festival's symbolic Lion Dance and parade. Likening it to the Fourth of July, the mayor declared that due to the danger and chance of injury, no permit would be issued for the use of pyrotechnics. Several Chinatown community groups joined together to challenge the 1998 decision. First they protested the decision, and then they devised alternative proposals for supervised and sanctioned use of firecrackers. In response, the city first offered to allow the fireworks at a site location off the parade route, then when community groups finally agreed, city officials announced that it was too late to make the necessary arrangements with the local police and fire departments. Chinese New Year was celebrated without an organized fireworks display. To some members of the community it was taken as an illustration of their political marginality, not as a benevolent safety concern.

THE BOARD OF ESTIMATES AND THE NEW CITY CHARTER

All budgetary matters used to be controlled by the Board of Estimates. Prior to 1989, the board was made up of five elected representatives, one from each borough of the city. It acted as a de facto legislative body, controlling the city's budget and appropriations. In 1981 the New York Civil Liberties Union filed federal suit on behalf of three Brooklyn residents claiming that the Board of Estimates violated the constitutional norm of one person, one vote. Staten Island, with only 350,000 residents, had the same representation and voting power on the board as did Brooklyn, with more than two million inhabitants. After a series of suits, a federal appeals court ruled in 1986 against the city. Mayor Koch established a Charter Revision Commission to reallocate the powers of city government, but the city also appealed this decision, and the case wound its way all the way to the Supreme Court. The Supreme Court agreed to hear the case, and on March 22, 1989, it ruled that the structure of New York City government violated the constitution of the United States. The Charter Revision Commission, which had stalled for so long, was forced to reconstruct New York City political institutions (McNickle 1993:313–314).

> The symphony of pattering feet, the staccato of typewriter keys, and the blinding beacons of photocopier light all indicated a rather desperate sense of urgency, and with good reason. In their infinite wisdom, the commission had originally promised to finish the charter by June 1989. The chairman of the commission, Frederick Schwartz—son of toy manufacturer F.A.O. Schwartz—valiantly vowed to complete the job, even if it meant staying overtime until the document was done. And "Fritz," as he liked to be called, insisted that he would keep his promise of dismantling the Board of Estimates and increasing minority representation, while keeping the public involved and informed throughout the process. (*A. Magazine* V. 1; July 31, 1990:28)

Despite the lofty rhetoric of inclusiveness, the reports were not translated into Chinese (or any other Asian language), and when a coalition of Asian-American, Latino, and African-American community agencies asked for a year to educate their supporters to the changes, they were given only thirty days (ibid.). The Asian American Legal Defense and Education Fund (AALDEF) and Chinatown Voter Education Alliance offered recommendations to the commission as to the optimal size of the to-be-created City Council districts so that they might best help the Chinese and Asian-American community, but after meeting with the commission to present their ideas, they were informed that that the district sizes had already been decided upon. This left the agencies bitter about the closed nature of the decision process about how the new districts would be shaped.

OTHER POLITICAL PLAYERS

City Council

The mayor currently shares power with the City Council, the borough presidents, and the comptroller. The City Council is the city's legislative body. Prior to 1991, the council had very little legislative power. Currently, it enacts local laws and has the power to oversee the functioning of city agencies. Although the council is charged with the power to make laws for the city, without the support of the mayor there is little likelihood of an initiative taking hold. In addition, the mayor is able to govern by issuing executive orders. The council's power is also circumscribed by the ability of the New York State legislature to intervene in the governing of the city. The state legislature can do so in three ways: first, it can directly pass New York City legislation after the City Council passes a home-rule request; second, it can enact laws that apply to cities with "one million inhabitants"; third, the state body can create regional authorities to take over functions that were once the province of the city's government (Eichenthal 1990:90–91). An example of this last method would be the creation of the Port Authority, a regional body that oversees several bridges, tunnels, and transit hubs.

Comptroller

The comptroller is given the power to oversee and investigate expenditure of city funds. Really, the comptroller is the city's chief fiscal officer. In this position the comptroller can critique the mayor's policy and budgetary decisions. Although the comptroller has little ability to put forth his or her own agenda, he or she can act as a watchdog against the mayor and generate criticism or public approbation of the mayor's actions in order to change city policy.

Borough Presidents

The borough presidents use to be significant sources of patronage jobs. In the 1980s they were powerful actors in issues surrounding economic development. Specifically, they had control over land use, tax abatements and subsidies. Borough presidents were able to use these powers to gain political support. And, as David Eichenthal writes, "Borough presidents have also retained popular support through constituent services by local community boards" (1990:99). Community board members are appointed by the borough presidents and are used as advocacy groups for each neighborhood to voice their views to the City Council. For example, in the early 1990s Manhattan Borough President Ruth Messinger hired David Wong as community liaison to the Chinatown area. Mr. Wong was responsible for attending community board meetings in Chinatown and for working with Chinatown community leaders to understand their needs and interests. To illustrate how these institutions and offices affect Chinese-American participation and influence, we now turn to the dispute over redistricting City Council seats, and several city elections that recount efforts by Chinese Americans to run for city positions.

REAPPORTIONMENT OF CITY COUNCIL DISTRICTS

The city's new charter expanded the number of City Council seats from thirty-five to fifty-one, with the express intent of crafting district lines to increase minority representation.[6] This set off fierce battles in different city neighborhoods as to how to redraw the districts and who would be favored in the next City Council elections. The Chinese community in Lower Manhattan was no exception. With only an estimated eight thousand voters in 1991, clearly Chinatown would have to be part of a multiracial district.[7] No fewer than three factions claiming to represent Chinatown residents began asserting their ideas for how the district should be shaped.

One group, Lower East Siders for a Multiracial District, led by Carlos Chino Garcia and Elaine Chan, supported "mapping to maximize minority representation." The district they envisioned stretched from the Brooklyn Bridge north to 14th Street and included the most eastern census tracts of the area and Chinatown. Since no ethnic minority in this area has the population to create a district reflective of their own group, they believed that a mixed Lower East Side district would provide a large enough cohort of Latino, African-American, and Asian voters to elect a minority candidate. Such a district would keep together people with shared economic and social interests, including better schools and responsive bilingual programs, access to health care, and affordable housing for low- and middle-income families (*New York Times* April 16, 1991:A22). The group's leaders acknowledge that the Chinese community seeks greater power and the successful election of an Asian candidate, but they argue that their plan will best serve the political interests of the Chinese community because it brings together groups with similar concerns. This proposed district would be composed of 36 percent Asians, 34 percent Hispanics, 9 percent black, and 21 percent whites. Other proposals would lump Chinatown residents with areas to its west, creating a district with a majority of higher-income, nonminority voters whose number would increase with the completion of Battery Park City (ibid.).

Margaret Chin and Doris W. Koo led the drive to create a predominantly Asian-American district by combining Chinatown with white neighborhoods of SoHo, TriBeCa, and Battery Park City. This plan would create a district where the population was 39.3 percent white, 5.4 percent black, 16.6 percent Hispanic, and 38.4 percent Asian (*New York Times* April 30, 1991:B1). Constituents in this area had twice chosen Ms. Chin as the Democratic State Committeewoman from the 61st. Assembly District (ibid.), thus she clearly felt that she would have a strong base for future political endeavors. Ms. Chin hoped to run for the City Council seat created in this manner.

The third redistricting plan that concerned Chinatown was one that sought to maximize Hispanic votes. Antonio Pagan spearheaded the Puerto Rican–Hispanic Political Council, which aimed to craft a district that included Tompkins Square Park, Astor Place and Loisaida (a heavily Hispanic part of the Lower East Side). It would be 37 percent Hispanic, 16.8 percent Asian, 35 percent white, and about 9.9 percent black (ibid.). Mr. Pagan was outspoken against the other plans: "We're both all over the place. But we're opposed to an Asian-Latino district. It defeats the purpose of minority empowerment and allows the incumbent to win by getting the votes of other groups" (ibid.).

The plan that was finally adopted was the one advocated by Margaret Chin, although with slight alterations that increased the percentage of white voters to about 45 percent of the district (*New York Times* May 7, 1991:B7). In the first test of these new districts, Margaret Chin ran against Kathryn Freed in the Democratic primaries the following September, and lost. No Chinese or Asian American has been elected from District 1 despite the attempts of those involved in reapportionment.[8] Maps 7.1 and 7.2 illustrate the City Council districts and their representatives in 1980 before redistricting, and then in 1996.

Clearly the plurality of plans advocated by Chinatown players weakened their collective bargaining power. They were unable to present a united front against other interests and plans for how the district should be drawn. The district in question is composed of more than 30 percent Chinese but because they are not clearly united, and in part because they have lower incomes than white residents in the district, it is less necessary to cater to them for electoral returns. This would seem to support Rosenstone and Hansen (1993) and Levitt's and Olson's (1996) research on the importance of mobilization for political incorporation and participation.

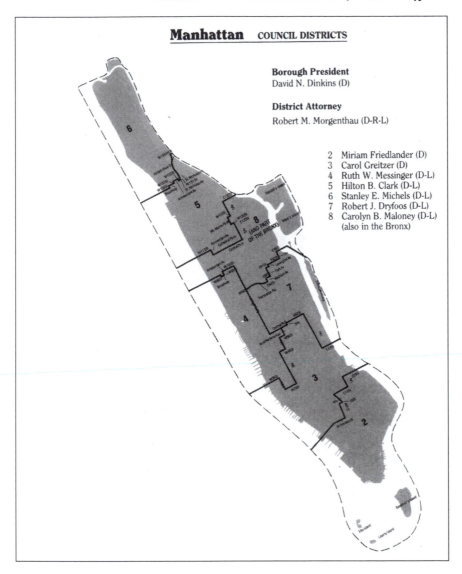

Manhattan   COUNCIL DISTRICTS

Borough President
David N. Dinkins (D)

District Attorney
Robert M. Morgenthau (D-R-L)

2   Miriam Friedlander (D)
3   Carol Greitzer (D)
4   Ruth W. Messinger (D-L)
5   Hilton B. Clark (D-L)
6   Stanley E. Michels (D-L)
7   Robert J. Dryfoos (D-L)
8   Carolyn B. Maloney (D-L)
     (also in the Bronx)

MAP 7.1 CITY COUNCIL DISTRICTS PRIOR TO REDISTRICTING

ELECTORAL POLITICS

In the 1997 City Council election Jennifer Lim ran in the Democratic primary against Kathryn Freed and lost. Her campaign tried to target groups that she felt Freed neglected: Chinatown residents and Lower East Side minority groups. Lim spent hours visiting housing projects, senior centers, and religious gatherings in order to introduce herself and her ideas.

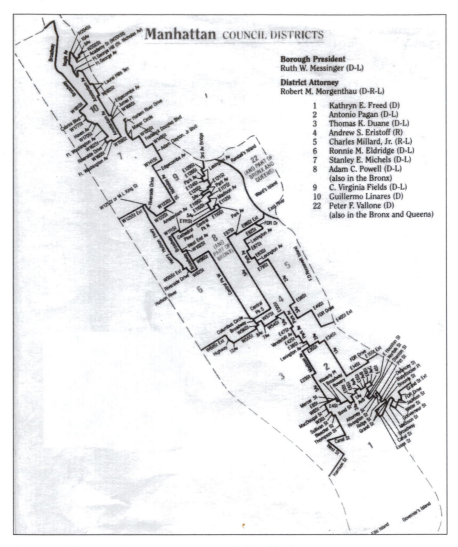

MAP 7.2 CITY COUNCIL DISTRICTS AFTER REDISTRICTING

She posted herself outside busy subway stations and handed campaign literature to commuters. She worried that it was difficult to mobilize Chinatown residents to vote. As she feared, turnout for the September primary was abysmally low and even lower for Chinatown residents whom she had counted on to defeat the incumbent. During the run-up to the primary, Lim often stated that the biggest problem for Chinatown candidates was getting through the primaries when so many Chinatown residents were registered as independents. It is possible that Jenny Lim, in running against Freed, was able to lay the groundwork for a run in 2001. If she chooses to run again she will have greater name recognition and will have learned from her first experience. Because of newly imposed term limits on city officials, Freed is prohibited from running again.

In 1987 Dorothy Chin Brandt became the first Chinese American elected to public office in all of Manhattan. In the same election Peter Tom (also Chinese) also won a judgeship in Civil Court. Judge Brandt has been active in Chinatown affairs through her job as director of the Asian American Federation, an offshoot of the United Way. She had sought a Civil Court position in an earlier election and had gained support from Democratic party leaders but lost by 138 votes in the Democratic primary that year. In 1987 she returned to the party leaders who had supported her earlier attempt and sought their support. She received their endorsement once again, and this time won the primary in a crowded field of Democratic candidates.9

In 1995 Doris Ling-Cohan was elected Civil Court judge in New York City. After a four-year campaign effort, Ling-Cohan became the first Chinese-American public official elected in a district that includes Chinatown (Geron 1995). In interviews with Judge Ling-Cohan, it is clear that she takes this accomplishment seriously. Doris Ling-Cohan was born and raised in Chinatown. She had sixteen years of experience in public interest law and is a founding member of the New York Asian Women's Center, a social service agency that assists battered women and victims of domestic violence. She has also taught law at the City University of New York School of Law and at New York University Law. The difficulties she met along the way to seeking office illustrate some of the hurdles that minority candidates face.

There were issues over the accessibility of bilingual ballots; they were not available in Chinatown polling sites as required. Also, as part of the process of getting on the ballot, she visited Democratic political clubs throughout the city to seek their support. Civil Court in New York City has jurisdiction over money, property, and personal property actions where the sum involved does not exceed $10,000. Judges are elected for ten-year terms (Smith, T.E. 1973). While she eventually received support from a majority of Democratic clubs, Ling-Cohan credits her victory to her strong ties to the Chinese and Asian-American community. She asserts that she had strong grassroots support from a variety of groups in Chinatown. Although many could not directly advocate on her behalf because of their not-for-profit status, instead they held candidate forums and urged community members to register to vote and then reminded them to get to the polls on election day. Ling-Cohan also received advice and support from those who have mounted or aided campaigns in Asian-American districts on the West Coast (Geron 1995).

The Chinese community in Manhattan seems to confirm outsiders' perceptions that the Chinese are internally focused and divided. Almost every attempt at political activity seems to bring out an array of conflicting interests within the community. While there are plenty of divisions among Chinese Americans in Monterey Park, the splits have to do with policy issues like the progrowth and slow-growth divide, and between Republican and Democratic parties. Although divisive, these issues assume that the Chinese are part of the city's political processes. In fact it is through the Monterey Park City Council that many of these issues are decided. In New York, the divisions reflect a conflict over how incorporated the group should be with city political institutions, and if so, with which other groups should political alliances be forged. Why is New York City different from Monterey Park?

ANALYSIS

An important study from the Center for Urban Research at the City University of New York Graduate Center examines six immigrant groups in New York City—Dominicans, Jamaicans, Chinese, Italians, Soviets, and Ecuadorians—to find the extent to which they participate in electoral politics. They find some support for the "immigrant apathy hypothesis," which predicts that immigrants will vote at lower rates than American-born groups.[10] However, they find that this is true for some immigrant groups more than others, and they attribute differences to socioeconomic status variables and to the political appeals which are made to some groups and not others (Levitt and Olsen 1996).

McNickle illustrates the importance of ethnicity in New York City politics historically. He traces the power of coalition-building between Jewish and Italian voters in mayoral elections of the early twentieth century (McNickle 1993:Chs. 1, 2). Ironically, during this period, voter turnout and electoral influence were *higher* in immigrant neighborhoods of the city (Tuckel and Maisel 1994). Levitt's and Olsen's work finds that "immigrant apathy" is a more appropriate description for New York City's current immigrant population.

For the Chinese population Levitt and Olsen (1996) find that voter turnout by foreign-born Chinese is a full 10 percent lower than for the city as a whole: 27 percent versus 37 percent. This is despite the high rates of naturalization in Chinese communities: 44.2 percent. Levitt and Olsen attribute the lack of turnout to low socioeconomic status and the high percentage of foreign-born residents in Chinese neighborhoods. They speculate that the participation figures could reflect the lack of direct appeals from any candidate in any election to the Chinese community of New York City (ibid.:13). Since the Chinese community is split in their party affiliation, it seems logical that candidates would look elsewhere for ethnic blocs of support. The low levels of politicization may also be attributed to internal dynamics within Chinatown and to the way that leaders interact with the larger political institutions of New York City, a factor that they do not take into account.

As is the case in Malaysia, it is possible that electoral incentives could hold the key to both increasing political participation in the Chinese community and to effecting greater influence in local decisions. In the 1993 New York City mayoral election between Rudolph Giuliani and David Dinkins, Giuliani beat Dinkins by less than 44,000 votes. Of an Asian-American community of a half-million, approximately sixty thousand were registered to vote. Polls and party registration data showed that the community has become more Democratic over time as the population grows younger. Betty Liu Ebron, columnist for the *Daily News*, noted (October 21, 1994) that "Asians may hold the key to this mayoral race—We're talking about Asian Americans, barely 2 percent of the voters. Except this year, a few thousand voters can make a difference." However, she was wrong. Asian Americans and Chinese Americans might have had a chance to make a difference, but it appears that Dinkins did not take advantage of this possible constituency. As *A. Magazine* (vol. 3 no.1 March 31, 1994:10) noted, "for all of Dinkins' eleventh-hour campaigning, he didn't show hide nor hair to the community that all too often falls between the cracks of this city's two-tone rainbow." Peter Lau of the Chinatown Voters Alliance argued that Giuliani did better outreach in the Chinese community. "It's obvious. You walk around Chinatown, all you see is Giuliani posters, no Dinkins banners, signs, or anything" (ibid.). However, Guiliani most avidly courted Hispanic voters, Puerto Ricans and Dominicans, in the realization that the shrunken white population would not be enough to win him office (Waldinger 1995:7).

Ironically perhaps, during David Dinkins's tenure he maintained community liaisons for different segments of the city. This meant that he had an office of Asian American Affairs, which facilitated communication with Chinatown. Giuliani closed this office, although Angelica Tang serves as Executive Director of the Mayor's Office of Immigrant and Language Services, a catchall office designed somewhat to replace Dinkins's community oriented bureaucracy. Ruth Messinger, Manhattan Borough President until 1997, maintained community liaisons. David Wong served in that capacity for Chinatown. His job description included running the community boards, working with City Council representatives, and serving on the Asian American Advisory Board. The board was comprised of about forty people chosen by Ms. Messinger with recommendations from community leaders. Some of the tasks that the board dealt with included creating a Chinatown tourism council and doing outreach to schools, housing projects, and community organizations.

PROVISION OF SOCIAL BENEFITS

One of the things that not-for-profit organizations are best at is providing social benefits to the community. An issue of primary importance to the Chinatown community is education. Distraught with the current bilingual education programs in the New York City public schools, a group of parents and education activists in 1993 began plans for a magnet school which would be bilingual and bicultural in Mandarin and English. The planning committee for the proposed school, the Shuang Wen Academy (roughly translated as a dual-language academy), was made up of the following: Ray Chin, President of the Chinese American Insurance Association and head of New York City's Commission on Human Rights; Cambao De Duong, President of the Indochina Sino-American Senior Citizens Center and Deputy Director of the Chinatown Manpower Project, Inc.; Julia Dutka, Professor at Baruch College; Larry Lee, Director of the Victim Services' Family, Clinical, and Community Services Division; Cao K. O., Executive Director of the Asian American Federation of New York; and Jacob Wong, Chairperson of the New York Chinese Educators Committee.[11] The committee members' affiliations illustrate that they are part of the social service corps of professionals active in addressing Chinatown's interests.

The proposed school's mission is the development of dual language and dual cultural identities for the students. Whereas the Chinese-English bilingual programs in the public schools are designed as a short-term bridge to ease language barriers to learning for new immigrants, the Shuang Wen Academy is committed to developing students' language and cultural literacy in both Chinese and English. Funding for the school was approved by and given seed money from the Fund for New York City Public Education, New Visions II, a network of innovative schools which begin with parent or community initiatives but which are then incorporated into local school districts. Shuang Wen Academy will be part of Community School District 1 and has been incorporated by the Board of Regents of the University of the State of New York's Education Department. While the committee was able to obtain funding and got a green light from the Board of Education, what proved most difficult was finding a space in which to open the proposed school. One elementary school on the edge of Chinatown on the Lower East Side originally agreed to house the program, and it was slated to open in the fall of 1997. Over the summer the school decided that it was uncomfortable with the arrangement, and backed out. Space was finally arranged in a Chelsea school with extra room, but the organizers are disappointed that it is further away from the target community in Chinatown than the first school was.[12]

CONCLUSION

What the New York case study shows is that despite institutional incentives for political participation—there is a system of elections in which the Chinese could participate to elect either a Chinese candidate or one whom they feel represents their interests—voter turnout from Chinese Americans is quite low at 27 percent. It is difficult to find even anecdotal evidence of Chinese influence in local politics. This can be explained by understanding that there are few direct electoral incentives for politicians to mobilize the Chinese community. While they are 30 percent of the local election district, not all are able to vote; party affiliation is split; and many voters cannot even participate in primary elections because so many are registered as independents.

The Chinese economic elites, in the form of the kinship leaders, have traditionally emphasized cultural insularity, in part perhaps to maximize their own power and prestige in the community. Social service leaders are hampered by 501(c)3 status and face collective action problems in mobilizing the community for one particular set of goals. When confronted with this situation, social activists have elected to work with each other to provide social benefits to the community, for example, the creation of Shuang Wen Academy. This bypasses most of the key political institutions of the city, as well as the old-guard leadership of the kinship associations. Only if there is greater comingling of interests and players, if the economic elite turn more toward political incorporation, or if social service leaders can forge successful coalitions, first with other Chinatown forces, and then possibly with neighboring Latino groups, will the Chinatown community see a rise in participatory activity.

8

Conclusion

SUMMARY OF CONCLUSIONS

After a closer examination of the Chinese communities in Indonesia, peninsular Malaysia, New York, and Los Angeles, it is necessary to return to the initial questions and the hypotheses to see if the case studies help untangle the puzzle. The starting point for this study was the observation that for Chinese communities overseas, levels of political participation are not correlated with socioeconomic variables such as income or education. In addition, Chinese overseas exact political influence in places where political institutions are least receptive to Chinese communal participation. The questions that were posed to address these puzzles were as follows: When or under what conditions do Chinese communities become active in the political processes of their adopted countries? Does political influence stem from group mobilization? And what role do communal organizations and their leaders play in determining the nature and scope of participation and influence?

The case studies illustrate that there is a dichotomy between participation and influence, and the book attempts to provide an explanation for this. Wealth and status are important in effecting influence, but the openness of the political system does not seem to impact levels of participation. Politicization of the community as a unit does not necessarily lead to greater political influence unless there are also political incentives to be gained in reaching out to the community. Briefly, the answers to the questions above are: (1) in open political systems, Chinese communities will be more active in the political process when there is direct mobilization by elites for electoral purposes. In closed political systems, this is less likely to occur. (2) Influence does not necessarily stem from greater group politicization. In more open political systems, influence is achieved through a mix of individual networking and group mobilization for electoral purposes. In closed political systems, especially where there is extensive state guidance in the course of economic development, influence is a product of individual networking for financial benefits. (3) Ethnic organizations and leaders within the Chinese community do play a vital role in impacting both the nature and scope of participation and influence, and results vary depending on the type of association and leadership that are at the fore-front; business groups are more effective at achieving influence, whereas social service agencies are better at community mobilization.

When business leaders seek influence in the political process, it is often for individual financial reasons. They are well positioned to achieve influence in the political process because of the economic incentives they can offer political elites. For the majority of the Chinese overseas, their political position is affected by a different set of processes. Social service activists' position rests with meeting the needs of the community through the provision of social benefits and services; this gives them a basis for facilitating politicization of the Chinese based on ethnic concerns. However, in order to mobilize a majority of the community, leaders must overcome the collective action problem. There is rarely consensus within a community as to what preferred policies are, which candidates to sup-port, or how programs should be implemented at the community level. This is clearly illustrated in Malaysia, where it was harder to rally support from a broad segment of the Chinese population for Chinese-vernacular schools than it was to gather support for expanded citizenship rights at the time of independence. Divisions are also evident in Southern Calif-ornia from the results of the most recent Monterey Park election. Likewise, in all of the case studies examined here, the Chinese commu-nities are divided by class, language, and acculturation differences, which makes it hard for social activists to achieve a groundswell of support on any particular issue. In addition, social service elites are constrained by institutional factors.

Even if they are successful in mobilizing a significant portion of the community behind a particular goal, by itself mobilization does not nec-essarily lead to influence. Because not-for-profit agencies (or NGOs in Malaysia and Indonesia) are constrained by government regulation, there are severe limits as to the types of political behavior they can sponsor. In the United States this is manifest by 501(c)3 status, which prohibits agen-cies from partisan political activity. As such, a group like the Organization of Chinese Americans can hold candidate forums but not endorse a par-ticular candidate or party. In Malaysia and Indonesia, NGO activity is strictly watched by the government and leaders can, and have been, arrested for activity threatening to the state apparatus. These limitations impact the degree of influence that they can effect, despite some suc-cessful efforts at increasing community awareness and politicization.

Overall, Chinese communities in the United States face very different challenges and institutional constraints from their counterparts in Southeast Asia. In the United States pluralism is the ideal, and conflict is institutionalized through competitive elections and interest group activity. In Malaysia, consociationalism is the presumed model whereby conflict is ideally channeled through ethnically based political parties. In Indonesia under Suharto, there were few formal institutional outlets to express conflict.[1] Now the system appears to be wide open to all sorts of political organization. There are new political parties, new advocacy groups, and new media outlets. It is too soon to know how Sino-Indonesians will fit within this more pluralist system. The case studies show that Chinese associations may be viewed as adaptive mechanisms to the policies of the state. One of the major points that this work hopes to convey in comparing Chinese communities in two very different regions of the world is the direct relationship between the nature of government policies and institutions and the way in which the communal interests are expressed and organized.

This concluding chapter reexamines the case studies in a comparative framework in order better to understand the relationship between the political institutions in each case, the community elites, and the variation in politicization and influence from different Chinese communities overseas. While some generalizations can be made across cases, such as the leadership divisions within the communities and the threat of discrimination, yet it is the differences among the four communities that help answer the questions posed here. Ultimately, conclusions are drawn about the importance of political rights for minority groups and the implications for domestic and international politics in the United States and Southeast Asia.

SOUTHEAST ASIA RECONSIDERED

THE IMPORTANCE OF ELECTIONS

The Indonesian and Malaysian case studies graphically illustrate the fundamental importance of elections in structuring and impacting the way that minority communities interact with the larger polity. While elections are crucial to maintaining regime legitimacy in both Indonesia and Malaysia, the stakes involved in electoral politics in the two nations are quite different. In Indonesia, elections under Suharto, were used as a tool of mass mobilization. The Chinese, in this respect, were treated no differently from the rest of Indonesia's population. Elections and the facade of democratic institutions are a secondary mechanism for enhancing the state's legitimacy.[2] In the run-up to general elections in Indonesia, there used to be mass rallies for Golkar, the ruling party. Decked out in bright gold attire, government employees and private-sector workers were given time off to participate in mass demonstrations. This gearing-up for elections has also coincided with violence, as was the case in the winter and spring of 1997, when PDI supporters of Megawati were forced out of sight. The fact that elections were held regularly during the New Order was a source of pride for Suharto, and they were used to justify *Pancasila* democracy and the ultimate goal of stability and development. As Liddle (1996) notes:

> Pancasila is intended to be an indigenizing modifier. . . . The point of this indigenization is to buttress the assertion that the New Order version of elections and election-related institutions is both genuinely Indonesian and authentically democratic, though admittedly different from the history and current practice of the Western democracies. (43–44)

The other goal of this indigenizing process was to eradicate political differences based on class or ethnicity. This facilitated Suharto's goal of producing an economically developed Indonesia and an Indonesian identity. In this respect there were no electoral incentives to mobilize the Chinese community for political gain through elections. Since the Chinese in Indonesia are subject to scapegoating by some Islamist leaders and are often targets for unrest and economic envy, it could well have been a liability for an opposition party, most probably Partai Demokrasi Indonesia (Indonesian Democracy Party, PDI, now the dominant party) to mobilize Chinese for electoral support. Likewise, even Suharto, who built his own family's wealth through connections with wealthy Chinese business leaders, has in times of political crisis distanced himself from his Chinese partners. One effect of having wealthy Chinese as the beneficiaries of state-led economic development was that there were fewer prominent indigenous Indonesian business leaders poised to threaten the Suharto family's preeminence.

It is unclear if President Wahid and Vice President Megawati will have the political will to curtail the power of the Sino-Indonesian business interests left over from Suharto's regime. There is much debate in Indonesia right now about how to restructure the economy so that the same large conglomerates are not the only ones to benefit from political connections and renewed economic growth. What do the economic and political changes mean for politicization for Indonesia's (nontycoon) embattled Chinese minority? As the chapter on Indonesia shows, partic-

ipation was once limited to networking through quasi-autonomous interest groups such as the business organizations outside of KADIN and
through religious identification and accepted religious institutions. The
most effective method was for wealthy Chinese to maintain (personal)
economic or business links to Suharto; this was mutually beneficial for
Suharto's family and for particular Chinese tycoons.

In Malaysia, elections play a much greater role in illustrating the nature
and impact of Chinese input in the political arena. While the ruling
National Front parties have, like Golkar in Indonesia, won over two-thirds
majorities in national elections, to a greater extent, elections in Malaysia
are vigorously contested. In order to maintain the unity of the BN coalition, the Chinese cannot be completely marginalized, and as the chapter
on Malaysia notes, it is during electoral campaigns that UMNO and Malay
political leaders seem to pay the most attention to their Chinese counterparts. This helps explain why the Chinese participate at fairly consistent
rates, yet, despite similar socioeconomic standing, they have seen their
influence in the political process erode since 1969.

Prior to the 1969 riots, there were electoral incentives for Malay political elites to work with wealthy Chinese businessmen (through MCA).
They needed to maintain Chinese support for MCA for two reasons: (1) to
successfully thwart the communist insurgency; and (2) to consolidate and
husband financial strength after independence. Likewise, social activists,
such as those at the forefront of *Dongjiaozhong,* were willing in the 1960s
to compromise on some goals, such as full government recognition and
funding of Chinese schools, in order to get expanded citizenship rights,
allowing a larger number of Chinese in Malaysia at the time to qualify as
citizens. This was one of the few unifying issues in the Chinese community. Thus it was easier for MCA to rally support in the early days after
Independence from a wide spectrum of the Chinese population.

Since 1969 the political and economic landscape has changed substantially. First, and perhaps most importantly, NEP has created an upper-
and middle-class Malay constituency. This means that there is less need
for Malay elites to cater to Chinese business interests for financial support.
Secondly, Chinese businesses, which were once family and community
centered, have been part of a shift from internally generated funding to
external borrowing and an increased dependence on state or public financing. Family businesses that once relied on their kinship association or the
hui guan for investment support have turned to political elites, and party
involvement in business enterprises has increased exponentially. Thus
Chinese business networks have become more closely tied with state
development goals. This has facilitated links between Chinese business

leaders like the Kuok brothers and Malay leaders. There is no longer any reason for ethnic business leaders to work exclusively through their co-ethnics in politics.

Electorally, there is also less need for politicians to reach out to the Chinese community for support. Since BN has won over two thirds majority in Parliament, it is able to change the Constitution at will. One of the things that it has used this power for is to create new electoral districts. After almost every election, the number of constituencies has been increased. For example, for the 1995 election the number of seats in Parliament were increased to a total of 192. This is twelve more seats than there had been previously. New constituencies are generally drawn in rural areas where Malays are the majority and where UMNO has most of its support. This marginalizes the Chinese in two ways: first, it violates the principle of one person one vote, or the notion that all votes have equal weight. Second, it serves to keep the number of Chinese elected officials to a minimum because it is not likely that the BN would run a Chinese candidate in a rural Malay district.

Social activists are faced with divisions in the Chinese community, making it more difficult to rally support for ethnic-centered concerns such as Chinese-vernacular education. Likewise, instead of working through MCA, education activists like Kua Kia Soong have allied themselves with the Democratic Action Party. The DAP, in turn, is limited by its lack of access to government posts and resources. This does not bode well for increased attention to Chinese education.

The DAP, as vocal opposition, along with (limited) electoral incentives, can play an important role in increasing political participation by Chinese in Malaysia. A snapshot of voter-turnout rates in three different states across time is shown in Table 8.1. Terengganu is a largely rural state with a preponderance of Malay residents. While its population has seen little

TABLE 8.1 VOTER TURNOUT IN MALAYSIAN ELECTIONS						
STATE	1959	1964	1969	1978	1982	1990[1]
Terengganu	70.3%	77.4%	74.6%	76.2%	80.28%	78–87%
Penang	73.2%	83.5%	77.5%	79.2%	77.27%	74–81%
Selengor	73.6%	73.6%	65.8%	74.3%	72.8%	62–71%[2]

[1] Voter-turnout statistics after 1982 are difficult to come by. The figures listed for the 1990 election are based on estimations by Harold Crouch (1996a).

[2] These figures are actually for the Federal Territory of Kuala Lumpur, not Selengor Province.

(Data compiled from Vasil 1972, Rachagan 1980, Khong 1990, NSTP Research and Information Services 1990, Crouch 1996a.)

growth, the number of seats it has in Parliament has risen from six in 1959 to eight in 1990. Likewise, voter turnout has increased from about 70 percent in 1959 to somewhere in the 80 percent range by 1990. In Selengor, a state with a large Chinese population and which has seen enormous population growth over the years due to urbanization, voter turnout has hovered in the low 70 percent range. Penang, also a state with a large Chinese population, is a stronghold of the DAP. Voter-turnout rates are higher than in Selengor by 5 to 10 percent. This may reflect several differences between Penang and a state like Selengor. First, there is greater per capita representation in Penang than in Selengor, and the strength of the DAP seems to result in more hotly contested elections. The DAP ran a vigorous campaign there in the 1990 elections, forcing BN parties (MCA and Gerakan) to work especially hard at appealing to Chinese voters.

Thus what the Malaysia and Indonesian case studies illustrate is the pivotal role that even moderately competitive elections can play in facilitating Chinese political participation. Yet the electoral process in Malaysia since 1969 shows that community mobilization does not necessarily lead to influence on education policy. These countries illustrate that the best way to affect particular policy outcomes is through individual networking. In Indonesia this takes the form of close business alliances between Chinese tycoons and Suharto's family and friends. In Malaysia this is manifest through close business ties between political party elites (Malay and Chinese) and Chinese business leaders. This sort of personal networking for economic benefits has little effect on the larger community's politicization or influence. Business leaders are unencumbered by the need to solicit community support or collective action.

THE UNITED STATES: "DIVERGENT DIASPORAS"—
MONTEREY PARK AND NEW YORK CITY

As in Indonesia, the Chinese are only a small percentage of the population in the United States and they currently tend to reside in large urban areas on the East and West Coast. San Francisco and New York have traditionally had the largest Chinese communities. The 1990 census shows that there were 7.2 million Asian Americans, representing about 3 percent of the population. This is up from about 1.5 million, or less than 1 percent of the population in 1970. Chinese Americans account for approximately one quarter of all Asian Americans (Lott 1991:58). The two most rapidly growing groups of immigrants in the United States over the last twenty years are from Latin America and Asia. These immigrants are seeking U.S. citizenship in larger numbers than ever before,[3] and Chinese represent the second-largest percentage of all immigrants in New York seeking citizenship; 7.9 percent of all applicants were of Chinese origin. Only Dominicans represented a larger percentage, at 10.3 percent (*New York Times* March 10, 1996:A1). California, too, is experiencing demographic shifts. Asians Americans and Latinos are a growing portion of the population; as of 1996 fully 10 percent of California's population was Asian American. In Monterey Park this figure is substantially higher: 40 percent of the population is of Chinese ancestry. These figures should suggest a growing power in the political arena, but that is only partially the case.

As measured by voter-turnout statistics and by studying the nature of coalition-building and organized political activity, the Chinese community in Monterey Park, California, has made large inroads into participatory activism. Approximately 32 percent of Chinese in Monterey Park vote, as oppose to 27 percent in New York City. Political activity such as coalition formation and the election of Chinese leaders to local offices shows that in Monterey Park Chinese community leaders have been somewhat more successful in politicization efforts than New York's Chinatown social service elites.

The combination of electoral, social, and economic incentives exists to a greater extent in Monterey Park than in New York City. While New York has often been described as being dominated by ethnic politics (Bellush 1990; McNickle 1993), smaller groups, such as the Chinese, are left competing with others for their share of the city's economic and political pie. Chinese in Monterey Park benefit both from their large percentage of the population, but even more so from the ability to make a difference within a smaller political arena. Chinese Americans have been elected to Monterey Park's City Council since 1982, when Lily Lee Chen was voted into office. Judy Chu, former mayor and currently still a City Councilwoman, is at the forefront of community activism in the San Gabriel Valley's Chinese networks.

In achieving electoral success within the local area, Chinese community groups in Monterey Park and neighboring communities have gained valuable political experience. Having worked with Latino groups after the 1990 census to recraft local election districts, the community is now organizing and educating community residents about the importance of the 2000 census and has lobbied against a "multiracial" category that might dilute its collective power. There is already talk in Monterey Park and the greater Los Angeles area about what possible reapportionment plans could be drafted to reflect the growth in population, power, and wealth of the metropolitan area's Asian-American population. The district that was created as a result of 1991's coalition with Latino groups did not result in electoral success for an Asian American outside of local Monterey Park positions. However, other political leaders, such as Antonio Villaraigosa, California Assembly member from the 45th district, have been mindful of their Asian-American constituents. Villaraigosa participated as keynote speaker at AP3CON's strategic planning conference and made it clear that he is aware of Asian American's growing power ambitions and that he is receptive to their concerns.

In New York, by contrast, there is less talk about the upcoming census and how the city's Chinese community might better cooperate to assert their own interests. If the community remains fractured there is little incentive for politicians to target them for electoral purposes. In New York, Chinese voters are divided between the Democratic and Republican parties by 48 percent to 20 percent, and 29 percent are registered as independents. In Los Angeles County the ratio is as follows: 41 percent are registered as Democrats, 36 percent, Republican, and 20 percent declined to give their party affiliation or were registered as independents (Muratsuchi 1991:24). These numbers indicate why politicians might be reluctant to mobilize the Chinese community in the United States: without a comprehensive understanding of the splits and the interests within the Chinese community, a politician would have difficulty knowing which community leaders to work with and how this would impact support for his or her candidacy. Similarly, since the community has traditionally been divided in its party affiliation, a Chinese-American candidate is faced with even greater hurdles in party-centered primaries. Ethnic appeals may draw only a third of potential constituents, and even this figure seems highly unlikely given the low rates of turnout to begin with in the Chinese community. Thus a Chinese American candidate might not make it to the general election, where he or she would have a better chance of getting community support. However, the 1996 presidential election may indicate that the balance is shifting. In the Los Angeles area 53 percent of the Chinese community voted for President Clinton, 40 percent for Bob Dole, and 4 percent for Ross Perot. In New York, the figures were as follows: 75 percent supported Clinton, 21 percent Dole, and 2 percent for Ross Perot. If party affiliation swings more solidly into either party camp, Chinese candidates will have an easier time running for office. It will also be interesting to see if the open primaries in California, which began in 1998, will have an impact on rates of turnout and candidacy among Chinese Americans.[4] This work suggests that it will have a positive effect on both of these matters.

As the three chapters on Chinese politicization and influence in the United States show, there are significant barriers to political participation. The first, and perhaps the most difficult to change, is the legacy of disenfranchisement that Chinese have faced in the United States. Chinese were first allowed to become U.S. citizens in 1943; until that time they were ineligible to vote and feared deportment if they mobilized for any sort of political, social, or economic justice. Since these historical barriers were removed, Chinese and other Asian immigrants have had some of the highest rates of naturalization of any immigrant group (Gall and Natividad 1995:351). The second significant barrier to participating in the American political arena is language proficiency. Because a large percentage of Chinese Americans are foreign-born, they are less likely to be fully proficient in English. "It is estimated that as many as 65 percent of Chinese Americans working in New York City's Chinatown do not speak English well or at all" (ibid.). While immigrants must have a basic understanding of English in order to become naturalized, this simple comprehension is inadequate to understand complicated electoral initiatives and voter information. Ballots in Chinese were used in New York City for the first time in 1994, and only a few years earlier in the Los Angeles area.

In New York City overall, Asians constitute 6 percent of eligible voters, but represent only 2 percent of the city's 3.4 million voters. It is estimated that 24 percent of all eligible Asian Americans were registered to vote in 1992, a rate that is substantially lower than for other groups in the city (see Table 8.2). Chinese-American voter registration in Los Angeles County is somewhat higher at around 35.5 percent (Muratsuchi 1991:24).

Social activists in both Monterey Park and New York City are constrained by 501(c)3 status, limiting the type of political activity that they can engage in. However, the prohibitions against partisan political behavior do not apply to AP3CON. At its strategy developing conference in the summer of 1997, different proposals were discussed as to how it could best maximize their political voice. The sense was that there needed to be an effort to cultivate and propose candidates, and that a louder voice should be asserted on issues of importance to the community.[5] No analogous organization has been formed in New York City.

TABLE 8.2 VOTER REGISTRATION IN NEW YORK CITY	
ETHNICITY	PERCENT OF ELIGIBLE VOTERS WHO ARE REGISTERED
Asian American	24%
White	77%
Black	81%
Hispanic	54%
(*Source:* Gall and Natividad 1995:352.)	

THE UNITED STATES AND SOUTHEAST ASIA IN PERSPECTIVE

Clearly there are tremendous demographic and political difference among the three nations and the four Chinese communities studied in this book. The most obvious differences are the percentage of the population that is Chinese, and the length of time the Chinese have resided in the nation in question. However, what this work hopes to show is that beyond these crucial variables, there is evidence showing that when there are electoral incentives for political elites to mobilize the community, then Chinese do participate in greater number than when there are weaker electoral concerns at stake. Likewise, there need to be social incentives for community elites to help mobilize support for particular interests. For instance, education leaders in Malaysia at Independence were willing to temper their demands for greater state recognition and funding for Chinese-vernacular education in order to push for expanded citizenship rights for Chinese in the new Malaysian nation. Most importantly, there was significant support from a wide percentage of the Chinese community for this trade-off. It is more difficult to find this sort of consensus today among Chinese in Malaysia or in the United States. In the United States and in Malaysia, elections are openly contested, but the "Chinese vote" is constrained by institutional impediments. In local Monterey Park elections, the Chinese, because of their percentage of the population, are a vital constituency. In New York City they are far less important, even in local elections, and rates of voter turnout and registration reflect this.

THE ROLE OF ELITES

This study focuses more on the role of elites than on the actions or preferences of individual members of the Chinese community. This is a result of both practical and theoretical concerns. Theoretically, Rosenstone and Hansen (1993), and Bernstein and Packard (1997) show how strong the correlation is between contact and political participation. Bernstein and Packard use path analysis, tested with data from the 1992 and 1994 National Election Studies, to confirm Rosenstone's, and Hansen's earlier analysis that contact from electoral mobilizers is one of the most important variables in determining electoral participation. Some of the reasons given for the importance of contact or mobilization are as follows: being asked to participate greatly increases expected solidarity rewards; doing others a favor or responding to a community leader's appeal can increase one's feeling of community identification or status; contact also reduces the costs of participation—an activist passes on information, such as bilingual brochures on registering and voting, and may even provide transportation or child care. The greater the effort on the behalf of mobilizers, the less effort it is for citizens to participate. This is not to say that community members always follow the lead of the elites, or even that there is consensus as to who constitutes the community's leaders; however, in understanding the nature of Chinese immigrant politicization, historically, it has been essential to study the myriad of kinship organizations and the power of associational leaders which structure life within the Chinese diaspora. This study merely attempts to update this analysis and to ask questions about political incorporation with the host society. This moves scholarship past a focus on the internal dynamics within the ethnic enclave to larger issues and processes at work. While some might argue that this work ignores the role of community members as actors, I have chosen to look at Chinese immigrants as being connected to a larger collectivity. In doing so, it is instructive to understand the interaction between those who take on the job of advocating on behalf of their co-ethnics and those whose political ambitions may be affected by the politicization of the community. There are practical reasons for this research focus as well. Administration of large-scale surveys about political issues would be deeply problematic, if not impossible, in Indonesia and Malaysia.

IMPLICATIONS

As this conclusion is being written, the investigation into Chinese "influence-buying" in the 1996 reelection of President Clinton still continues, and there is uncertainty over the Indonesian election results and over economic recovery. Wealthy Chinese business families were once credited for fueling economic growth in China and Southeast Asia over the last twenty years. Now that these economies are being reevaluated and younger Indonesians and Malaysians may not immediately achieve the levels of wealth that only two years ago seemed attainable for many, the Chinese may continue to find themselves in a precarious position. However, there is cause for hope. Democracy has taken hold in Indonesia, even if it is far from being perfected. Sino-Indonesians have greater opportunities to become full and active members of the Indonesian polity than ever before. While Malaysia does not seem poised on the brink of political reform, it is heartening that even with the economic turmoil of 1997 and 1998, Malaysian Chinese did not suffer at the hands of angry Malay mobs. One reason for the relative calm in Malaysia (as oppose to the chaos and violence in Indonesia) is that Malays perceived that the political system has their interests at heart. While this may be beneficial to Malaysian Chinese safety, it only reinforces the notion that Malays are the rightful rulers and that Malaysian Chinese *should* take a back seat to *bumiputras*. This is hardly a foundation on which greater democracy and transparency can be built.

THE ROLE OF THE PEOPLE'S REPUBLIC OF CHINA

There is one other reason for optimism about Chinese political incorporation in Southeast Asia. The People's Republic of China (PRC), while sometimes viewed as a power on the rise, has moderated its foreign policy over the last fifteen years. Although neighboring countries may question China's power ambitions, few countries believe that China is supporting communist insurgents outside the PRC's borders.

Turmoil in Indonesia in the 1960s produced pronouncements from Mao in the People's Republic of China about all Chinese being welcome to come "home": "We want none of our dear ones to suffer in foreign lands," one official announced in 1960. "It is our hope that they all come back to the arms of the Motherland" (*Los Angeles Times* February 28, 1998). China sent ships to Indonesia in 1960 and 1965 to transport ethnic Chinese back to China, and the PRC broke off diplomatic relations with Indonesia in 1967 and did not restore them until 1990. There has been no statement from Beijing about the 1998 targeting of Chinese in Indonesia for looting and persecution. The *Los Angeles Times* speculated that the Chinese government was fearful of exacerbating the problems in Indonesia and thus was overly cautious about its public statements. In the period after World War II, as the nations in Southeast Asia were negotiating transitions from colonialism, the threat of communist insurgencies, possibly sponsored by the Chinese Communist party, created a very different geo-strategic picture from today.

Knowing the history of the 1950s and 1960s in Southeast Asia, and understanding that China has growing power ambitions, one might believe that it would be more outspoken about both the monetary crisis and about the treatment of Chinese minority populations. China has certainly flexed its military muscle in Southeast Asia, namely in the Spratly Islands, and it has benefited greatly from investments from international conglomerates controlled by overseas Chinese families in Indonesia, Malaysia, and Singapore. Yet throughout the financial crisis and the discussions over Indonesia's plight, China has been studiously nonjudgmental. While China seems to want to assume regional military supremacy, it is reluctant to make any overture to either Chinese Indonesians or to Suharto's government because of a greater desire to maintain order in Asia, and because of its often-stated beliefs about respecting a nation's sovereignty. In addition, in the 1990s most Chinese in Indonesia are Indonesian citizens and few have any interest in fleeing to China or Taiwan.

China's reaction to current events in Indonesia and, to a lesser extent, Malaysia may have implications for two larger issues: security concerns in Asia Pacific, and questions about acculturation of Chinese overseas. China's hands-off attitude may reflect larger aims to cooperate within Asia as a counterweight to U.S. hegemony. The experience of the Cold War tends to color American perceptions of China's growing power so that any conflicts can be viewed as evidence of growing Chinese aggression. Instead, it is possible that the Chinese are willing to work with other nations in Asia to restimulate the economic gains of the past two decades. One might also find that China's reticence to reach out to ethnic Chinese in Southeast Asia will facilitate greater social incorporation of Chinese minorities in to their adopted home lands. More Chinese may acculturate instead of viewing themselves as a distinct group within the larger society.

In the United States there is fear that "Asian-donorgate" and the suspected espionage at Los Alamos indicate a new geostrategic rivalry between the United States and the PRC, with all the attendant trappings of the Cold War, spies, and shady weapons dealers. While much is made in the press about James Riady's connections to Chinese state interests, little is mentioned about the fact that in gaining access to the top echelons of the DNC, the Riady's Lippo Group might have increased clout at home in Indonesia with President Suharto. Despite this explanation, which is somewhat less dramatic, the fallout from the DNC fund-raising scandal may have implications for Chinese communities throughout the United States. Political officials may be more reluctant to reach out to their Chinese-American constituents for fear of potential scandal. If this does occur, then Chinese Americans will loose a valuable opportunity for increased political mobilization by political office-seekers.

Interestingly enough, when I was first interviewing community leaders in Los Angeles and New York, most made it clear that they saw little connection between John Huang, the Riadys, Ted Sioeng, and themselves. Most community activists remarked that national-level politics and intrigue had little to do with their immediate political battles at the local level.[6] As the media continued to focus on the issue, many activists realized that they too would suffer if improprieties were found. The growing realization of potential harm to the Asian-American community's political position escalated when the media attention did continue and the DNC began calling all donors with Asian surnames to return contributions.

The Organization for Chinese Americans has criticized the DNC for stereotyping all Asian Americans as immigrants ineligible to give to political campaigns, and the Asian American Legal Defense and Education Fund has also worked hard both in New York and in Washington to dispel this sort of singling out of Asian Americans. Leaders in the Chinese communities in Los Angeles and New York did not initially seem to believe that the scandal would have an impact on local politics or on their efforts to mobilize the community towards greater participation. It is not yet clear if this assumption is correct.

ANSWERING THE PUZZLE

The reason that socioeconomic status seems to have little correlation with political participation and that levels of influence are unrelated to community participation is that politicization is linked to the collective action problem. Social activists face this significant hurdle in mobilizing the community in support of political goals, but those seeking personal or business influence do not. Business leaders are not faced with the same need to provide social incentives to community members in order for them to achieve the economic benefits they seek. Politicians reach out to Chinese minorities when there are electoral reasons for doing so. This occurs in open political systems and in districts in which the Chinese represent enough of a constituency to matter electorally. In the absence of these conditions, Chinese business elites are still able to network with political leaders to influence policies beneficial to them.

Politicization, as examined through community activism and voter-turnout rates, does not seem to be correlated with influence. With the exception of Malaysia until the late 1960s, it is hard to find a connection between the political activities of the Chinese community and political outcomes favorable to them. Wealth and status are clearly correlated with political influence, as discussed above. Yet, contrary to much of the literature on American politics, the overall economic profile of the Chinese community does not seem to be connected with community politicization.

CHAPTER 1

1. Estimates of the number of people of Chinese descent living outside the People's Republic of China, Taiwan, and Hong Kong vary tremendously. The figure given here is based on statistics given in Pan 1999. Other sources consulted include *New York Times* (May 13, 1996): A10; "Asia Yearbook 1995," *Far Eastern Economic Review*.

2. For a good overview of this, see Louise de Rosario, "Network Capitalism: Personal Connections Help Overseas Chinese Investors," *Far Eastern Economic Review* 156(48) (December 2, 1993): 17.

3. I am referring here to the Democratic National Committee's fund-raising scandal involving Ted Siong, James Riady, John Huang, and others; and to the much publicized relationship between former president Suharto and a few Chinese tycoons, including Bob Hasan.

4. While there are many definitions of culture, the way it is used here is as follows: culture as public, shared meaning; "behaviors, institutions, and social structure are understood not as culture itself but as culturally constituted phenomena.... Culture, in short, marks a 'distinctive way of life' characterized in the subjective we-feelings of cultural group members (and outsiders) and is expressed through specific behaviors (customs and rituals)—both sacred and profane—which mark the daily, yearly, and life cycle rhythms of its members and reveal how people view past, present, and future events and understand choices they face" (Berger 1995; Ross 1997:45).

5. Within the Chinese diaspora there has been considerable tension between supporters of the Nationalist Party, the KMT (now in Taiwan), and those who support the PRC. Wong (1988:251) and Chan (1991:94–95) both give good accounts of the friction along these lines among Chinese in the United States. Similar splits occurred in Malaysia and Indonesia in the 1950s and 1960s. While this divide still exists, it may be masked by class differences between wealthier and better-educated immigrants from Taiwan and Hong Kong, and their poorer co-ethnics from the mainland. No group, however, opposes the government on the mainland with the same stridency of the 1950s.

6. Wang gives the example of Thailand here: Chinese have become active members of the ruling economic and political elite (1993:940).

7. For good work on questions of identity and globalization see Stuart Hall, "The Local and the Global: Globalization and Ethnicity" and "Old and New Identities: Old and New Ethnicities," both in *Culture, Globalization, and the World System: Contemporary Conditions for the Representation of Identity*, Anthony D. King, ed. (Binghamton: State University of New York at Binghamton, 1991).

8. This list of political categories is derived from a longer list in Samuel Huntington and Joan Nelson, *No Easy Choice: Political Participation in Developing Countries* (Cambridge, MA: Harvard University Press, 1976).

9. Reports often state that the Chinese control up to 75 percent of Indonesia's assets. This is a highly misleading figure. Although Sino-Indonesians do control a large portion of the economy, most assets are controlled by the Indonesian government and by multinational corporations.

10. One of the things that the chapter on Indonesia will discuss is the role that some Chinese have played within Golkar. The Chinese-developed think tank,

CSIS, used to be well connected to government officials. This link also reflects tension between Christian and Islamist players within Golkar.

11. This is not to be confused with the creation of state-owned enterprises. As will be explained further in the chapters on Indonesia and Malaysia, economic development in these countries over the last twenty years has loosely followed a Japanese model: creating close links between government bureaucracies, banks, and private businesses.

12. Although I did not have access to interviews with the small number of wealthy tycoons who exemplify personal networking, the connections between individuals like Mochtar Riady or Bob Hasan and Suharto are well documented. Likewise, there is ample material on key figures in Malaysia such as Robert Kuok, and in the United States there are almost daily reports on the campaign contributions to the Democratic National Committee during the 1996 election.

13. This is a similar definition to that used by Rosenstone and Hansen (1993:4).

14. Gary King's work on the problem of ecological inference (1997) highlights the difficulty in reconstructing individual behavior from aggregate data such as voter turnout surveys.

CHAPTER 2

1. Perhaps the equivalent Southeast Asian example of this was Indonesia's attempt in the 1960s to have all Sino-Indonesians take Indonesian names, and the further outlawing of Chinese language press and cultural institutions.

2. Gordon 1964: 70–71.

3. Gordon 1964: 81, 110.

4. Tamura 1994: 52.

5. For works of this type see James Clifford, "Diasporas," *Cultural Anthropology* 9, (1994) no. 3:302–338; Paul Gilroy, *"There Ain't No Black in the Union Jack": The Cultural Politics of Race and Nation* (London: Routledge, 1987); and Gilroy, *The Black Atlantic: Modernity and Double Consciousness* (Cambridge, MA: Harvard University Press, 1994); Nonini 1997: 203–228; Aihwa Ong, "Chinese Modernities: Narratives of Nation and of Capitalism," in *Underground Empires*, Ong and Nonini, eds. (New York: Routledge, 1994), 171–203.

6. Thailand provides the best example of acculturation of the Chinese with the Thai population. As early as the 1920s the Thai monarchy stressed culture over biology as the basis for "Thai-ness." In contrast to other nations where the Chinese have settled in large numbers, it was possible in Siam for immigrants to change their nationality and become Thai. To do so they had to become fluent in the Thai language, practice Buddhism, and renounce other citizenship (Charles F. Keyes, "Cultural Diversity and National Identity in Thailand," in *Government Policies and Ethnic Relations in Asia and the Pacific*, Brown and Ganguly, eds. (Cambridge, MA: MIT Press, 1997).

7. Keyes, "Cultural Diversity," 209.

8. The need to have a common understanding of the past has led to much misrepresentation, both about the aims of the Malaysian Communist Party in the 1940s and 1950s, and about the underlying causes of the 1969 riots. For good accounts of both events see Pek Koon Heng 1988 and David Brown 1994.

9. Nonini uses "regime" in his work as a form of the power-knowledge dynamic (Foucault 1978) inherent in three realms: families, capitalist work sites, and nation-states (Nonini 1997:204). That I will focus on the third aspect of this, the nation-state and its institutions, should not be taken as an indication that these other uses are not likewise crucial to notions of culture and identity.

10. The Democratic Action Party, or DAP, evolved as the main rival to MCA prior to the 1964 elections. As the chapter on Malaysia will illustrate, DAP has drawn considerable Chinese support away from MCA. This has occurred during periods when the Chinese have felt their interests particularly threatened, for example in 1969 and 1990.

11. Rather than raising questions about buying political influence in the United States, Riady's donations to the Democratic Party and President Clinton may well be an attempt to exert influence in Indonesia. This possibility will be explored further in Chapter Six.

CHAPTER 3

1. Daim Zainuddin served as finance minister from 1984 to 1991. He is given credit for helping Malaysia pull out of a recession in the mid-1980s and for crafting the policies that resulted in almost ten years of 8 percent annual economic growth. For more information on Daim, see Hiebert and Jayasankaran.

2. Secret societies were not actually secret (nor were they antigovernment) until they were banned in 1890. For more information on the secret societies in Malay, and for a more lengthy discussion on the Kapitan Cina system, see Pan 1999: 173.

3. Under British colonial rule the mainland or penisula of western Malaysia was known as "Malaya." After independence in the 1950s the country was named Malaysia. The provinces of Sabah and Sarawak on the island of Borneo were incorporated into Malaysia in the early 1960s to balance out the inclusion of (largely Chinese-dominated) Singapore into the nation.

4. For a more complete account of The Emergency period, see Pye 1956, and Heng 1988.

5. The Malaysian Indian Congress has represented Indians in Malaysia; however, Indians have lagged behind both Malay and Chinese in economic and political standing.

6. In 1970 the average per capita household income for Chinese was M$1,032 as compared with M$492 for Malay households.

7. Indians and the leaders of the Malaysian Indian Congress have often bristled at being such junior partners in the ruling coalition, and since NEP was ostensibly aimed at poverty alleviation, the Indian community hoped it would also raise their status.

8. For a good account of the actions taken under ISA, see Means 1991:211–213.

9. For works on consociationalism, see Arend Lijphart, *Democracy in Plural Societies* (New Haven: Yale University Press, 1977), and Cynthia H. Enloe, *Elite Conflict and Political Development* (Boston: Little, Brown and Co., 1973). For Malaysia in particular, see Horowitz 1985 and 1989.

10. For more on the government's harassment of Lim Kit Siang in 1976 under the Official State Secrets Act see Barraclough 1985: 797–822.

11. In 1969 after riots erupted following preliminary election results, voting was suspended before the election was completed. Voting was eventually allowed to continue and the period of emergency rule did not upset the regular pattern of elections (Means 1991:296).

12. As evidence of this, municipal elections, which were largely won by opposition parties, have not been held since 1960 (Jomo 1996:93).

13. Of course, there could be several mediating factors to explain these rates of participation: for example, rural turnout is generally higher than urban turnout in most democracies (Crouch 1996).

14. Lim Guan Eng, the current opposition leader, is serving time in jail for supporting a teenage girl's rape accusation against a powerful Malay politician.

15. Professional Chinese with whom I met in Kuala Lumpur and Penang in 1996 and early 1997 repeatedly expressed support for the status quo. They felt that although the government's policies clearly favored the Malays, politics was not a zero-sum game. As long as all were doing better, they could accept the unevenness of it. Most admitted some fear that riots like those in Tasikmalaya, West Java, the day after Christmas 1996 could also occur in Malaysia if the economic and political conditions took a turn for the worse. More recently, Malaysian Chinese followed with horror the violence and looting that occurred in Indonesia in 1998. While none thought that Malaysia would suffer the same chaos, many expressed fear that neither their persons nor their property were completely safe.

16. Tan Liok Ee argues that *Dongjiaozong* should not be viewed in this manner as a pressure group, but rather that the group poses a challenge to the ruling groups' policies on education and culture.

CHAPTER 4

1. No accurate statistics are kept on the number of people of Chinese descent in Indonesia. The last firm statistics on the number of ethnic Chinese are from the 1930 colonial census. Then, 1,233,000 Chinese lived in the Dutch East Indies. Later figures are just estimates.

2. Throughout January and February 1998, violent protest occurred across Indonesia, much of it aimed at the Chinese minority. While some of the rioting appeared to be largely spontaneous, some senior government and military officials have fueled anti-Chinese sentiment by making references to "rats" and "traitors" and by their failure to explain that rising prices and food shortages are not the fault of individual shopkeepers. Small-scale rioting and looting of Chinese property occurred in Central and East Java, Sumatra, Sulawesi, Lombok, Sumbawa, and Flores (www.indopubs.com/archives/0232. html). "Indonesia Alert: Economic Crisis Leads to Scapegoating of Ethnic Chinese," February 1998.

3. The choice of Bob Hasan for a cabinet position was highly controversial because Hasan would be in a position to police and oversee the industrial sectors in which he is heavily involved.

4. For a good account of the last few days in Suharto's palace, see Michael Vatkiotis and Adam Schwarz 1998.

5. In the spring of 1998 there was extensive media coverage of the riots and political turmoil in Indonesia. Information on the formation of new political parties comes specifically from Jay Soloman 1998, and from *Kompus* 1998.

6. There is in fact another party called PWBI (*Partai Warga Bangsa Indonesia*) whose members are Indonesian Chinese, but little is known about the party at this time.

7. There is some suggestion that the chairman of PBI (Nurdin Halim) was regarded by Chinese leaders in Jakarta as tainted by association with Suharto's late wife, Ibu Tien Suharto.

8. Election results were taken from Seth Mydans, "Indonesia President Accepts Assembly Election Results," *The New York Times* (August 4, 1999): A4.

9. The People's Consultative Assembly (MPR) is responsible for appointing the president. The MPR is made up of all the members of parliament plus two hundred additional appointees. Many of these appointees are military designees and holdovers from Suharto's regime.

10. For information on Wahid's election and on his cabinet appointments see: David Lamb, "Wahid Stressess Need for Investment in Indonesia," *Los Angeles Times* (October 25, 1999); Seth Mydans, "Indonesian Leader Forms 'Mix-

master' Cabinet," *New York Times* (October 27, 1999); Andrew MacIntyre, "Chemistry at the Top Could Prove Volatile," *Los Angeles Times* (October 24, 1999).

11. Even before the economic crisis hit Indonesia in the summer of 1997, Sino-Indonesians have been the subject of violence and discontent from the Muslim majority. For example, rioting occurred the day after Christmas 1996 in Tasikmalaya, West Java. Angered at the behavior of the local police toward teachers in an Islamic school, local residents took to the streets, looting and burning shops and churches of ethnic Chinese.

12. Pan 1999: 152.

13. The exceptions to this were smaller leftist parties with internationalist sentiments.

14. The word *peranakan* comes from the Malay word *anak,* or child. It suggests a child of mixed racial ancestry. Some *peranakans* may have had *pribumi* mothers. Early use of the word may also have referred to Muslim Chinese. Mary Somers Heidhues, "Indonesia," in Pan 1999: 153.

15. *Peranakan* was also used in a political context. The Dutch colonial government used the term to mean Indies-born, and it was a way of distinguishing between immigrant groups who were aliens and those who were Dutch subjects (Pan 1999: 153).

16. As an example of this jockeying, in 1963 Sukarno threw his weight behind *Baperki* by saying that there was no need for *peranakan* Chinese to "Indonesianize" their names to be good citizens, something that the assimilationists had been vigorously promoting (Coppel 1976:57).

17. There are different versions of the truth about October 1, 1965. Ruth McVey and Benedict Anderson wrote a speculative paper on the coup, which hotly disputes the official account that Beijing-backed communists propagated the conflict. They argue that the coup was an attempt by loyal (to Sukarno) officers to prevent Western-supported generals from collaborating with the US to overthrow Sukarno (McVey and Anderson, "A Preliminary Analysis of the October 1, 1965 Coup in Indonesia." Cornell University Modern Indonesia Project No. 52, 1971).

18. Like in Malaysia, state-led development has not meant the creation of state-owned enterprises. Rather, the government has developed regulatory bodies that oversee key export commodities and domestic production of important resources. There are close ties between state bureaucracies, banks, and private companies. For a comprehensive account of business developments and networks in Indonesia, see Irwan 1995 and Macintyre 1990.

19. For most of Suharto's rule these one hundred seats went to military appointees. In 1998 President Habibie decreased the military's seats to thirty-eight.

20. While in Central Java I witnessed a Golkar rally. Government employees and politically connected private firms' staff gathered in the town square wearing Golkar's brilliant color gold. I was told that these people were given little choice in choosing to attend the rally and that when they went to vote in elections they were also pressured to cast their ballot accordingly. Likewise, I was told that private business owners were encouraged to support Golkar or risk losing their license, store, or merchandise.

21. In light of this it is particularly significant that in the face of rising violence against the Chinese this winter, opposition leader Amien Rais of *Muhammadiya,* a popular figure in Indonesia today, condemned the anti-Chinese attacks in a speech on February 15, 1998 and called the Chinese "our brothers" who "have become part and parcel of this integrated nation" (www.indopubs.

com/archives/0232.html. "Indonesia Alert: Economic Crisis Leads to Scapegoating of Ethnic Chinese" Feb. 1998).

22. It should also be noted here that the Chinese are not the only Christians in Indonesia, and, there seems to be little solidarity based on religion between the Chinese and other Indonesian Christians.

23. This information was related to me in an article distributed to an internet group interested in Chinese overseas, and can be found at www.indopubs. com/archives/0232.html.

24. Officially, thirty protesters were killed by the troops, other estimates are that as many as one hundred were killed. op. cit.

25. In March 1998 Suharto named Hasan as the new Minister of Trade and Industry, a powerful post in which he can officially wield influence over economic decisions.

26. As the IMF has pressed Suharto to implement austerity measures in the wake of the 1997 fiscal crisis, connections between key economic elites and the ruling family have remained important. Bob Hasan, head of a cartel that controls Indonesia's $4 billion plywood export industry, along with cartels in cement and cloves, was to have his monopoly abolished as part of the IMF's program to open Indonesia's economy to free-market forces. The *New York Times* reports that the cartel was abolished in name only. "Mr. Hasan's group, known as Apkindo, immediately formed what it called a statistical research board. To pay for the board, Apkindo told exporters they would have to pay $5 for each cubic meter of plywood exports. The annual total of this de facto tax would be between $40 and $50 million" (*New York Times* March 5, 1998: A6). Hasan has denied that these restrictions exist and announced the cessation of the statistical research tax, but as the *Times* notes, "exporters are now waiting for his next direction" (ibid.).

27. It is possible that Suharto has favored Chinese interests precisely because supporting an indigenous *pribumi* class could lead to the development of a class that could challenge his supremacy.

28. For greater analysis of this period, see Coppel 1976: 33–38 and 44–46.

29. Harry Tjan at CSIS told me that conversion to Islam was increasingly common for Chinese, making intermarriage more possible. In addition, several people told me that religion was "not an issue for Chinese"—that in this area they were flexible, and that the issue of not eating pork was not so salient.

30. Singapore too has organized society along ethnic lines. For example: children learn their "home" language (Mandarin, Tamil, or Malay) in school. And, like Indonesia, Singapore claims to prohibit displays of ethnic chauvinism. A good reference for this is David Brown's (1994) chapter on Singapore. Despite this, during my time in Singapore, Malay and Indian citizens were quite open about their sense (and resentment) of Chinese superiority on the island.

CHAPTER 5

1. Although the Exclusion Acts prevented the Chinese already in the United States from becoming naturalized citizens, and despite the fact that these first Chinese migrants were almost exclusively male, it is likely that some were married to either Chinese or non-Chinese women and had children. From the existing secondary literature it is unclear how this second generation identified itself.

2. Between May 9 and May 27, the *Los Angeles Times* conducted a poll of 773 adult Chinese residents in Southern California. Surveys were done by Interviewing Services of America, Inc. in Mandarin, Cantonese, and English. Individuals were chosen from a sample of Chinese surnames from telephone

directories. All interviews were conducted over the telephone. For the results of the survey, see K. Connie Kang, "Chinese in the Southland: a Changing Picture," *Los Angeles Times* (June 29, 1997): A1.

3. Chinese Americans account for approximately one quarter of all Asian Americans (Lott 1991:58).

CHAPTER 6

1. These population figures are from 1995 city estimates; they reflect an increase of 1,116 persons since the 1990 census (http://ci.monterey-park.ca.us/geninfo.html).

2. Bill Reel wrote an insightful op-ed entitled "See Asian Americans for What They Are" that discusses the dangers of such "positive" prejudice, *New York Newsday* (March 16, 1997): G8.

3. Such social networks are prevalent in the Chinese community. There are kinship and business associations as well as social service agencies. These associations will be discussed at greater length later in this chapter, and again in Chapter Six.

4. Bernstein and Packard (1997) present empirical support for Rosenstone's and Hansen's (1993) theoretical work.

5. These numbers are based on the 1990 U.S. census; they are mostly likely quite a bit higher now.

6. The percent of Chinese who are registered to vote is based on information contained in Nakanishi (1987), a UCLA voter registration study of Asian Pacific Americans in the Los Angeles area.

7. Included in this category would be the business executives who maintain one foot in Asia and one foot in the United States. Aiwa Ong discusses these hypermobile migrants in her work on "transnational" capital and looks at how the forces of globalization have created this class of elites who move beyond U.S. and Asian boundaries (1996). In Mandarin these businessmen are called "*Tai Kun Fei Jen*" or spacemen (Waldinger and Tseng 1992:105).

8. Interestingly, in the middle of the 1950s Monterey Park was known to many in East Los Angeles as the "Mexican Beverly Hills" (Fong 1994:22).

9. On a smaller scale, this is also true in Flushing, Queens, New York.

10. Information on the Monterey Park Democratic Club was provided by Ruth and Erve Willner, longtime leaders of the club, during an interview on July 30, 1997.

11. Jeff Siu provided the author with much of the information about the Asian Pacific Democratic Club in an interview held on July 28, 1997.

12. Certainly there is something to be gained in running for political office, even if in doing so, one weakens others' likelihood of winning. Democracy values choice, and it is far better to have too many candidates competing than to have too few. In fact, having so many Chinese Americans running for office may signal a normalization of Chinese in politics!

13. Likewise, in New York City, Jennifer Lim's attempt to challenge Kathryn Freed's seat on the City Council was aided by a large dinner held on her behalf by her family association in a restaurant in Chinatown in the run-up to the democratic primary this fall.

14. In interviews conducted in both New York and Los Angeles, social service leaders expressed frustration at this constraint. Interviews in Los Angeles were held with Judy Chu, Sam Luk, Deborah Ching, Robert Kwan, Jeff Siu, and others.

15. Saito's account gives many of the details of the negotiations between the Asian American Coalition and Latino groups (Saito 1993).

16. For example, Stewart Kwoh (current director of the Asian Pacific American Legal Center) and Mike Eng (Judy Chu's husband and an attorney/political activist) attended law school at UCLA in the 1970s and from their experiences were prompted to open up a poverty law office after graduation (Saito 1997:137).

17. This figure was stated before the campaign finance inquiries began, and well before the DNC decided to return donations from contributors with Asian, particularly Chinese, surnames.

18. *The New Yorker* (March 14, 1997), in an investigative essay by Peter J. Boyer entitled "American Guanxi," details the connections between Ron Brown and Nora and Eugene Lum dating back to 1992.

CHAPTER 7

1. A census tract is a district of several thousand people used for census enumeration purposes.

2. For a comprehensive history of the CCBA, see "China Politics and the U.S. Chinese Communities" by Him Mark Lai in *Counterpoint*, Gee (ed.) 1965.

3. In Malaysia, the Chinese Chambers of Commerce served the same purpose as the CCBA.

4. In contrast to this, the Japanese Association of America was more outward-looking. It published material in English with the goal of swaying American public opinion in a positive direction (Chan 1991:68).

5. Many of those active in OCA come from working in social service agencies in Chinatown.

6. The council was given substantial legislative and budgetary authority, and a referendum allowed New Yorkers to approve the new charter, which they did by a margin of five to four (*New York Times* March 23, 1989, November 8, 1989).

7. By 1996 there were only approximately 10,000 registered voters in Chinatown, less than 10 percent of the actual population (Tomio Geron, "Voter Drives on in NY: Community Groups Register New Citizens, Organize to Increase Voter Turnout," *Asian Week* vol. 17; no. 47).

8. On February 26, 1997, a federal district court found the 12th Congressional District in New York, which included Manhattan's Chinatown and Sunset Park, Brooklyn—a neighborhood with an increasingly large Chinese population—to be unconstitutional and ordered that it be redrawn. As part of the Asian American Redistricting Coalition, AALDEF is urging that new plans keep these neighborhoods together as they constitute a "community of interest." Many residents of Sunset Park work in Chinatown and residents in both communities have similar income levels and speak the same dialects of Chinese. The 12th Congressional District had the largest concentration of Chinese Americans in any New York City congressional district (*Righting Wrongs*, newsletter published by the Asian American Legal Defense and Education Fund, July/August 1997:1).

9. Information on Dorothy Chin Brandt comes from interviews with her and from the *New York Daily News* September 17, 1987: 1.

10. This is generally attributed to lower socioeconomic status and because those recently enfranchised tend to vote at low rates (Levitt and Olsen 1996: 3). Lieske and Hillard see that this is possibly because voting is a civic activity that "mainstream" groups participate in (1984).

11. Committee members' affiliations are for identification purposes only and do not imply organizational endorsement of the proposed school.

12. Information on Shuang Wen Academy is based on interviews with Larry Lee and Jacob Wong, as well as through documentation from the school proposal and curriculum outline.

CHAPTER 8

1. Even without ethnic scapegoating, violence and riots may be a result of the lack of other means to express dissatisfaction with the regime.

2. Suharto's New Order regime, until the monetary crisis hit in the summer of 1997, was primarily based on and legitimated by its developmental goals. Successful economic growth for the last fifteen years made this possible, even in the face of corruption and blatant disregard for democratic processes and norms. The repeated rioting throughout Java and Sumatra during the end of 1997 and into early 1998, clearly reflects not only a sense of economic insecurity and scapegoating of the Chinese minority but also an expression of distrust and lack of support for the state apparatus.

3. The number of those seeking U.S. citizenship in 1995 jumped to just over 1million, up from 500,000 in 1994. In New York City alone, 141,235 immigrants sought citizenship, up from 80,000 in 1994 (*New York Times* March 10, 1996:A1). Reasons for this include fear of loosing benefits like Medicare and food stamps, and defensive reaction against the general feeling of invective aimed at immigrants.

4. Monterey Park city elections are all open to registered voters of any party. Thus one cannot tell from the 1999 City Council elections whether the statewide changes will impact Chinese-American voter turnout.

5. It seems important to note here that the activities of AP3CON do not necessarily represent *all* views of the community. Those who participated in the conference were interested in issues of social justice, education, and welfare concerns. There was little representation from business interests in the Chinese community. It is probably fair to estimate that participants would be largely supportive of liberal Democratic candidates who would have voted no on California Proposition 209 and who would have supported Proposition 210, a rise in the state minimum wage (such views would coincide with 76% and 66%, respectively, of Asian Americans in the 1996 elections) (www.sscnet.ucla.edu/ aasc/ccx/exitpoll.html).

6. Local Democratic party club leaders in Monterey Park said that John Huang had run a fund-raiser in their area but that he had not made a deep impression on them, and they did not see Huang or the Lums from Hawaii as speaking for the larger community of Chinese Americans.

A. *Magazine*. "A Rottenness in Monterey Park." Issue 10 (October 31, 1994): 21.

Abraham, Collin. "Manipulation and Management of Racial and Ethnic Groups in Colonial Malaya: A Case Study of Ideological Domination and Control." In *Ethnicity and Ethnic Relations in Malaysia*, Raymond Lee, ed. Center on Southeast Asian Studies, Northern Illinois University Occasional Paper, no. 12. 1986.

Almond, Gabriel. *A Civic Culture: Political Attitudes and Democracy in Five Nations*. Princeton, NJ: Princeton University Press, 1996.

Anderson, Benedict R. "Elections and Participation in Three Southeast Asian Countries." In *The Politics of Elections in Southeast Asia*, R. H. Taylor, ed. New York: Cambridge University Press, 1963.

———. *Imagined Communities: Reflections on the Origin and Spread of Nationalism*. London and New York: Verso Press, 1991.

Asian Pacific American Legal Center of Southern California and National Asian Pacific American Legal Consortium. *1996 Southern California Asian Pacific American Exit Poll Report*. Los Angeles, California, 1996.

Banfield, Edward. *Big City Politics*. New York: Random House, 1965.

———, and James Q. Wilson. *City Politics*. Cambridge, MA: Harvard University Press, 1962.

Bard, Mitchell. "The Influence of Ethnic Interest Groups on American Middle East Policy." In *The Domestic Sources of American Foreign Policy*, Charles W. Kegley, Jr. and Eugene R. Wittkopf, eds. New York: St. Martins Press, 1988, 57–70.

Barns, Samuel H. "Electoral Behavior and Comparative Politics." In *Comparative Politics Rationality, Culture, and Structure*, Lichbach and Zuckerman, eds. New York: Cambridge University Press, 1997.

Barraclough, Simon. "The Dynamics of Coercion in the Malaysian Political Process." *Modern Asian Studies* vol. 19, issue 4 (1985).

Barth, Fredrik, ed. *Ethnic Groups and Boundaries: The Social Organization of Cultural Difference*. London: Allen and Unwin, 1969.

Barzel, Yoram, and Eugene Silberberg. "Is the Act of Voting Rational?" *Public Choice* 16 (1973):51–58.

Bau, Ignatius. "Immigrant Rights: A Challenge to Asian Pacific American Political Influence." *Asian American Policy Review* vol. V (Spring 1995).

Bellush, Jewel. "Clusters of Power: Interest Groups." In *Urban Politics New York Style*, Bellush and Netzer, eds. New York: M. E. Sharpe, 1990.

Berger, Bennett M. *An Essay on Culture: Symbolic Structure and Social Structure*. Berkeley: University of California Press, 1995.

Bernstein, Robert A., and Edward Packard. "Paths to Participation in Electoral Politics: The Importance of Mobilization." Paper presented at the Annual Meeting of the American Political Science Association. Washington, D.C., August 1997.

Blanc, Christina Szanton. "'Sisterhood' and Politics: Reflections on Some New Identities and Communities of Philippine Women across Multiple Diasporas." Presented at Institute of Southeast Asian Studies, Singapore, Conference on Diasporas in Southeast Asia. December 5–7, 1996.

Bobo, Lawrence, and Franklin D. Gilliam, Jr. "Race, Sociopolitical Participation, and Black Empowerment." *American Political Science Review* vol. 84, no. 2 (June 1990).

Boyer, Peter J. "American Guanxi." *The New Yorker* (April 14, 1997): 48–61.

Brown, David. *The State and Ethnic Politics in Southeast Asia.* New York: Routledge, 1994.

Bucuvalas, Michael John. "Ethnicity and the Nature of Political Participation, Difference in the Correlates of Participation among the European Ethnic Groups of Upper Manhattan." Columbia University Dissertation, 1978.

Cain, Bruce, John Ferejohn, and Morris Fiorina. *The Personal Vote.* Cambridge, MA: Harvard University Press, 1987.

Castles, Stephen, and Godula Kosack. *Immigrant Workers and Class Structure in Western Europe.* Oxford, England: Oxford University Press, 1973.

———. "How the Trade Unions Try to Control and Integrate Immigrant Workers in the German Federal Republic." *Race* 15, no. 4, 497–515.

Cattell, Stuart. *Health, Welfare, and Social Organization in Chinatown, New York City.* New York: Community Service Society of New York, 1962.

Cerny, Philip G. *Social Movements and Protest in France.* London: Frances Pinter, 1982.

Chan, Sucheng. *Asian American: An Interpretive History.* Boston: Twayne, 1991.

Chen, Nina. "Crooked Voting Lines: Supreme Court's Decision to Axe Racial Redistricting Could be a Setback for Asian Americans." *AsianWeek* vol. 16, no. 45 (July 7, 1995): 1.

Chesneaux, Jean. *Popular Movements and Secret Societies in China, 1840–1950.* Stanford, CA: Stanford University Press, 1976.

Chew, Kong Huat. "Chinese Education in Malaysia." In *Malaysian Ethnic Relations Report #1*, Stewart Gardner, ed. Sociology Working Paper, School of Comparative Social Sciences, Universiti Sains Malaysia, Pulau Pinang, Malaysia, 1975.

Chiu, Wing. "New and Improved? New York City's Charter According to Fred Schwartz." *A. Magazine* vol. 1, no. 0 (July 31, 1990): 28.

Cho, Wendy K. Tam. "Naturalization, Socialization, Participation: Immigrants and (Non-) Voting." *Journal of Politics* (1999).

"City Promises to End Bias against Chinese-Indonesian," *Tempo* (June 12, 1998) (http://www.tempo.co.id/har/12 juni–8.html).

"Clout in the Capital." *Asian Week* vol. 17, no. 39 (1996).

Cohen, Margot. "'Us' and 'Them.'" *Far Eastern Economic Review* (February 12, 1998a): 16–17.

———. "To the Barricades." *Far Eastern Economic Review* (May 14, 1998b).

———. "Turning Point." *Far Eastern Economic Review* (July 30, 1998c).

Coppel, Charles A. "Patterns of Chinese Political Activity in Indonesia." In *The Chinese in Indonesia*, J.A.C. Mackie, ed. Australia: Australian Institute of International Affairs, 1976.

Crissman, Lawrence. "Segmentary Structure of Urban Overseas Chinese." *Man* vol. 2, issue 2 (1967).

———. "Segmentary Organization of Urban Overseas Chinese Communities." *Man* 2(2) (1972):185–204.

Crouch, Harold A. *Malaysia's 1982 General Election*. Singapore: Institute of Southeast Asian Studies Press, 1982.

———. *The Army and Politics in Indonesia*, rev. ed. Ithaca, NY: Cornell University Press, 1986, 1988.

———. *Government and Society in Malaysia*. Ithaca, NY: Cornell University Press, 1996a.

———. "Malaysia: Do Elections Make a Difference?" In *The Politics of Elections in Southeast Asia*, R. H. Taylor, ed. New York: Cambridge University Press, 1996b.

———, Lee Kam Hing, and Michael Ong. *Malaysian Politics and the 1978 Election*. Kuala Lumpur: Oxford University Press, 1980.

Dahl, Robert A. *Modern Political Analysis*, 2nd ed. New Jersey: Prentice-Hall, 1970.

Drogin, Bob. "FBI Unable to Build Case against Scientist Linked to China Leaks" and "Espionage: Officials Try to Determine if Wen Ho Lee Passed along Classified Information." *Los Angeles Times* (Sunday, March 14, 1999a): A22.

———. "Scientist in China Spy Case Offers a Defense." *Los Angeles Times* (May 7, 1999b): A1.

Dugger, Celia W. "Immigrant Voters Reshape Politics." *New York Times* (March 10, 1996): B1.

Dusenbery, Verne. "Diasporic Imagings and the Conditions of Possibility: Sikhs and the State in Southeast Asia." Paper presented at the Social Science Research Council and Institute of Southeast Asian Studies conference on Disaporas in Southeast Asia. Singapore, December 5–7, 1996.

Eichenthal, David R. "The Other Elected Officials" and "Changing Styles and Strategies of the Mayor." In *Urban Politics New York Style*, Bellush and Netzer, eds. New York: M.E. Sharpe, 1990, 63–107.

Elijera, Bert. "Bilingual Voting under Attack: Bill Would Undo Mandate for Multilingual Ballots." *AsianWeek* vol. 17, no. 40 (May 31, 1996): 8.

———. "The Chinese Beverly Hills" *Asian Week* vol. 17, no. 39 (May 24, 1996).

Erie, Steven P. *Rainbow's End: Irish American and the Dilemma of Urban Machine Politics, 1840–1985*. Berkeley: University of California Press, 1988.

Fitzgerald, Stephen. *China and the Overseas Chinese: A Study of Peking's Changing Policy*. Cambridge: Cambridge University Press, 1972.

Fong, Timothy. *The First Suburban Chinatown: The Remaking of Monterey Park, California*. Philadelphia: Temple University Press, 1994.

Foucault, Michel. *History of Sexuality*. New York: Pantheon Books, 1978.

————. *Discipline and Punish: The Birth of the Prison*. New York: Vintage Books, 1979.

Freedman, Maurice. "Overseas Chinese Associations: A Comment." *Comparative Studies in Society and History* vol. 3, issue 4 (1961).

————. "Immigrants and Associations: The Chinese in 19th Century Singapore." *Comparative Society and History* vol. 3, (1962a): 25–48.

————. "Overseas Chinese Associations: A Comment." *Comparative Society and History* vol. 3 (1962b): 478–480.

————. "Chinese Kinship and Marriage in Early Singapore." *Journal of Southeast Asian History* vol. 3(3) (1962c): 65–73.

————. *The Study of Chinese Societies: Essays*. Stanford, CA: Stanford University Press, 1979.

Friel, Terry. "Indonesian Military May Hold Palace Key." *The Japan Times* (June 4, 1999): 21.

Fung, Margaret. "Guinier's Electoral Reforms Would Undermine American Ideal: Asian American Voters." *New York Times* (April 22, 1994): A26.

Gall, Susan, and Irene Natividad, eds. *Asian American Almanac*. Washington, DC: Gale Research, 1995.

Garcia, Carlos Chino, and Elaine Chan. "A Multiracial Council District Best Reflects Lower East Side." *New York Times* (April 16, 1991): A22.

Geron, Tomio. "Representation, At Last: New York's Chinatown Elects Its First Public Official." *AsianWeek* vol. 1, no. 47 (July 17, 1995): 9.

————. "Voter Drives on in NY: Community Groups Register New Citizens, Organize to Increase Voter Turnout." *AsiaWeek* vol. 1, no. 47 (July 26, 1996): 11.

Gilley, Bruce. "Over to You." *Far Eastern Economic Review* (March 19, 1998): 10–14.

Glazer, Nathan. "Ethnic Groups in America: From National Culture to Ideology." In Monroe Berger, Theodore Abel, and Charles H. Page, eds., *Freedom and Control in Modern Society*. New York: Van Nostrand, 1954.

————, and Daniel P. Moynihan. *Beyond the Melting Pot*. Cambridge, MA: MIT Press, 1963.

Gomez, Edmund Terence. *Money Politics in the Barisan Nasional*. Kuala Lumpur, Malaysia: Forum Books, 1991.

————. *Corporate Involvement of Malaysian Political Parties*. Australia: Center for Southeast Asian Studies, 1994.

Gordon, Milton M. *Assimilation in American Life: The Role of Race, Religion, and National Origin*. New York: Oxford University Press, 1964.

Greif, Stuart William. *Indonesians of Chinese Origin: Assimilation and the Goal of "One Nation One People."* New York: Professors' World Peace Academy, 1988.

Hall, Kenneth R. *Maritime Trade and State Development in Early Southeast Asia*. Honolulu: University of Hawaii Press, 1985.

Hall, Peter. "The Role of Interests, Institutions, and Ideas in the Comparative Political Economy of Industrialized Nations." In *Comparative Politics Rationality, Culture, and Structure*, Lichbach and Zuckerman, eds. New York: Cambridge University Press, 1997.

Hamilton, Charles. "Political Access, Minority Participation, and the New Normalcy." In *Minority Report, What Has Happened to Blacks, Hispanics, American Indians, and other Minorities in the Eighties*, Leslie W. Dunbar, ed. New York: Pantheon Books, 1984.

Handlin, Oscar. *The Uprooted.* Boston: Little, Brown and Company, 1951.

Hansen, John Mark. *Gaining Access: Congress and the Farm Lobby 1919–1981.* Chicago: University of Chicago Press, 1991.

Harsono, Andreas. "Accounts of Gang Rape of Chinese Women Emerge from Jakarta Riots" *Huaren 1998.* (http://www.huaren.org/focus/id/061398–02.html).

Heidhues, Mary Somers. "Indonesia." In *Encyclopedia of Chinese Overseas,* Lynn Pan, ed. Cambridge, MA: Harvard University Press, 1999, 151–168.

Heng, Pek Koon. *Chinese Politics in Malaysia: A History of the MCA.* Singapore: Oxford University Press, 1988.

———. "The Chinese Business Elite of Malaysia." In *Southeast Asian Capitalists,* McVey, ed. Ithaca, NY: Studies on Southeast Asia Program, 1992.

———. "Malaysia." In *Encyclopedia of Chinese Overseas,* Lynn Pan, ed. Cambridge, MA: Harvard University Press, 1999, 172–182.

Heyer, Virginia. "Patterns of Social Organization in New York's Chinatown." Ph.D. Dissertation. Ann Arbor, MI: University Microfilms, 1953.

Hiebert, Murray, and S. Jayasankaran. "Consummate Insider." *Far Eastern Economic Review* (February 19, 1998a).

———. "Mixed Signals." *Far Eastern Economic Review* (May 21, 1998b).

———. "After the Fall." *Far Eastern Economic Review* (September 17, 1998c).

———. "Bruised but Unbowed." *Far Eastern Economic Review* (October 8, 1998d).

———. "A Single Spark." *Far Eastern Economic Review* (October 29, 1998e).

Hill, Hal, ed. *Unity and Diversity: Regional Economic Development in Indonesia since 1970.* New York: Oxford University Press, 1989.

———, ed. *Indonesia's New Order: The Dynamics of Socio-Economic Transformation.* Honolulu: University of Hawaii Press, 1994.

Hodder, Rupert. *Merchant Princes of the East: Cultural Delusions, Economic Success and the Overseas Chinese in Southeast Asia.* New York: John Wiley and Sons, 1996.

Horowitz, Donald. *Ethnic Groups in Conflict.* Berkeley: University of California Press, 1985.

———. "Incentives and Behavior in the Ethnic Politics of Sri Lanka and Malaysia." *Third World Quarterly* (October 1989):18–35.

Horton, John. "The Politics of Diversity in Monterey Park, CA." In *Structuring Diversity: Ethnographic Perspectives on the New Immigration,* Lamphere, ed. Chicago: University of Chicago Press, 1992.

Huntington, Samuel. *Clash of Civilizations and the Remaking of World Order.* New York: Simon & Schuster, 1996.

———, and Joan M. Nelson. *No Easy Choice: Political Participation in Developing Countries.* Cambridge, MA: Harvard University Press, 1976.

Idid, Syed Arabi, and Mazni Buyong. *Malaysia's General Election 1995: People, Issues and Media Use.* Kuala Lumpur: Asia Foundation and Universiti Kebangsaan Malaysia Bangi, 1995.

Ireland, Patrick. *The Policy Challenge of Ethnic Diversity: Immigrant Politics in France and Switzerland.* Cambridge, MA: Harvard University Press, 1994.

Irwan, Alexander. "Business Networks and the Regional Economy of East and Southeast Asia in the Late Twentieth Century." Binghamton, NY: SUNY at Binghamton unpublished dissertation, 1995.

Jalali, Rita, and Seymour Martin Lipset. "Racial and Ethnic Conflicts: A Global Perspective." In *Political Science Quarterly* vol. 107, no. 4. (Winter 1992/93).

Jawhar, Mohamed. "Malaysia in 1995: High Growth, Big Deficit, Stable Politics." *Asian Survey* vol. xxxvi, no. 2 (February 1996).

Jayasankaran, S. "High Wire Act." *Far Eastern Economic Review* (October 9, 1997a).

———. "Eye of the Storm." *Far Eastern Economic Review* (October 16, 1997b).

———. "Hit the Brakes." *Far Eastern Economic Review* (December 17, 1997c).

———. "Malaysia: Surprise Attack." *Far Eastern Economic Review* (November 18, 1999).

Jenkins, Shirley. "New Immigrants: Ethnic Factors in Governance and Politics." In *Urban Politics New York Style*, Bellush and Netzer, eds. New York: M.E. Sharpe, 1990.

Jesudason, James. "Statist Democracy and the Limits to Civil Society in Malaysia." *Journal of Commonwealth and Comparative Politics* vol. 33, no. 3 (1995).

Jomo, K.S. "Elections' Janus Face: Limitations and Potential in Malaysia." In *The Politics of Elections in Southeast Asia*, E. H. Taylor, ed. New York: Cambridge University Press, 1996.

Kahn, Joel S., and Francis Loh Kok Wah. *Fragmented Vision: Culture and Politics in Contemporary Malaysia.* Honolulu: University of Hawaii Press, 1992.

Katznelson, Ira. *Black Men, White Cities.* London: Oxford University Press, 1973.

———. "Working-Class Formation: Constructing Cases and Comparisons." In *Working Class Formation: Nineteenth Century Patterns in Western Europe and the United States*, Katznelson and Aristide Zolberg, eds. Princeton, NJ: Princeton University Press, 1986.

———. "Structure and Configuration in Comparative Politics." In *Comparative Politics: Rationality, Culture, and Structure*, Lichbach and Zuckerman, eds. New York: Cambridge University Press, 1997.

King, Gary. *A Solution to the Ecological Inference Problem: Reconstructing Individual Behavior From Aggregate Data.* Princeton, NJ: Princeton University Press, 1997.

Kim, Pan S. "A Status Report on Asian Americans in Government" *Asian American Policy Review* vol. IV (1994).

Kitschelt, Herbert. "Political Opportunity Structures and Political Protest: Anti-Nuclear Movements in Four Democracies." *British Journal of Political Science* 16 (1986).

Klinken, Gerry van. "The May Riots." *Inside Indonesia* May 29, 1998 for Refugee Review Tribunal (http://insideindonesia.org/digest/dig63html).

Kompas Online. "Stagnating Assimilation Process Pushed Forming of Parpindo" Tuesday, June 9, 1998a (http://www.kompas.com/9806/09/ENGLISH/stag. html).

———. "Nurcholish Madjid: Diversity a National Asset" June 25, 1998b (http:// www.kompas.com/9806/25/ENGLISH/nurc.html).

Kua Kia Soon. *A Protean Saga: The Chinese Schools of Malaysia.* Kuala Lumpur, Malaysia: Resource and Research Center Selangor Chinese Assembly Hall, 1990.

———. *Malaysian Political Realities.* Petaling Jaya, Malaysia: Orieng Group Sdn. Bhd., 1992.

Kuo, Chia-ling. *Social and Political Change in New York's Chinatown: The Role of Voluntary Associations.* New York: Praeger Publishers, 1977.

Kwong, Peter. *Chinatown, NY: Labor and Politics, 1930–1950.* New York: Monthly Review Press, 1979.

———. *The New Chinatown.* New York: Hill and Wang Publishers, 1996.

Lai, Him Mark. "The United States." In *Encyclopedia of Chinese Overseas,* Lynn Pan, ed. Cambridge, MA: Harvard University Press, 1999, 261–73.

Laitin, David D. *Hegemony and Culture: Politics and Religious Change among the Yoruba.* Chicago: University of Chicago Press, 1986.

———. "Marginality: A Microperspective." *Rationality and Society* vol. 7, no. 1 (January 1995).

Lamphere, Louise, ed. *Structuring Diversity: Ethnographic Perspectives on the New Immigration.* Chicago, IL: University of Chicago Press, 1992.

Lane, Robert E. "The Way of the Ethnic in Politics." In *Ethnic Group Politics,* Bailey and Katz, eds. Ohio: Charles E. Merrill, 1969.

Lee, Felicia R. "Fiery Debate at Redistricting Forum." *New York Times* (May 7, 1991a): B7.

———. "Blocs Battle to Draw Chinatown's New Council Map." *New York Times* (April 30, 1991b): B1.

Lee, Raymond, ed. *Ethnicity and Ethnic Relations in Malaysia.* Center on Southeast Asian Studies, Monograph Series on Southeast Asia, Northern Illinois University, Occasional Paper no. 12, 1986.

Lee, Taeku. "The Backdoor and the Backlash: Campaign Finance and the Politicization of Chinese-Americans." Paper presented at the American Political Science Association Annual Meeting, Boston, MA, September 1998.

Levi, Margaret. "A Model, A Method, and a Map: Rational Choice in Comparative and Historical Analysis." In *Comparative Politics: Rationality, Culture, and Structure,* Lichbach and Zuckerman, eds. New York: Cambridge University Press, 1997.

Levitt, Melissa, and David Olson. "Immigration and Political Incorporation: But Do They Vote?" Unpublished paper presented at Northeast Political Science Association Annual Meeting, Boston, MA, November 1996.

Lichbach, Mark I., and Alan S. Zuckerman, eds. *Comparative Politics: Rationality, Culture, and Structure.* New York: Cambridge University Press, 1997.

Liddle, R. William. *Ethnicity, Party, and National Integration: An Indonesian Case Study.* New Haven: Yale University Press, 1970.

————, ed. *Political Participation in Modern Indonesia*. Monograph Series no. 19. New Haven: Yale University Southeast Asia Studies, 1973.

————. "A Useful Fiction: Democratic Legitimation in New Order Indonesia." In *The Politics of Elections in Southeast Asia*, R. H. Taylor, ed. New York: Cambridge University Press, 1996.

Lien, Pei-te. "Ethnicity and Political Participation: a Comparison Between Asian and Mexican Americans." *Political Behavior* vol. 16 (1994).

————. *The Political Participation of Asian Americans: Voting Behavior in Southern California*. New York: Garland Publishing, 1997.

————. "Who Votes in Multiracial American? An Analysis of Voting Registration and Turnout by Race and Ethnicity, 1990–1996." Paper prepared for delivery at the 1998 Annual Meeting of the American Political Science Association, Boston, September 3–6, 1998.

Lieske, Joel A., and Jan William Hillard. "The Racial Factor in Urban Elections" *The Western Political Quarterly* vol. 37, issue 4 (1984).

Lim, Y.W.C., and L.A.P. Gosling, eds. *The Chinese in Southeast Asia*. Singapore: Maruzen Asia, 1988.

Lott, Juanita T. "Policy Implications of Population Changes in the Asian American Community." *Asian American Policy Review* vol. II (Spring 1991).

Macintyre, Andrew. *Business and Politics in Indonesia*. Australia: Allen and Unwin Pty. Ltd., 1990.

Mackie, J.A.C., ed. *The Chinese in Indonesia*. Australia: Australian Institute of International Affairs, 1976.

————, and George Hicks. "Overseas Chinese: a Question of Identity." *Far Eastern Economic Review* vol. 157 (July 14, 1994).

————, and Andrew Macintyre. "Chapter One." In *Indonesia's New Order: The Dynamics of Socioeconomic Transformation*, Hill, ed. Honolulu: University of Hawaii Press, 1994.

Mahathir, Bin Mohamad. *The Malay Dilemma*. Singapore: D. Moore for Asian Pacific Press, 1970.

Malaysian Chinese Association. "Chinese Community Towards & Beyond 1990." A political seminar organized by Malaysian Chinese Association Headquarters, June 28, 1987.

Malaysian Yearbook of Statistics. Kuala Lumpur: Government of Malaysia Office of Publications, 1996.

Mallarangeng, Rizal, and R. William Liddle. "Indonesia in 1995: The Struggle for Power and Policy." *Asian Survey* vol. xxxvi, no. 2 (February 1996).

McAdam, Doug, Sidney Tarrow, and Charles Tilly. "Toward an Integrated Perspective on Social Movements and Revolution." In *Comparative Politics: Rationality, Culture, and Structure*, Mark I. Lichbach and Alan S. Zuckerman, eds. New York: Cambridge University Press, 1997.

McBeth, John, and Margot Cohen. "Red Menace." *Far Eastern Economic Review* (November 2, 1995a): 18–19.

————. "An Indonesian Miti?" *Far Eastern Economic Review* (December 21, 1995b): 60.

————. "Political Engineering." *Far Eastern Economic Review* (July 4, 1996a): 14–15.

———. "Streets of Fire." *Far Eastern Economic Review* (August 8, 1996b): 14–16.

———. "Suharto's Test." *Far Eastern Economic Review* (November 20, 1997).

———. "Double or Nothing." *Far Eastern Economic Review* (February 26, 1998a): 14–17.

———. "The Line of Fire, Army's Choice Is Between Suharto and Saving the Country." *Far Eastern Economic Review* (May 21, 1998b) interactive edition (http://www.feer.com/Restricted/98may_21/indonesia.html).

———. "Dawn of a New Age." *Far Eastern Economic Review* (September 17, 1998c).

———, and Fanny Lioe. "Clement Times Suharto Frees Prisoners, Lightens Coup-Era Blacklist." *Far Eastern Economic Review* (August 24, 1995): 20–21.

———, and Michael Vatikiotis. "Into the Void." *Far Eastern Economic Review* (June 4, 1998).

McKinley James C., Jr. "Primary Day; New Voices to Mold Power Balance in the New City Council." *New York Times* (Sept. 13, 1991): B5.

McNickle, Chris. *To Be Mayor of New York; Ethnic Politics in the City.* New York: Columbia University Press: 1993.

McVey, Ruth. *Southeast Asian Capitalists.* Ithaca, NY: Cornell University Press, 1992.

Means, Gordon P. *Malaysian Politics: The Second Generation.* Singapore: Oxford University Press, 1991.

Milbrath, Lester W. *Political Participation: How and Why Do People Get Involved in Politics?* Chicago: Rand McNally & Co., 1965.

Moe, Terry. "The New Economics of Organization." *American Journal of Political Science* 28 (Nov. 1984): 739–777.

Montinola, Gabriella, Yingyi Qian, and Barry Weingast. "Federalism, Chinese Style." *World Politics* (October 1995).

Moynihan, Daniel Patrick. *Ethnicity: Theory and Experience.* Cambridge, MA: Harvard University Press, 1975.

Munro-Kua, Anne. *Authoritarian Populism in Malaysia.* New York: St. Martin's Press, 1996.

Muratsuchi, Albert Y. "Voter Registration in Asian and Pacific Islander Communities: An Agenda from the 1990s." *Asian American Policy Review* vol. II (Spring 1991).

Mydans, Seth. "Indonesia President Accepts Assembly Election Results." *The New York Times* (August 4, 1999): A4.

Nakanishi, Don T. *The UCLA Asian Pacific American Voter Registration Study.* Asian Pacific American Legal Center, 1987.

———. "An Emerging Electorate: The Political Education of Asian Pacific Americans." *Asian American Policy Review* (Spring 1990).

Nee and Nee. *Longtime Californ': A Documentary Study of an American Chinatown.* Stanford, CA: Stanford University Press, 1986.

Ng, Beoy Kui. "The New Economic Policy (NEP) 1970–1990." In *Encyclopedia of the Chinese Overseas*, Lynn Pan, ed. Cambridge, MA: Harvard University Press, 1999.

Nonini, Donald M. "Shifting Identities, Positioned Imaginaries: Transnational Traversals and Reversals by Malaysian Chinese." In *Ungrounded Empires: The Cultural Politics of Modern Chinese Transnationalism*, Ong and Nonini, eds. New York: Routledge, 1997, 203–228.

North, Douglass. *Institutions, Institutional Change and Economic Performance.* New York: Cambridge University Press, 1990.

NSTP Research and Information Services. *Elections in Malaysia: A Handbook of Facts and Figures on the Elections of 1955–1986.* Kuala Lumpur, 1990.

Olson, Mancur. *The Logic of Collective Action.* Cambridge: Harvard University Press, 1965.

Ong, Aihwa. "Metropolitan Futures: Male Migration, the Media, and Emerging Transnational Publics." Paper presented at the Institute of Southeast Asian Studies, Singapore: Conference on Southeast Asian Diasporas, December 5–7, 1996.

Ong, Paul, Edna Bonacich, and Lucie Cheng, eds. *The New Asian Immigration in Los Angeles and Global Restructuring.* Philadelphia, PA: Temple University Press, 1994.

Ong, Paul, and Tania Azores. "Asian Immigrants in Los Angeles: Diversity and Divisions." In *The New Asian Immigration in Los Angeles and Global Restructuring,* Ong, Bonacich, and Cheng, eds. Philadelphia, PA: Temple University Press, 1994, 100–133.

————, and John M. Liu. "U.S. Immigration Policies and Asian Migration." In Ong, Bonacich, and Cheng, eds. Philadelphia, PA: Temple University Press, 1994, 45–74.

Onghokham. "Roots of Anti-Chinese Sentiment." In *The Jakarta Post* (June 1, 1998).

Pan, Lynn, ed. *The Encyclopedia of the Chinese Overseas.* Cambridge, MA: Harvard University Press, 1999.

Parenti, Michael. "Ethnic Politics and the Persistence of Ethnic Identification." In *Ethnic Group Politics.* Bailey and Katz, eds. Ohio: Charles E. Merrill, 1969.

Parry, Richard Lloyd. "The Suharto Shadow." *The New York Times Magazine* (July 18, 1999): 38–41.

Pereira, Brendan, Douglas Wong, Edward Tang, Susan Sim, and Derwin Pereira. "Plan to Set up Chinese Political Party." *The Straits Times* (June 6, 1998a).

————. "Equal Treatment for Chinese." *The Straits Times* (June 7, 1998b).

————. "Wary Welcome for New Parties." *The Straits Times* (June 8, 1998c).

Pereira, Derwin. "Mob Violence in East Java 'Instigated by Radicals.'" *The Straits Times* (July 22, 1998).

Piore, Michael J. *Birds of a Passage.* London: Cambridge University Press, 1979.

Portes, Alejandro, and Ruben G. Rumaut. *Immigrant America: A Portrait.* Berkeley, CA: University of California Press, 1990.

Purcell, Victor. *The Chinese in Southeast Asia.* London: Oxford University Press, 1965.

Pye, Lucian W. *Guerrilla Communism in Malaya: Its Social and Political Meaning.* Princeton, NJ: Princeton University Press 1956.

————. *Asian Power and Politics: The Cultural Dimension of Authority.* Cambridge, MA: Harvard University Press, 1985.

Rachagan, Sothi. "The Development of the Electoral System." In *Malaysian Politics and the 1978 Election*, Crouch, Lee, and Ong, eds. Kuala Lumpur: Oxford University Press, 1980.

————. *Law and the Electoral Process in Malaysia.* Kuala Lumpur, Malaysia: Oxford University Press, 1993.

Razak Report, Paragraph 12. Malaysia: Government of Malaysia, Department of Education, 1956.

Roberts, Sam. "Redistricting Oddities Reflect Racial and Ethnic Politics." *New York Times* (May 7, 1991): B1.

Rocamora, J. Eliseo. "Political Participation and the Party System: The PNI Example." In *Political Participation in Modern Indonesia.* Monograph Series no. 19, Liddle, ed. New Haven, CT: Yale University Souteast Asia Studies, 1973.

Rogers, David. "Community Control and Decentralization." In *Urban Politics New York Style*, Bellush and Netzer, eds. New York: M.E. Sharpe, 1990.

Rogers, Gerry. *A General Problem and its Implications in India.* Geneva: International Institute for Labor, ILO, 1993.

Rosenstone, Steven J., and John Mark Hansen. *Mobilization, Participation, and Democracy in America.* New York: Macmillan, 1993.

Ross, Marc Howard. "Culture and Identity in Comparative Political Analysis." In *Comparative Politics: Rationality, Culture, and Structure*, Lichbach and Zuckerman, eds. New York: Cambridge University Press, 1997.

Saito, Leland T. "Asian Americans and Latinos in San Gabriel Valley, California: Ethnic Political Cooperation and Redistricting 1990–92." *Amerasia Journal* vol. 19:2 (1993).

————, and John Horton. "The New Chinese Immigration and the Rise of Asian American Politics in Monterey Park, California." In *The New Asian Immigration in Los Angeles and Global Restructuring*, Ong, Bonacich, and Cheng, eds. Philadelphia, PA: Temple University Press, 1994.

Sayre, Wallace, and Herbert Kaufman. *Governing New York.* New York: Russell Sage, 1959, 1960, and 1965 editions.

Schattschneider, E.E. *Politics, Pressures, and the Tariff.* New York: Prentice-Hall, 1935.

Schelling, Thomas C. *Micromotives and Macrobehavior.* New York: WW Norton, 1978.

Schmitter, Barbara Heisler, and Martin O. Heisler. *From Foreign Workers to Settlers?* Beverly Hills, CA: Sage Publisher, 1986.

Seagrave, Sterling. *Lords of the Rim: The Invisible Empire of the Overseas Chinese.* New York: G.P. Putnam's Sons, 1995.

Sieh Lee Mei Ling. "The Transformation of Malaysian Business Groups." In *Southeast Asian Capitalists*, Ruth McVey, ed. Ithaca, NY: Studies on Southeast Asia Program, 1992.

Sim, Shao Chee. "Social Service Needs of Chinese Immigrant High School Students in New York City." *Asian American Policy Review* vol. III (Winter 1993).

Siu, Paul C.P. *The Chinese Laundryman: A Study in Social Isolation*, John Kuo Wei Tchen, ed. New York: New York University Press, 1987.

Skeldon, Ronald, ed. *Reluctant Exiles? Migration from Hong Kong and the New Overseas Chinese*. London: M.E. Sharpe, 1994.

———. "The Last Half Century of Chinese Overseas (1945–1994): Comparative Perspectives." *International Migration Review* vol. xxix, no. 2.

Skinner, G. William *Leadership and Power in the Chinese Community of Thailand*. Ithaca, NY: Cornell University Press, 1958.

———. "Change and Persistence in Chinese Culture Overseas." *Journal of South Seas Society* vol. 16 (1 & 2) (1960):86–100.

———. "Overseas Chinese Leadership: Paradigm for a Paradox." In *Leadership and Authority*, Gehan Wijeyewardene, ed. Singapore: University of Malaya Press, 1968, 191–207.

Smith, Christopher J. "Asian New York: The Geography and Politics of Diversity" *International Migration Review* vol. XXIX, no. 1 (1992).

Smith, Thelma E., ed. *Guide to the Municipal Government of the City of New York*. New York: Meilan Press, 1973.

Solomon, Jay. "Indonesia's Ethnic Chinese End Long Political Silence." *The Wall Street Journal* (June 8, 1998).

The Straits Times (Singapore). "What Does the Future Hold for Indonesia's Chinese?" (April 19, 1999).

Suryadinata, Leo. *Peranakan's Search for National Identity: Biographical Studies of 7 Indonesian Chinese*. Singapore: Times Academic Press, 1993.

———. *Political Thinking of the Indonesian Chinese 1900–1995: A Source Book*. 2nd ed. Singapore: Singapore University Press, 1997.

———. *Interpreting Indonesian Politics*. Singapore: Times Academic Press, 1998.

Tamayo, William, Stewart Kwoh, and Robin Tomo. *The Voting Rights of Asian Pacific Americans*. Los Angeles: LEAP Asian Pacific American Public Policy Institute, 1991.

Tamura, Eileen. *Americanization, Acculturation, and Ethnic Identity: The Nisei Generation in Hawaii*. Urbana, IL: University of Illinois Press, 1994.

Tan Liok Ee. "Dong Jiao Zong and the Challenge to Cultural Hegemony." In *Fragmented Vision: Culture and Politics in Contemporary Malaysia*, Kohn and Loh, eds. Honolulu: University of Hawaii Press, 1992.

Tarrow, Sidney. *Struggling to Reform: Social Movements and Policy Change during Cycles of Protest*. Ithaca, NY: Cornell University Press, Western Societies Program Occasional Paper no. 15, New York Center for International Studies, 1983.

———. *Democracy and Disorder: Social Conflict, Political Protest, and Democracy in Italy 1965–1975*. New York: Oxford University Press, 1989.

———. *Power in Movement: Social Movements, Collective Action and Politics*. New York: Cambridge University Press, 1994.

Taylor, R.H., ed. *The Politics of Elections in Southeast Asia*. New York: Cambridge University Press, 1996.

Tesoro, Jose Manuel. "How and Why Indonesia's Third-Largest City Descended into Chaos." *Asiaweek* (May 22, 1998).

Tilly, Charles. *From Mobilization to Revolution*. Reading, MA: Addison-Wesley, 1978.

Truman, David. *The Governmental Process*, 2nd ed. New York: Alfred A. Knopf, 1971.

Tuckel, Peter, and Richard Maisel. "Voter Turnout among European Immigrants to the United States." *Journal of Interdisciplinary History* XXIV (3) (1994): 407–430.

UCLA Asian American Studies Center. *1996 National Asian Pacific American Political Almanac*. 7th ed. Los Angeles, CA: 1996.

Uhlaner, Carole J. "Rational Turnout: The Neglected Role of Groups." *American Journal of Political Science* 33 (1989): 390–422.

Uriely, Natan. "Rhetorical Ethnicity of Permanent Sojourners." *International Sociology* vol. 9, issue 4 (1994).

Vasil, R.K. *The Malaysian General Election of 1969*. Singapore: Oxford University Press, 1972.

Vatikiotis, Michael R. J. *Indonesian Politics Under Suharto: Order, Development, and Pressure for Change*. New York: Routledge, 1993.

———. "The Reform Tango." *Far Eastern Economic Review* (November 5, 1998).

———, and Adam Schwarz. "A Nation Awakes." *Far Eastern Economic Review* (June 4, 1998).

Verba, Sidney, and Norman H. Nie. *Participation in America: Political Democracy and Social Equality*. New York: Harper & Row Publishers, 1972.

———, Jae-on Kim. *Participation and Political Equality*. Cambridge: Cambridge University Press, 1978.

———, Kay Lehman Schlozman, and Henry E. Brady. *Voice and Equality: Civic Voluntarism in American Politics*. Cambridge: Harvard University Press, 1995.

Viteritti, Joseph P. "The New Charter: Will It Make a Difference?" In *Urban Politics New York Style*, Bellush and Netzer, eds. New York: M. E. Sharpe, 1990.

Waldinger, Roger. "From Ellis Island to LAX: Immigrant Prospects in the American City." Taken from http://www.nyu.edu/urban/research/immigration/ immigration.html. 1995.

———, and Yenfen Tseng. "Divergent Diasporas: The Chinese Communities of New York and Los Angeles." *Revue Europeenne des Migrations Internationales* vol. 8, no. 3 (1992).

Wanandi, Jusuf. "The Road Ahead." *Far Eastern Economic Review* (July 30, 1998).

Wang, Gungwu. "Greater China and the Chinese Overseas." *China Quarterly* 136 (December 1993).

Wang, L. Ling-chi. "The Politics of Ethnic Identity and Empowerment: The Asian American Community Since the 1960s." *Asian American Policy Review* (Spring 1991).

Watchman. "Watchman: A Hard Rain." *A. Magazine* vol. 3, no. 1 (March 3, 1994): 10.

Watson, Keith. "The Problem of Chinese Education in Malaysia and Singapore." *Journal of Asian and African Studies* vol. 8, issue 1–2 (1973).

Weiner, Myron. "Security, Stability, and International Migration." *International Security* vol. 17, no. 3 (Winter 1992/93).

Weiss, Melford S. *Valley City: A Chinese Community in America.* Cambridge, MA: Schenkman, 1974.

Wibisono, Christiano. "The Bank Central Asia Trajedy and the Indonesian Chinese," *Suara Pembarun Daily* (Reprinted from *Huaren*, June 1, 1998) (http://www.huaren.org/focus/id/06069:–01.html).

Willman, David, Alan C. Miller, and Glenn F. Bunting. "What Clinton Knew; How a Push for New Fundraising Led to Foreign Access, Bad Money, and Questionable Ties." *Los Angeles Times* (December 21, 1997): A1.

Wilson, James Q. *The Amateur Democrat: Club Politics in Three Cities.* Chicago: University of Chicago Press, 1962.

Winzeler, Robert L. "Overseas Chinese Power, Social Organization, and Ethnicity in Southeast Asia: An East Coast Malayan Example." In *Ethnicity and Ethnic Relations in Malaysia*, Lee, ed. Center on Southwest Asian Studies Northern Illinois University, Occasional Paper no. 12, 1986.

Wolfinger, Raymond E., and Steven J. Rosenstone. *Who Votes?* New Haven: Yale University Press, 1980.

Wong, Bernard. *Patronage, Brokerage and Entrenpeneurship and the Chinese Community of New York.* New York: AMS Press, 1988.

Wu, Frank H. "Constructive Engagement: Foreign Policy, Local Politics on the Agenda at High-Powered Conference." *Asian Week* vol. 17, no. 36 (May 3, 1996): 10.

Yep, Kathy. "The Power of Collective Voice." *Asian American Policy Review* vol. IV (Spring 1994).

Zangwill, Israel. *The Melting Pot: A Drama in Four Acts.* New York: MacMillan Press, 1909.

Zimmerman, Emily, Hongsook Eu, and David Daykin. "The Lower East Side Community District 3, Manhattan." Report prepared for The City of New York Human Resources Administration, Research Division, United Way of New York, 1993.